CHELSEA HOUSE PUBLISHERS
Modern Critical Views

HENRY ADAMS
EDWARD ALBEE
A. R. AMMONS
MATTHEW ARNOLD
JOHN ASHBERY
W. H. AUDEN
JANE AUSTEN
JAMES BALDWIN
CHARLES BAUDELAIRE
SAMUEL BECKETT
SAUL BELLOW
THE BIBLE
ELIZABETH BISHOP
WILLIAM BLAKE
JORGE LUIS BORGES
ELIZABETH BOWEN
BERTOLT BRECHT
THE BRONTËS
ROBERT BROWNING
ANTHONY BURGESS
GEORGE GORDON, LORD BYRON
THOMAS CARLYLE
LEWIS CARROLL
WILLA CATHER
CERVANTES
GEOFFREY CHAUCER
KATE CHOPIN
SAMUEL TAYLOR COLERIDGE
JOSEPH CONRAD
CONTEMPORARY POETS
HART CRANE
STEPHEN CRANE
DANTE
CHARLES DICKENS
EMILY DICKINSON
JOHN DONNE & THE
    17th-CENTURY POETS
ELIZABETHAN DRAMATISTS
THEODORE DREISER
JOHN DRYDEN
GEORGE ELIOT
T. S. ELIOT
RALPH ELLISON
RALPH WALDO EMERSON
WILLIAM FAULKNER
HENRY FIELDING
F. SCOTT FITZGERALD
GUSTAVE FLAUBERT
E. M. FORSTER
SIGMUND FREUD
ROBERT FROST

ROBERT GRAVES
GRAHAM GREENE
THOMAS HARDY
NATHANIEL HAWTHORNE
WILLIAM HAZLITT
SEAMUS HEANEY
ERNEST HEMINGWAY
GEOFFREY HILL
FRIEDRICH HÖLDERLIN
HOMER
GERARD MANLEY HOPKINS
WILLIAM DEAN HOWELLS
ZORA NEALE HURSTON
HENRY JAMES
SAMUEL JOHNSON
BEN JONSON
JAMES JOYCE
FRANZ KAFKA
JOHN KEATS
RUDYARD KIPLING
D. H. LAWRENCE
JOHN LE CARRÉ
URSULA K. LE GUIN
DORIS LESSING
SINCLAIR LEWIS
ROBERT LOWELL
NORMAN MAILER
BERNARD MALAMUD
THOMAS MANN
CHRISTOPHER MARLOWE
CARSON MCCULLERS
HERMAN MELVILLE
JAMES MERRILL
ARTHUR MILLER
JOHN MILTON
EUGENIO MONTALE
MARIANNE MOORE
IRIS MURDOCH
VLADIMIR NABOKOV
JOYCE CAROL OATES
SEAN O'CASEY
FLANNERY O'CONNOR
EUGENE O'NEILL
GEORGE ORWELL
CYNTHIA OZICK
WALTER PATER
WALKER PERCY
HAROLD PINTER
PLATO
EDGAR ALLAN POE

POETS OF SENSIBILITY &
    THE SUBLIME
ALEXANDER POPE
KATHERINE ANNE PORTER
EZRA POUND
PRE-RAPHAELITE POETS
MARCEL PROUST
THOMAS PYNCHON
ARTHUR RIMBAUD
THEODORE ROETHKE
PHILIP ROTH
JOHN RUSKIN
J. D. SALINGER
GERSHOM SCHOLEM
WILLIAM SHAKESPEARE (3 vols.)
    HISTORIES & POEMS
    COMEDIES
    TRAGEDIES
GEORGE BERNARD SHAW
MARY WOLLSTONECRAFT SHELLEY
PERCY BYSSHE SHELLEY
EDMUND SPENSER
GERTRUDE STEIN
JOHN STEINBECK
LAURENCE STERNE
WALLACE STEVENS
TOM STOPPARD
JONATHAN SWIFT
ALFRED LORD TENNYSON
WILLIAM MAKEPEACE THACKERAY
HENRY DAVID THOREAU
LEO TOLSTOI
ANTHONY TROLLOPE
MARK TWAIN
JOHN UPDIKE
GORE VIDAL
VIRGIL
ROBERT PENN WARREN
EVELYN WAUGH
EUDORA WELTY
NATHANAEL WEST
EDITH WHARTON
WALT WHITMAN
OSCAR WILDE
TENNESSEE WILLIAMS
WILLIAM CARLOS WILLIAMS
THOMAS WOLFE
VIRGINIA WOOLF
WILLIAM WORDSWORTH
RICHARD WRIGHT
WILLIAM BUTLER YEATS

Further titles in preparation.

Modern Critical Views

DANTE

Modern Critical Views

DANTE

Edited with an introduction by

Harold Bloom

Sterling Professor of the Humanities
Yale University

1986
CHELSEA HOUSE PUBLISHERS
New York
New Haven   Philadelphia

PROJECT EDITORS: Emily Bestler, James Uebbing
ASSOCIATE EDITOR: Maria Behan
EDITORIAL COORDINATOR: Karyn Gullen Browne
EDITORIAL STAFF: Perry King, Bert Yaeger
DESIGN: Susan Lusk

Cover by Robin Peterson

Printed and bound in the United States of America

Library of Congress Cataloging in Publication Data

Dante.
      (Modern critical views)
      Bibliography: p.
      Includes index.
      1. Dante Alighieri, 1265–1321—Criticism and
interpretation—Addresses, essays, lectures.
I. Bloom, Harold.   II. Title.   III. Series.
PQ4390.D27   1986   851'.1   85–28063
ISBN 0–87754–665–7

Chelsea House Publishers
Harold Steinberg, Chairman and Publisher
Susan Lusk, Vice President
A Division of Chelsea House Educational Communications, Inc.
133 Christopher Street, New York, NY 10014

Contents

Editor's Note

This volume gathers together a representative selection of the best Dante criticism of the past thirty years, arranged in the chronological order of its publication. The editor acknowledges the invaluable assistance of Ms. Cathy Caruth, who introduced him to some of the essays collected here. His "Introduction" follows the approach to Dante of Ernst Robert Curtius, who is not represented here only because this book seeks to present the practical criticism of Dante, particularly as inspired by the exegetical principles of Charles S. Singleton and Erich Auerbach, rather than the theoretical speculations of Curtius. Nevertheless, the "Introduction" ventures to question aspects of their approach to Dante, while invoking the complex stance of Curtius towards the difficult question of Dante's originality.

The chronological sequence begins with Singleton's classic essay on the distinction between the allegory of the poets and the allegory of the theologians, with Dante's allegory assimilated to the latter. Two of Erich Auerbach's seminal essays on the Christian trope of *figura*, and Dante's relation to that trope, then follow. The discussion by R. E. Kaske of the splendidly perverse allusion to the "DXV" by Beatrice in *Purgatorio* XXXII also now has classic status, being an ingenious instance of learning and insight applied to Dante at his most difficult. Francis X. Newman's equally essential demonstration of an Augustinian element in the structure of the *Commedia* rounds out this introductory group of essays, all of which map the contexts of Dante's poem.

The remaining commentaries address themselves to specific dimensions of Dante's work, beginning with Marguerite Mills Chiarenza on the *Paradiso*, and her crucial insight that: "In the *Paradiso* it is the poet who struggles while the pilgrim is safe." John Freccero's powerful reading of the Medusa (*Inferno* IX) follows, with its important suggestion that Dante views petrification as "an interpretive as well as moral threat." With Robert Durling's discussion of "Seneca, Plato, and the Microcosm," the focus shifts to Dante's lyric poetry and then relates the group of "stony rhymes" to the *Commedia*. David Quint returns us to the *Inferno* with his analysis of epic tradition and a thematic crossroads in Canto IX.

Freccero, certainly the central Dante critic of his generation, is represented by a second essay, his exquisite analysis of the poetics of the *Purgatorio* as a process of Dante's maturation out of and away from the precursor, Virgil. With the reading of the Paolo and Francesca episode (*Inferno* V) by Susan Noakes, we receive a remarkably fresh account of what is perhaps the best-known passage in Dante. Teodolinda Barolini's exegesis of "textuality and truth" in *Purgatorio* XXIV illuminates Dante by raising again, as Freccero does, everything that is problematic about a poet's relation to his precursors. In the essay following, by Kenneth Gross, an interpretation of a single word (for "counterpass") in the *Inferno* (Canto XXVIII) opens out into a revealing meditation upon Dante's poetics of pain and punishment.

The final essay, by Giuseppe Mazzotta, printed here for the first time, relates the *Vita Nuova* to *Inferno* XXVII in order to trace Dante's powerful and characteristic exploration of both the limits and the dangers of rhetoric in the language of love. In some sense, Mazzotta returns Dante full circle to his own poetic origins, and so brings this book to its appropriate close.

Introduction

I

Dante, by common consent, stands with the supreme Western masters of literary representation: the Yahwist, Homer, Chaucer, Shakespeare, Cervantes, Milton, Tolstoi, Proust. Our ideas as to how reality can be represented by literary language depend, to a considerable extent, on this ninefold. Perhaps it can also be said that these writers have formed a large part of our experience of what is called reality. Certain aspects of reality might not be nearly so visible, had we not read these nine masters of mimesis. Setting the Yahwist and Homer aside as being both ancient and hypothetical, only Shakespeare, again by common consent, is judged to be Dante's rival as a great Original in representation. But Shakespearean representation has naturalized us in its domain. Dante is now an immensely difficult poet partly because we are so much at home with Shakespeare.

Erich Auerbach, who with Charles S. Singleton and John Freccero makes up a celestial trinity of Dante interpreters, gave us the definitive opening description of Dante's ways of representing reality:

> . . . Dante in the *Comedy* transcended tragic death by identifying man's ultimate fate with the earthly unity of his personality, and . . . the very plan of the work made it possible, and indeed confronted him with the obligation, to represent earthly reality exactly as he saw it. Thus it became necessary that the characters in Dante's other world, in their situation and attitude, should represent the sum of themselves; that they should disclose, in a single act, the character and fate that had filled out their lives . . .
>
> . . . from classical theory Dante took over only one principle, the *sibi constare*, or consistency, of his persons; all other tenets had lost their literal meaning for him . . . Dante's vision is a tragedy according to Aristotle's definition. In any event it is far more a tragedy than an epic, for the descriptive, epic elements in the poem are not autonomous, but serve other purposes, and the time, for Dante as well as his characters, is not the epic time in which destiny gradually unfolds, but the final time in which it is fulfilled.

If time is the final time, past all unfolding, then reality indeed can be represented in a single act that is at once character and fate. Dante's personages can reveal themselves totally in what they say and do, but they cannot change *because* of what Dante has them say and do. Chaucer, who owed Dante more than he would acknowledge, nevertheless departed from Dante in this, which is precisely where Chaucer most influenced Shakespeare. The Pardoner listens to himself speaking, listens to his own tale, and is darkly made doom-eager through just that listening. This mode of representation expands in Shakespeare to a point that no writer since has reached so consistently. Hamlet may be the most metamorphic of Shakespeare's people (or it may be Cleopatra, or Falstaff, or who you will), but as such he merely sets the mode. Nearly everyone of consequence in Shakespeare helps inaugurate a mimetic style we all now take too much for granted. They, like us, are strengthened or victimized, reach an apotheosis or are destroyed, by themselves reacting to what they say and do. It may be that we have learned to affect ourselves so strongly, in part because involuntarily we imitate Shakespeare's characters. We never imitate Dante's creatures because we do not live in finalities; we know that we are not fulfilled.

A literary text can represent a fulfilled reality only if it can persuade itself, and momentarily persuade us, that one text can fulfill another. Dante, as Auerbach demonstrated, relied upon the great Christian trope of *figura*, whose basis was the insistence that the Christian New Testament had fulfilled what it called "the Old Testament," itself a phrase deeply offensive to normative Jews who continue to trust in the Covenant as set forth in the Hebrew Bible. But the Hebrew Bible indeed must be the Old Testament, if Christianity is to retain its power. What must the New Testament be, if Dante's poem is to develop and maintain its force?

Auerbach, quoting the Church Father Tertullian's comments upon the renaming of Oshea, son of Nun, by Moses as Jehoshua (Joshua, Jesus), speaks of Joshua as "a figure of things to come." The definition of this figure of prophecy or *figura* by Auerbach is now classic: "*Figura* is something real and historical which announces something else that is real and historical." Equally classic is Auerbach's formulation of "figural interpretation":

> Figural interpretation establishes a connection between two events or persons, the first of which signifies not only itself but also the second, while the second encompasses or fulfills the first. The first two poles of the figure are separate in time, but both, being real events or figures, are within time, within the stream of historical life. Only the understanding of the two persons or events is a spiritual act, but this spriitual act deals

with concrete events whether past, present, or future, and not with concepts or abstractions; these are quite secondary, since promise and fulfillment are real historical events, which have either happened in the incarnation of the word, or will happen in the second coming.

What happens when figural interpretation is transferred from sacred to secular literature? When Dante takes the historical Virgil and reads him as a *figura* of which Dante's character, Virgil, is the fulfillment, are we seeing the same pattern enacted as when Tertullian reads Joshua as the *figura* of which Jesus Christ was the fulfillment? Auerbach's answer is "yes," but this is a dialectical affirmative: "Thus Virgil in the *Divine Comedy* is the historical Virgil himself, but then again he is not; for the historical Virgil is only a *figura* of the fulfilled truth that the poem reveals, and this fulfillment is more real, more significant than the *figura*." Auerbach, writing on *figura* back in 1944, thought back to his book on Dante as poet of the secular world (1929), from which I quoted earlier, and insisted that he had acquired "a solid historical grounding" for his view of fifteen years before.

I am not certain that the earlier Auerbach is not to be preferred to the later. In secularizing *figura*, Auerbach dangerously idealized the relationship between literary texts. Appropriating the historical Virgil is not an idealizing gesture, as John Freccero shows in his superb essay, "Manfred's Wounds and the Poetics of the *Purgatorio*." Poetic fathers die hard, and Dante understood that he had made the historical Virgil the *figura*, and his own Virgil the fulfillment, partly in order to suggest that he himself was the poet Virgil's true fulfillment. Great poets are pragmatists when they deal with precursors; witness Blake's caricature of Milton as the hero of his poem *Milton*, or James Merrill's loving and witty portrayal of Stevens and Auden in *The Changing Light at Sandover*. Dante's Virgil is no more the historical Virgil than Blake's Milton is the historical Milton. If texts fulfill one another, it is always through some self-serving caricature of the earlier text by the later.

II

Charles S. Singleton, carefully reminding us that "Beatrice is not Christ," expounds Dante's use of the principle of analogy which likens the advent of Beatrice to the advent of Christ:

> Thus it is that the figure of a rising sun by which Beatrice comes at last to stand upon the triumphal chariot is the most revealing image which the poet might have found not only to affirm the analogy of her advent to

Christ's in the present tense, but to stress, in so doing, the very basis upon which that analogy rests: the advent of light.

Whitman, certainly a poet antithetical to Dante, opposed himself to the rising sun as a greater rising sun:

> Dazzling and tremendous how quick the sun-rise would kill me,
> If I could not now and always send sun-rise out of me.

> We also ascend dazzling and tremendous as the sun,
> We found our own O my soul in the calm and cool of the daybreak.

This is not analogy but a subversive mode akin to Nietzsche's, and learned from Emerson. The figure of the Whitmanian sun here is not an advent of Christ ("a great defeat" Emerson called that advent) but is "now and always," a perpetual dawning ("we demand victory," as Emerson said for his Americans, prophesying Whitman). The figure of Beatrice, to Whitman, might as well have been the figure of Christ. Can we, with Singleton, accept her as an analogy, or is she now the principal embarrassment of Dante's poem? As a fiction she retains her force, but does not Dante present her as more than a fiction? If Dante wrote, as Singleton says, the allegory of the theologians rather than the allegory of the poets, how are we to recapture Dante's sense of Beatrice if we do not accept the analogy that likens her advent to Christ's?

Singleton's answer is that Beatrice is the representation of Wisdom in a Christian sense, or the light of Grace. This answer, though given in the allegorical language of the theologians rather than that of the poets, remains a poetic answer because its analogical matrix is light rather than Grace. Dante persuades us not by his theology but y his occult mastery of the trope of light, in which he surpasses even the blind Milton among the poets:

> There is a light up there which makes the Creator visible to the creature,
> who finds his peace only in seeing Him.
>
> (*Paradiso* XXX, 100–102)

This, as Singleton says, is the Light of Glory rather than the Light of Grace, which is Beatrice's, or the Natural Light, which is Virgil's. Dante's peculiar gift is to find perpetually valid analogies for all three lights. Since his poem's fiction of duration is not temporal, but final, all three modes of light must be portrayed by him as though they were beyond change. And yet an unchanging fiction cannot give pleasure, as Dante clearly knew. What does he give us that more than compensates for his poem's apparent refusal of temporal anguish?

Auerbach, in his essay on St. Francis of Assisi in the *Commedia*, turned to *figura* again as his answer. To the medieval reader, according to Auerbach, the representations of forerunning and after-following repetitions were as familiar as the trope of "historical development" is (or was, to those who believe that Foucault forever exposed the trope). To us, now, "forerunning and after-following repetitions" suggest, not *figura* and its fulfillment, but the Freudian death-drive as the "fulfillment" of the compulsion-to-repeat. The repetition-compulsion perhaps is the final Western *figura*, prophesying our urge to drive beyond the pleasure principle. That is to say, for us the only text that can fulfill earlier texts, rather than correct or negate them, is what might be called "the text of death," which is totally opposed to what Dante sought to write.

III

What saves Dante from the idealizing lameness that necessarily haunts the allegorizing of the theologians? The earlier Auerbach was on the track of the answer when he meditated upon Dante's originality in the representation of persons. As seer, Dante identified character and fate, *ethos* and *daemon*, and what he saw in his contemporaries he transferred precisely to the three final worlds of *Inferno*, *Purgatorio*, and *Paradiso*. Dante's friends and enemies alike are presented, without ambiguity or ambivalence, as being consistent with themselves, beyond change, their eternal destinies over-determined by their fixed characters.

There are endless surprises in his poem for Dante himself, as for us, but there are no accidents. Farinata standing upright in his tomb, as if of Hell he had a great disdain, is heroic because he is massively consistent with himself, in his own tomb, can be nothing but what he is. His marvelous disdain of Hell represents a kind of necessity, what Wallace Stevens called the inescapable necessity of being that inescapable animal, oneself. Such a necessity is presented by Dante as being the judgment of Heaven upon us.

In Shakespeare, there are always accidents, and character can be as metamorphic as personality. Hamlet yields himself up to accident, at the last, perhaps because he has all but exhausted the possibilities for change that even his protean character possesses. This is our mode of representation, inherited by us from Shakespeare, and we no longer are able to see how original it originally was. Shakespeare therefore seems "natural" to us, even though we live in the age of Freud, who suspected darkly that there were no accidents, once we were past infancy. Dante no longer can be naturalized in our imaginations. His originality has not been lost for us, and yet his difficulty or strangeness for us is probably not caused by his authentic originality.

The allegory of the theologians simply is not an available mode for us, despite the labors of Auerbach and Singleton. Freccero has replaced them as the most relevant of Dante critics because he has returned Dante to what may be the truest, because least idealizing, allegory of the poets, which is the agon of poet against poet, the struggle for imaginative priority between forerunner and latecomer. Despite a marvelous parody by Borges, theologians are not primarily agonists. Dante understood that poets were. The light of glory, the light of grace, the light of nature are not competing lights, and yet all tropes for them necessarily compete, and always with other tropes.

Singleton, rejecting the allegory of the poets, said that it would reduce Dante's Virgil to a mere personification of Reason:

> For if this is the allegory of poets, then what Virgil does, like what Orpheus does, is a fiction devised to convey a hidden meaning which it ought to convey all the time, since only by conveying that other meaning is what he does justified at all. Instead, if this action is allegory as theologians take it, then this action must always have a literal sense which is historical and no fiction; and thus Virgil's deeds as part of the whole action may, in their turn, be as words signifying other things, but they do not have to do this all the time, because, being historical, those deeds exist simply in their own right.

But what if Virgil, as allegory of the poets, were to be read not as Reason, the light of nature, but as the trope of that light, reflecting among much else the lustres of the tears of universal nature? To say farewell to Virgil is to take leave not of Reason, but of the pathos of a certain natural light, perhaps of Wordsworth's "light of common day." Dante abandons Virgil not so as to substitute grace for reason, but so as to find his own image of voice, his own trope for all three lights. In the oldest and most authentic allegory of the poets, Virgil represents not reason but poetic fatherhood, the Scene of Instruction that Dante must transcend if he is to complete his journey to Beatrice.

IV

The figure of Beatrice, in my own experience as a reader, is now the most difficult of all Dante's tropes, because sublimation no longer seems to be a human possibility. What is lost, perhaps permanently, is the tradition that moves between Dante and Yeats, in which sublimated desire for a woman can be regarded as an enlargement of existence. One respected feminist critic has gone so far as to call Beatrice a "dumb broad," since she supposedly contemplates the One without understanding Him. What James Thurber grimly celebrated as the War between Men and Women has claimed many recent literary casualties, but none perhaps so unmerited as Dante's Beatrice. Dante, like tradition, thought that God's Wisdom, who daily played before His feet, was a woman, even as Nietzsche, with a gesture beyond irony, considered Truth to be a woman, presumably a deathly one. We possess art in order not to perish from the truth, Nietzsche insisted, which must mean that the aesthetic is a way of not being destroyed by a woman. Dante hardly would have agreed.

Beatrice is now so difficult to apprehend precisely because she participates both in the allegory of the poets and in the allegory of the philosophers. Her advent follows Dante's poetic maturation, or the vanishing of the precursor, Virgil. In the allegory of the poets, Beatrice is the Muse, whose function is to help the poet remember. Since remembering, in poetry, is the major mode of cognition, Beatrice is Dante's power of invention, the essence of his art. That means she is somehow the highest of the Muses, and yet far above them also, since in Dante's version of the allegory of the poets, Beatrice has "a place in the objective process of salvation," as Ernst Robert Curtius phrased it. Curtius rightly emphasized the extent of Dante's audacity:

> Guido Guinicelli (d. 1276) had made the exaltation of the beloved to an angel of paradise a topos of Italian lyric. To choose as guide in a poetic vision of the otherworld a loved woman who has been thus exalted is still within the bounds of Christian philosophy and faith. But Dante goes much further than this. He gives Beatrice a place in the objective process of salvation. Her function is thought of as not only for himself but also for all believers. Thus, on his own authority, he introduces into the Christian revelation an element which disrupts the doctrine of the church. This is either heresy—or myth.

It is now customary to speak of Dante as *the* Catholic poet, even as Milton is called *the* Protestant poet. Perhaps someday Kafka will be named as *the* Jewish writer, though his distance from normative Judaism was infinite. Dante and Milton were not less idiosyncratic, each in his own time, than Kafka was in ours, and the figure of Beatrice would be heresy and not myth if Dante had not been so strong a poet that the Church of later centuries has been happy to claim him. Curtius centered upon Dante's vision of himself as a prophet, even insisting that Dante expected the prophecy's fulfillment in the immediate future, during his own lifetime. Since Dante died at the age of fifty-six, a quarter-century away from the "perfect" age of eighty-one set forth in his *Convivio*, the literal force of the prophecy presumably was voided. But the prophecy, still hidden from us, matters nevertheless, as Curtius again maintains:

> Even if we could interpret his prophecy, that would give it no meaning for us. What Dante hid, Dante scholarship need not now unriddle. But it must take seriously the fact that Dante believed that he had an apocalyptic mission. This must be taken into consideration in interpreting him. Hence the question of Beatrice is not mere idle curiosity. Dante's system is built up in the first two cantos of the *Inferno*, it supports the entire *Commedia*. Beatrice can be seen only within it. The Lady Nine has become a cosmic power which emanates from two superior powers. A hierarchy of celestial powers which intervene in the process of history— this concept is manifestly related to Gnosticism: as an intellectual construction, a schema of intellectual contemplation, if perhaps not in origin. Such constructions can and must be pointed out. We do not know what Dante meant by Lucia. The only proper procedure for the commentator, then, is to admit that we do not know and to say that neither the ophthalmological explanation nor the allegorical interpretations are satisfactory. Exegesis is also bound to give its full weight to all the passages at the end of the *Purgatorio* and in the *Paradiso* which are opposed to the identification of Beatrice with the daughter of the banker Portinari. Beatrice is a myth created by Dante.

Very little significant criticism of Dante has followed this suggestion of Curtius, and a distorted emphasis upon Dante's supposed orthodoxy has been the result. Curtius certainly does not mean that Dante was a Gnostic, but he does remind us that Dante's Beatrice is the central figure in a purely personal gnosis. Dante indeed was a ruthless visionary, passionate and willful, whose poem triumphantly expresses his own unique personality. The *Commedia*, though one would hardly know this from most of its critics (Freccero is the sublime exception), is an immense trope of pathos or power, the power of the individual who was Dante. The pathos of that personality is most felt, perhaps, in the great and final parting of Beatrice from her poet, in the middle of Canto XXXI of the *Paradiso*, at the moment when her place as guide is transferred to the aged St. Bernard:

Already my glance had taken in the whole general form of Paradise but had not yet dwelt on any part of it, and I turned with new-kindled eagerness to question my Lady of things on which my mind was in suspense. One thing I intended, and another encountered me: I thought to see Beatrice, and I saw an old man, clothed like that glorious company. His eyes and his cheeks were suffused with a gracious gladness, and his aspect was of such kindness as befits a tender father. And "Where is she?" I said in haste; and he replied: "To end thy longing Beatrice sent me from my place; and if thou look up into the third circle from the highest tier thou shalt see her again, in the throne her merits have assigned to her."

Without answering, I lifted up my eyes and saw her where she made for herself a crown, reflecting from her the eternal beams. From the highest region where it thunders no mortal eye is so far, were it lost in the depth of the sea, as was my sight there from Beatrice; but to me it made no difference, for her image came down to me undimmed by aught between.

"O Lady in whom my hope has its strength and who didst bear for my salvation to leave thy footprints in Hell, of all the things that I have seen I acknowledge the grace and the virtue to be from thy power and from thy goodness. It is thou who hast drawn me from bondage into liberty by all those ways, by every means for it that was in thy power. Preserve in me thy great bounty, so that my spirit, which thou hast made whole, may be loosed from the body well-pleasing to thee." I prayed thus; and she, so far off as she seemed, smiled and looked at me, then turned again to the eternal fount.

It is difficult to comment upon the remorseless strength of this, upon its apparent sublimation of a mythmaking drive that here accepts a restraint which is more than rhetorical. Freud in his own great *summa*, the essay of 1937, "Analysis Terminable and Interminable," lamented his inability to cure those who could not accept the cure:

A man will not be subject to a father-substitute or owe him anything and he therefore refuses to accept his cure from the physician.

Dante too would not owe any man anything, not even if the man were Virgil, his poetic father. The cure had been accepted by Dante from his physician, Beatrice. In smiling and looking at him, as they part, she confirms the cure.

CHARLES S. SINGLETON

Two Kinds of Allegory

In his *Convivio* Dante recognizes two kinds of allegory: an "allegory of poets" and an "allegory of theologians." And in the interpretation of his own poems in that work he declares that he intends to follow the allegory of poets, for the reason that the poems were composed after that manner of allegory.

It is well to recall that there is an unfortunate lacuna in the text of the *Convivio* at just this most interesting point, with the result that those words which defined the literal sense, as distinguished from the allegorical, are missing. But no one who knows the general argument of the whole work will, I think, make serious objection to the way the editors of the accepted critical text have filled the lacuna.

The passage in question, patched by them, reads as follows:

> Dico che, sì come nel primo capitolo è narrato, questa sposizione conviene essere literale e allegorica. E a ciò dare a intendere, si vuol sapere che le scritture si possono intendere e deonsi esponere massimamente per quattro sensi. L'uno si chiama litterale [e questo è quello che non si stende più oltre la lettera de le parole fittizie, sì come sono le favole de li poeti. L'altro si chiama allegorico] e questo è quello che si nasconde sotto'l manto di queste favole, ed è una veritade ascosa sotto bella menzogna: sì come quando dice Ovidio che Orfeo facea con la cetera mansuete le fiere, e li arbori e le pietre a sè muovere; che vuol dire che lo savio uomo con lo strumento de la sua voce fa[r]ia mansuescere e umiliare li crudeli cuori, a fa[r]ia muovere a la sua volontade coloro che non hanno vita di scienza e d'arte: e coloro che non hanno vita ragionevole alcuna sono quasi come pietre. E perchè questo nascondimento fosse trovato per li savi, nel penultimo trattato si mosterrà. Veramente li teologi questo senso

From *Commedia: Elements of Structure*. Copyright © 1954 by Harvard University Press.

prendono altrimenti che li poeti; ma però che mia intenzione è qui lo modo de li poeti seguitare, prendo lo senso allegorico secondo che per li poeti è usato.

I say that, as is narrated in the first chapter, this exposition is to be both literal and allegorical. And to make this clear, one should know that writing can be understood and must be explained mainly in four senses. One is called the literal [and this is the sense that does not go beyond the letter of the fictive words, as are the fables of the poets. The other is called allegorical], and this is the sense that is hidden under the cloak of these fables, and it is a truth hidden under the beautiful lie; as when Ovid says that Orpheus tamed the wild beasts with his zither and caused the trees and the stones to come to him; which signifies that the wise man with the instrument of his voice would make cruel hearts gentle and humble, and would make those who do not live in science and art do his will; and those who have no kind of life of reason in them are as stones. And the reason why this concealment was devised by wise men will be shown in the next to the last treatise. It is true that theologians understand this sense otherwise than do the poets; but since it is my intention here to follow after the manner of the poets, I take the allegorical sense as the poets are wont to take it.

Dante goes on here to distinguish the customary third and fourth senses, the moral and the anagogical. However, in illustration of these no example from "the poets" is given. For both senses, the example in illustration is taken from Holy Scripture. It is, however, evident from the closing words of the chapter that in the exposition of the poems of the *Convivio*, the third and fourth senses will have only an incidental interest and that the poet is to concern himself mainly with the first two.

It was no doubt inevitable that the conception of allegory which Dante here calls the allegory of poets should come to be identified with the allegory of the *Divine Comedy*. This, after all, is a formulation of the matter of allegory by Dante himself. It distinguishes an allegory of poets from an allegory of theologians. Now poets create and theologians only interpret. And, if we must choose between Dante as theologian and Dante as poet, then, I suppose, we take the poet. For the *Divine Comedy*, all are agreed, is the work of a poet, is a poem. Why, then, would its allegory not be allegory as the poets understood it—that is, as Dante, in the *Convivio*, says the poets understood it? Surely the allegory of the *Comedy* is the allegorical of poets in which the first and literal sense is a fiction and the second or allegorical sense is the true one.

Indeed, with some Dante scholars, so strong has the persuasion been that such a view of the allegory of the *Divine Comedy* is the correct one that it has brought them to question the authorship of the famous letter to Can Grande. This, in all consistency, was bound to occur. For the Letter, in pointing out the allegory of the *Commedia*, speaks in its turn of the usual four senses. But the example of allegory which it gives is not taken from Ovid nor indeed from the work of any poet. Let us consider this famous and familiar passage:

> Ad evidentiam itaque dicendorum sciendum est quod istius operis non est simplex sensus, ymo dici potest polisemos, hoc est plurium sensuum; nam primus sensus est qui habetur per litteram, alius est qui habetur per significata per litteram. Et primus dicitur litteralis, secundus vero allegoricus sive moralis sive anagogicus. Qui modus tractandi, ut melius pateat, potest considerari in hiis versibus: "In exitu Israel de Egypto, domus Jacob ed populo barbaro, facta est Iudea sanctificatio eius, Israel potestas eius." Nam si ad litteram solam inspiciamus, significatur nobis exitus filiorum Israel de Egypto, tempore Moysis; si ad allegoriam, nobis significatur nostra redemptio facta per Christum; si ad moralem sensum significatur nobis conversio anime de luctu et miseria peccati ad statum gratie: si ad anagogicum, significatur exitus anime sancte ab huius corruptionis servitute ad eterne glorie libertatem. Et quanquam isti sensus mistici variis appellentur nominibus, generaliter omnes dici possunt allegorici, cum sint a litterali sive historiali diversi. Nam allegoria dicitur ab "alleon" grece, quod in latinum dicitur "alienum," sive "diversum."

> To elucidate, then, what we have to say, be it known that the sense of this work is not simple, but on the contrary it may be called polysemous, that is to say, "of more senses than one"; for it is one sense that we get through the letter, and another which we get through the thing the letter signifies; and the first is called literal, but the second allegorical or mystic. And this mode of treatment, for its better manifestation, may be considered in this verse: "When Israel came out of Egypt, and the house of Jacob from a people of strange speech, Judaea became his sanctification, Israel his power." For if we inspect the letter alone, the departure of the children of Israel from Egypt in the time of Moses is presented to us; if the allegory, our redemption wrought by Christ; if the moral sense, the conversion of the soul from the grief and misery of sin to the state of grace is presented to us; if the anagogical, the departure of the holy soul from the slavery of this corruption to the liberty of eternal glory is presented to us. And although these mystic senses have each their special denominations, they may all in general be called allegorical, since they differ from the literal and historical. Now allegory is so called from "alleon" in Greek, which means in Latin "alieum" or "diversum."

and the Letter continues directly as follows:

> Hiis visis, manifestum est quod duplex oportet esse subiectum, circa quod currant alterni sensus. Et ideo videndum est de subiecto huius operis, prout ad litteram accipitur; deinde de subiecto, prout allegorice sententia-

tur. Est ergo subiectum totius operis, litteraliter tantum accepti, status animarum post mortem simpliciter sumptus; nam de illo et circa illum totius operis versatur processus. Si vero accipiatur opus allegorice, subiectum est homo prout merendo et demerendo per arbitrii libertatem iustitie premiandi et puniendi obnoxius est.

When we understand this we see clearly that the subject round which the alternative senses play must be twofold. And we must therefore consider the subject of this work as literally understood, and then its subject as allegorically intended. The subject of the whole work, then, taken in the literal sense only is "the state of souls after death" without qualification, for the whole progress of the work hinges on it and about it. Whereas if the work be taken allegorically, the subject is "man as by good or ill deserts, in the exercise of the freedom of his choice, he becomes liable to rewarding or punishing justice."

Now this, to return to the distinction made in the *Convivio*, is beyond the shadow of a doubt, the "allegory of theologians." It is their kind of allegory not only because Holy Scripture is cited to illustrate it, but because since Scripture is cited, the first or literal sense cannot be fictive but must be true and, in this instance, historical. The effects of Orpheus' music on beasts and stones may be a poet's invention, setting forth under a veil of fiction some hidden truth, but the Exodus is no poet's invention.

All medievalists are familiar with the classical statement of the "allegory of theologians" as given by St. Thomas Aquinas toward the beginning of the *Summa Theologica*:

Auctor Sacrae Scripturae est Deus, in cuius potestate est ut non solum voces ad significandum accommodet, quod etiam homo facere potest, sed etiam res ipsas. Et ideo cum in omnibus scientiis voces significent, hoc habet proprium ista scientia, quod ipsae res significatae per voces, etiam significant aliquid. Illa ergo prima significatio, qua voces significant res, pertinet ad primum sensum, qui est sensus historicus vel litteralis. Illa vero significatio qua res significatae per voces, iterum res alias significant, dicitur sensus spiritualis, qui super litteralem fundatur et eum supponit.

The author of Holy Scripture is God, in whose power it is to signify His meaning, not by words only (as man also can do) but also by things themselves. So, whereas in every other science things are signified by words, this science has the property that the things signified by the words have themselves also a signification. Therefore that first signification whereby words signify things belongs to the first sense, the historical or literal. That signification whereby things signified by words have themselves also a signification is called the spiritual sense, which is based on the literal and presupposes it.

St. Thomas goes on to subdivide the second or spiritual sense into the usual three: the allegorical, the moral, and the anagogical. But in his first division into two he has made the fundamental distinction, which St. Augustine expressed in terms of one meaning which is *in verbis* (in words) and another meaning which is *in facto* (in things). And, in reading his words, one may surely recall Dante's in the Letter: "nam primus sensus est qui habetur per litteram, alius est qui habetur per significata per litteram" ("for it is one sense that we get through the letter, and another which we get through the thing the letter signifies").

An allegory of poets and an allegory of theologians: the Letter to Can Grande does not make the distinction. The Letter is speaking of the way in which a poem is to be understood. And in choosing its example of allegory from Holy Scripture, the Letter is clearly looking to the kind of allegory which is the allegory of theologians; and is thus pointing to a poem in which the first and literal sense is to be taken as the first and literal sense of Holy Scripture is taken, namely as an historical sense. The well-known jingle on the four senses began, one recalls, "Littera *gesta* docet . . ." ("The literal teaches *conduct*").

But, before going further, let us ask if this matter can have more than antiquarian interest. When we read the *Divine Comedy* today, does it matter, really, whether we take its first meaning to be historical or fictive, since in either case we must enter into that willing suspension of disbelief required in the reading of any poem?

Indeed, it happens to matter very much, because with this poem it is not a question of one meaning but of two meanings; and the nature of the first meaning will necessarily determine the nature of the second—will say how we shall look for the second. In the case of a fictive first meaning, as in the "allegory of poets," interpretation will invariably speak in terms of an outer and an inner meaning, of a second meaning which is conveyed but also, in some way, deliberately concealed under the "shell" or the "bark" or the "veil" of an outer fictive meaning. This allegory of the poets, as Dante presents it in the *Convivio*, is essentially an allegory of "this for that," of "this figuration in order to give (and also to conceal) that meaning." Orpheus and the effects of his music yield the meaning that a wise man can tame cruel hearts. It should be noted that here we are not concerned with allegory as expressed in personification, but of an allegory of action, of event.

But the kind of allegory to which the example from Scriptures given in the Letter to Can Grande points is not an allegory of "this for that," but an allegory of "this *and* that," of this sense plus that sense. The verse in Scripture which says "When Israel went out of Egypt," has its first meaning in denoting a real historical event; and it has its second meaning because that historical event itself, having the Author that it had, can signify yet another event: our Redemption through Christ. Its first meaning is a meaning *in verbis;* its other meaning is a meaning *in facto,* in the event itself. The words have a real meaning in pointing to a real event; the event, in its turn, has meaning because events wrought by God are themselves as words yielding a meaning, a higher and spiritual sense.

But there was a further point about this kind of allegory of Scriptures: it was generally agreed that while the first literal meaning would always be there, *in verbis,* the second or spiritual meaning was not always to be found in all the things and events that the words pointed to. Some events yielded the second meaning, some did not. And it is this fact which best shows that the literal historical meaning of Scriptures was not necessarily a sense in the service of another sense, not therefore a matter of "this for that." It is this that matters most in the interpretation of the *Divine Comedy.*

The crux of the matter, then, is this: If we take the allegory of the *Divine Comedy* to be the allegory of poets (as Dante understood that allegory in the *Convivio*) then we shall be taking it as a construction in which the literal sense ought always to be expected to yield another sense because the literal is only a fiction devised to express a second meaning. In this view the first meaning, if it does not give another, true meaning, has no excuse for being. Whereas, if we take the allegory of the *Divine Comedy* to be the allegory of theologians, we shall expect to find in the poem a first literal meaning presented as a meaning which is not fictive but true, because the words which give that meaning point to events which are seen as historically true. And we shall see these events themselves reflecting a second meaning because their author, who is God, can use events as men use words. *But,* we shall not demand at every moment that the event signified by the words be in its turn as a word, because this is not the case in Holy Scripture.

One should have no difficulty in making the choice. The allegory of the *Divine Comedy* is so clearly the "allegory of theologians" (as the Letter to Can Grande by its example says it is) that one may only wonder at the continuing efforts made to see it as the "allegory of poets." What indeed increases the wonder at this effort is that every attempt to treat the first meaning of the poem as a fiction devised to convey a true but hidden meaning has been such a clear demonstration of how a poem may be forced to meanings that it cannot possibly bear as a poem.

It seems necessary to illustrate the matter briefly with a single and obvious example. All readers of the *Comedy,* whatever their allegorical credo, must recognize that Virgil, for instance, if he be taken statically, in isolation from the action of the poem, had and has, as the poem would see him, a real historical existence. He was a living man and he is now a soul dwelling in Limbo. Standing alone, he would have no other, no second meaning, at all. It is by having a role in the action of the poem that Virgil takes on a second meaning. And it is at this point that the view one holds of the nature of the first meaning begins to matter. For if this is the allegory of poets, then what Virgil does, like what Orpheus does, is a fiction devised to convey a hidden meaning which it ought to convey all the time, since only by conveying that other meaning is what he does justified at all. Instead, if this action is allegory as theologians take it, then this action must always have a literal sense which is historical and no fiction; and thus Virgil's deeds as part of the whole action may, in their turn, be as words signifying other things; but they do not have to do this all the time, because, being historical, those deeds exist simply in their own right.

But can we hesitate in such a choice? Is it not clear that Virgil can not and does not always speak and act as Reason, with a capital initial, and that to try to make him do this is to try to rewrite the poem according to a conception of allegory which the poem does not bear within itself?

If, then, the allegory of the *Divine Comedy* is the allegory of theologians, if it is an allegory of "this and that," if its allegory may be seen in terms of a first meaning which is *in verbis* and of another meaning which is *in facto*, what is the main outline of its allegorical structure?

In the simplest and briefest possible statement it is this: the journey to God of a man through three realms of the world beyond this life is what is given by the literal meaning. It points to the event. The event is that journey to God through the world beyond. "Littera *gesta* docet." The words of the poem have their first meaning in signifying that event, just as the verse of Psalms had its first meaning in signifying the historical event of the Exodus.

And then just as the event of the Exodus, being wrought by God, can give in turn a meaning, namely, our Redemption through Christ; so, in the event of this journey through the world beyond (an event which, as the poem sees it, is also wrought by God) we see the reflection of other meanings. These, in the poem, are the various reflections of man's journey to his proper end, not in the life after death, but here in this life, as that journey was conceived possible in Dante's day—and not only in Dante's day. The main allegory of the *Divine Comedy* is thus an allegory of action, of event, an event given by words which in its turn reflects, (*in facto*), another event. Both are journeys to God.

What, then, of the *Convivio*? Does not its "allegory of poets" contradict this "allegory of theologians" in the later work? It does, if a poet must always use one kind of allegory and may not try one in one work and one in another. But shall we not simply face this fact? And shall we not recognize that in this sense the *Convivio* contradicts not only the *Divine Comedy* in its allegory, but also the *Vita Nuova* where there is no allegory. The *Convivio* is Dante's attempt to use the "allegory of poets." And to have that kind of allegory and the kind of figure that could have a role in it—to have a Lady Philosophy who was an allegory of poets—he was obliged to rob the "donna pietosa" of the *Vita Nuova* of all real existence. And in doing this he contradicted the *Vita Nuova*.

The *Convivio* is a fragment. We do not know why Dante gave up the work before it was hardly under way. We do not know. We are, therefore, free to speculate. I venture to do so, and suggest that Dante abandoned the *Convivio* because he came to see that in choosing to build this work according to the allegory of poets, he had ventured down a false way; that he came to realize that a poet could not be a poet of rectitude and work with an allegory whose first meaning was a disembodied fiction.

The Letter to Can Grande declares that the end of the whole *Comedy* is "to remove those living in this life from the state of misery and lead them to the state of felicity." A poet of rectitude is one who is interested in directing the will of men to God. But a disembodied Lady Philosophy is not a *machina* which can bear the weight of lifting man to God because, in her, man finds no part of his own weight. Lady Philosophy did not, does not, will not, exist in the flesh. As she is constructed in the *Convivio* she comes to stand for Sapientia, for created Sapientia standing in analogy to uncreated Sapientia Which is the Word. Even so, she is word without flesh. And only the word made flesh can lift man to God. If the allegory of a Christian poet of rectitude is to support any weight, it will be grounded in the flesh, which means grounded in history—and will lift up from there. In short, the trouble with Lady Philosophy was the trouble which Augustine found with the Platonists: "But that the Word was made flesh and dwelt among us I did not read there."

Dante, then, abandons Lady Philosophy and returns to Beatrice. But now the way to God must be made open to all men: he constructs an allegory, a *machina*, that is, in which an historical Virgil, an historical Beatrice, and an historical Bernard replace that Lady in an action which is given, in its first sense, not as a beautiful fiction but as a real, historical event, an event remembered by one who was, as a verse of the poem says, the scribe of it. Historical and, by a Christian standard, beautiful as an

allegory because bearing within it the reflection of the true way to God in
this life—a way given and supported by the Word made flesh. With its first
meaning as an historical meaning, the allegory of the *Divine Comedy* is
grounded in the mystery of the Incarnation.

In his commentary on the poem written some half century after
the poet's death, Benvenuto da Imola would seem to understand the
allegory of the *Divine Comedy* to be the "allegory of theologians." To
make clear to some doubting reader the concept by which Beatrice has a
second meaning, he points to Rachel in Holy Scripture:

> Nec videatur tibi indignum, lector, quod Beatrix mulier carnea accipiatur
> a Dante pro sacra theologia. Nonne Rachel secundum historicam veritatem
> fuit pulcra uxor Jacob summe amata ab eo, pro qua habenda custodivit
> oves per XIIII annos, et tamen anagogice figurat vitam contemplativam,
> quam Jacob mirabiliter amavit? Et si dicis: non credo quod Beatrix vel
> Rachel sumantur unquam spiritualiter, dicam quod contra negantes prin-
> cipia non est amplius disputandum. Si enim vis intelligere opus istius
> autoris, oportet concedere quod ipse loquatur catholice tamquam perfectus
> christianus, et qui semper et ubique conatur ostendere se christianum.

> Let it not seem improper to you, reader, that Beatrice, a woman of flesh,
> should be taken by Dante as sacred Theology. Was not Rachel, according
> to historical truth, the beautiful wife of Jacob, loved exceedingly by him,
> to win whom he tended the sheep for fourteen years, and yet she figures
> the contemplative life which Jacob loved marvelously well? And if you
> say, I do not believe that Beatrice or Rachel ever had such spiritual
> meanings, then I say that against those who deny first principles there is
> no further disputing. For if you wish to understand the work of this
> writer, it is necessary to concede that he speaks in a catholic way as a
> perfect Christian and who always and everywhere strives to show himself
> a Christian.

Dr. Edward Moore once pointed, in a footnote, to these remarks
by the early commentator and smiled at them as words that throw "a
curious light on the logical processes of Benvenuto's mind." But Benvenuto's
words have, I think, a way of smiling back. And to make their smile more
apparent to a modern reader one might transpose them so:

> Let it not seem improper to you, reader, that this journey of a living man
> into the world beyond is presented to you in its first sense as literally and
> historically true. And if you say: "I do not believe that Dante ever went
> to the other world," then I say that with those who deny what a poem
> asks be granted, there is no further disputing.

ERICH AUERBACH

Figural Art in the Middle Ages

The figural interpretation, or to put it more completely, the figural view of history was widespread and deeply influential up to the Middle Ages, and beyond. This has not escaped the attention of scholars. Not only theological works on the history of hermeneutics but also studies on the history of art and literature have met with figural conceptions on their way, and dealt with them. This is particularly true of the history of art in connection with medieval iconography, and of the history of literature in connection with the religious theater of the Middle Ages. But the special nature of the problem does not seem to have been recognized; the figural or typological or phenomenal structure is not sharply distinguished from other, allegorical or symbolical, forms. A beginning is to be found in T. C. Goode's instructive dissertation on Gonzalo de Berceo's *El Sacrificio de la Misa* (Washington, 1933); although he does not go into fundamental questions, H. Pflaum shows a clear understanding of the situation in his *Die religiose Disputation in der europäischen Dichtung des Mittelalters* (Geneva-Florence, 1935). Recently (in *Romania*, LXIII) his sound understanding of the word *figure* enabled him to give a correct interpretation of some Old French verses that had been misunderstood by the editor and to restore the text. Perhaps other examples have escaped me, but I do not think that there is any systematic treatment of the subject. Yet such an investigation strikes me as indispensable for an understanding of the mixture of spirituality and sense of reality which characterizes the European Middle Ages and which seems so baffling to us.

From *Scenes from the Drama of European Literature.* Copyright © 1959 by Meridian Books.

In most European countries figural interpretation was active up to the eighteenth century; we find traces of it not only in Bossuet as might be expected, but many years later in the religious authors whom Groethuysen quotes in *Les Origines de la France bourgeoise*. A clear knowledge of its character and how it differed from related but differently structured forms would generally sharpen and deepen our understanding of the documents of late antiquity and the Middle Ages, and solve a good many puzzles. Might the themes that recur so frequently on early Christian sarcophagi and in the catacombs not be figures of the Resurrection? Or to cite an example from Mâle's great work, might not the legend of Maria Aegyptiaca, the representations of which in the Toulouse Museum he describes, be a figure of the people of Israel going out of Egypt, hence to be interpreted exactly as the Psalm *In exitu Israel de Aegypto* was generally interpreted in the Middle Ages?

But individual interpretations do not exhaust the importance of the figural method. No student of the Middle Ages can fail to see how it provides the medieval interpretation of history with its general foundation and often enters into the medieval view of everyday reality. The analogism that reaches into every sphere of medieval thought is closely bound up with the figural structure; in the interpretation of the Trinity that extends roughly from Augustine's *De Trinitate* to St. Thomas, I,q.45, art. 7, man himself, as the image of God, takes on the character of a *figura Trinitatis*. It is not quite clear to me how far aesthetic ideas were determined by figural conceptions—to what extent the work of art was viewed as the *figura* of a still unattainable fulfillment in reality. The question of the imitation of nature in art aroused little theoretical interest in the Middle Ages; but all the more attention was accorded to the notion that the artist, as a kind of figure for God the Creator, realized an archetype that was alive in his spirit. These, as we see, are ideas of Neoplatonic origin. But the question remains: to what extent were this archetype and the work of art produced from it regarded as figures for a reality and truth fulfilled in God? I have found no conclusive answer in the texts available to me here and the most important works of the specialized literature are lacking. But I should like to quote a few passages which happen to be at hand, and which point somewhat in the direction I have in mind. In an article on the representation of musical tones in the capitals of the Abbey of Cluny (*Deutsche Vierteljahrsschrift*, 7, p. 264) L. Schrade quotes an explanation of the word *imitari* by Remigius of Auxerre: *scilicet persequi, quia veram musicam non potest humana musica imitari* ("that is, to follow after, for the music of man cannot imitate the true music"). This is probably based on the notion that the artist's work is an imitation or at least a shadowy figuration of a true and likewise sensuous reality (the music of the heavenly choirs). In the *Purgatorio* Dante praises the works of art created by God himself, representing examples of virtues and vices, for their perfectly fulfilled sensuous truth, beside which human art and even nature pales (*Purg.*, 10 and 12); his invocation to Apollo (*Par.*, 1) includes the lines:

> O divina virtù, se mi ti presti
> tanto che l'ombra del beato regno
> segnata nel mio capo io manifesti

(O divine Virtue, if thou dost so far lend thyself to me, that I make manifest the shadow of the blessed realm imprinted on my brain.)
(Temple Classics ed., p. 5.)

Here his poetry is characterized as an *umbra* of truth, engraved in his mind, and his theory of inspiration is sometimes expressed in statements that may be explained along the same lines. But these are only suggestions; an investigation purporting to explain the relation between Neoplatonic and figural elements in medieval aesthetics would require broader foundations. Still, the present remarks suffice, I believe, to show the need for distinguishing the figural structure from the other forms of imagery. We may say roughly that the figural method in Europe goes back to Christian influences, while the allegorical method derives from ancient pagan sources, and also that the one is applied primarily to Christian, the other to ancient material. Nor shall we be going too far afield in terming the figural view the predominantly Christian-medieval one, while the allegorial view, modeled on pagan or not inwardly Christianized authors of late antiquity, tends to appear where ancient, pagan, or strongly secular influences are dominant. But such observations are too general and imprecise, for the many phenomena that reflect an intermingling of different cultures over a thousand years do not admit of such simple classifications. At a very early date profane and pagan material was also interpreted figurally; Gregory of Tours, for example, uses the legend of the Seven Sleepers as a figure for the Resurrection; the waking of Lazarus from the dead and Jonah's rescue from the belly of the whale were also commonly interpreted in this sense. In the high Middle Ages, the Sybils, Virgil, the characters of the *Aeneid*, and even those of the Breton legend cycle (e.g., Galahad in the quest for the Holy Grail) were drawn into the figural interpretation, and moreover there were all sorts of mixtures between figural, allegoric, and symbolic forms. All these forms, applied to classical as well as Christian material, occur in the work which concludes and sums up the culture of the Middle Ages: the *Divine Comedy*. But I shall now attempt to show that basically it is the figural forms which predominate and determine the whole structure of the poem.

At the foot of the mountain of Purgatory, Dante and Virgil meet a man of venerable mien, whose countenance is illumined by four stars signifying the four cardinal virtues. He inquires sternly into the legitimacy of their journey and from Virgil's respectful reply—after he has told Dante to kneel before this man—we learn that it is Cato of Utica. For after explaining his divine mission, Virgil continues as follows (*Purg.*, 1, 70–5):

> Or ti piaccia gradir la sua venuta.
> libertà va cercando, che è sì cara,
> come sa chi per lei vita rifiuta.
> Tu il sai, chè non ti fu per lei amara
> in Utica la morte, ove lasciasti
> la vesta che al gran dì sarà sì chiara.

(Now may it please thee to be gracious unto his coming: he seeketh freedom, which is so precious, as he knows who giveth up life for her.

Thou knowest it; since for her sake death was not bitter to thee in Utica, where thou leftest the raiment which at the great day shall be so bright.)

(Temple Classics ed., p. 7.)

Virgil goes on, asking Cato to favor him for the sake of the memory of Marcia, his former wife. This plea Cato rejects with undiminished severity; but if such is the desire of the *donna del ciel* (Beatrice), that suffices; and he orders that before his ascent Dante's face be cleansed of the stains of Hell and that he be girded with reeds. Cato appears again at the end of the second canto, where he sternly rebukes the souls just arrived at the foot of the mountain, who are listening in self-forgetfulness to Casella's song, and reminds them to get on with their journey.

It is Cato of Utica whom God has here appointed guardian at the foot of Purgatory: a pagan, an enemy of Caesar, and a suicide. This is startling, and the very first commentators, such as Benvenuto of Imola, expressed their bewilderment. Dante mentions only a very few pagans who were freed from Hell by Christ; and among them we find an enemy of Caesar, whose associates, Caesar's murderers, are with Judas in the jaws of Lucifer, who as a suicide seems no less guilty than those others "who have done themselves violence" and who for the same sin are suffering the most frightful torments in the seventh circle of Hell. The riddle is solved by the words of Virgil, who says that Dante is seeking freedom, which is so precious as you yourself know who have despised life for its sake. The story of Cato is removed from its earthly and political context, just as the stories of Isaac, Jacob, etc., were removed from theirs by the patristic exegetes of the Old Testament, and made into a *figura futurorum*. Cato is a *figura*, or rather the earthly Cato, who renounced his life for freedom, was a *figura*, and the Cato who appears here in the *Purgatorio* is the revealed or fulfilled figure, the truth of that figural event. The political and earthly freedom for which he died was only an *umbra futurorum*: a prefiguration of the Christian freedom whose guardian he is here appointed, and for the sake of which he here again opposes all earthly temptation; the Christian freedom from all evil impulses, which leads to true domination of self, the freedom for the acquisition of which Dante is girded with the rushes of humility, until, on the summit of the mountain, he actually achieves it and is crowned by Virgil as lord over himself. Cato's voluntary choice of death rather than political servitude is here introduced as a *figura* for the eternal freedom of the children of God, in behalf of which all earthly things are to be despised, for the liberation of the soul from the servitude of sin. Dante's choice of Cato for his role is explained by the position "above the parties" that Cato occupies according to the Roman authors, who held him up as a model of virtue, justice, piety, and love of freedom. Dante found him praised equally in Cicero, Virgil, Lucan, Seneca, and Valerius Maximus; particularly Virgil's *secretosque pios his dantem iura Catonem* (*Aeneid*, 8, 670) ("the righteous in a place apart, with Cato their lawgiver"), coming as it did from a poet of the Empire, must have made a great impression on him. His admiration for Cato may be judged from several passages in the *Convivio*, and in his *De Monarchia* (2, 5) he has a quotation from Cicero saying that Cato's voluntary death should be judged in a special light and connecting it with the examples of Roman political virtue to which Dante attached so much importance; in this passage Dante tries to show that Roman rule was legitimized by Roman virtue; that it fostered the justice and freedom of all mankind. The chapter contains this sentence: *Romanum imperium de fonte nascitur pietatis* ("the Roman Empire springs from the fount of justice").

Dante believed in a predetermined concordance between the Christian story of salvation and the Roman secular monarchy; thus it is not surprising that he should apply the figural interpretation to a pagan Roman— in general he draws his symbols, allegories, and figures from both worlds without distinction. Beyond any doubt Cato is a *figura*; not an allegory like the characters from the *Roman de la Rose*, but a figure that has become the truth. The *Comedy* is a vision which regards and proclaims the figural truth as already fulfilled, and what constitutes its distinctive character is precisely that, fully in the spirit of figural interpretation, it attaches the truth perceived in the vision to historical, earthly events. The character of Cato as a severe, righteous, and pious man, who in a significant moment in his own destiny and in the providential history of the world sets freedom above life, is preserved in its full historical and personal force; it does not become an allegory for freedom; no, Cato of Utica stands there as a unique individual, just as Dante saw him; but he is lifted out of the tentative earthly state in which he regarded political freedom as the highest good (just as the Jews singled out strict observance of the Law), and transposed into a state of definitive fulfillment, concerned no longer with the earthly works of civic virtue or the law, but with the *ben dell'intelletto*, the highest good, the freedom of the immortal soul in the sight of God.

Let us attempt the same demonstration in a somewhat more difficult case. Virgil has been taken by almost all commentators as an allegory for reason—the human, natural reason which leads to the right earthly order, that is, in Dante's view, the secular monarchy. The older commentators had no objection to a purely allegorical interpretation, for they did not, as we do today, feel that allegory was incompatible with authentic poetry. Many modern critics have argued against this idea, stressing the poetic, human, personal quality of Dante's Virgil; still, they have been unable either to deny that he "means something" or to find a satisfactory relation between this meaning and the human reality. Recently (and not only in connection with Virgil) a number of writers (L. Valli and Mandonnet, for example) have gone back to the purely allegorical or symbolic aspect and attempted to reject the historical reality as "positivistic" or "romantic." But actually there is no choice between historical and hidden meaning; both are present. The figural structure preserves the historical event while interpreting it as revelation; and must preserve it in order to interpret it.

In Dante's eyes the historical Virgil is both poet and guide. He is a poet and a guide because in the righteous Aeneas' journey to the underworld he prophesies and glorifies universal peace under the Roman Empire, the political order which Dante regards as exemplary, as the *terrena Jerusalem*; and because in his poem the founding of Rome, predestined seat of the secular and spiritual power, is celebrated in the light of its future mission. Above all he is poet and guide because all the great poets who came after him have been inflamed and inspired by his work; Dante not only states this for himself, but brings in a second poet, Statius, to proclaim the same thing most emphatically: in the meeting with Sordello and perhaps also in the highly controversial verse about Guido Cavalcanti (*Inf.*, 10, 63) the same theme is sounded. In addition, Virgil is a guide because, beyond his temporal prophecy, he also—in the Fourth Eclogue—

proclaimed the eternal transcendent order, the appearance of Christ which would usher in the renewal of the temporal world without, to be sure, suspecting the significance of his own words, but nevertheless in such a way that posterity might derive inspiration from his light. Virgil the poet was a guide because he had described the realm of the dead—thus he knew the way thither. But also as a Roman and a man, he was destined to be a guide, for not only was he a master of eloquent discourse and lofty wisdom but also possessed the qualities that fit a man for guidance and leadership, the qualities that characterize his hero Aeneas and Rome in general: *iustitia* and *pietas*. For Dante the historical Virgil embodied this fullness of earthly perfection and was therefore capable of guiding him to the very threshold of insight into the divine and eternal perfection; the historic Virgil was for him a *figura* of the poet-prophet-guide, now fulfilled in the other world. The historical Virgil is "fulfilled" by the dweller in limbo, the companion of the great poets of antiquity, who at the wish of Beatrice undertakes to guide Dante. As a Roman and poet Virgil had sent Aeneas down to the underworld in search of divine counsel to learn the destiny of the Roman world; and now Virgil is summoned by the heavenly powers to exercise a no less important guidance; for there is no doubt that Dante saw himself in a mission no less important than that of Aeneas: elected to divulge to a world out of joint the right order, which is revealed to him upon his way. Virgil is elected to point out and interpret for him the true earthly order, whose laws are carried out and whose essence is fulfilled in the other world, and at the same time to direct him toward its goal, the heavenly community of the blessed, which he has presaged in his poetry— yet not into the heart of the kingdom of God, for the meaning of his presage was not revealed to him during his earthly lifetime, and without such illumination he had died an unbeliever. Thus God does not wish Dante to enter His kingdom with Virgil's help; Virgil can lead him only to the threshold of the kingdom, only as far as the limit which his noble and righteous poetry was able to discern. "Thou first," says Statius to Virgil, "didst send me towards Parnassus to drink in its caves, and then didst light me on to God. Thou didst like one who goes by night, and carries the light behind him, and profits not himself, but maketh persons wise that follow him. . . . Through thee I was a poet, through thee a Christian." And just as the earthly Virgil led Statius to salvation, so now, as a fulfilled figure, he leads Dante: for Dante too has received from him the lofty style of poetry, through him he is saved from eternal damnation and set on the way of salvation; and just as he once illumined Statius, without himself seeing the light that he bore and proclaimed, so now he leads Dante to the threshold of the light, which he knows of but may not himself behold.

Thus Virgil is not an allegory of an attribute, virtue, capacity, power, or historical institution. He is neither reason nor poetry nor the Empire. He is Virgil himself. Yet he is not himself in the same way as the historical characters whom later poets have set out to portray in all their historical involvement, as for example, Shakespeare's Caesar or Schiller's Wallenstein. These poets disclose their historical characters in the thick of their earthly existence; they bring an important epoch to life before our eyes, and look for the meaning of the epoch itself. For Dante the meaning of every life has its place in the providential history of the world, the general lines of which are laid down in the Revelation which has been given to every Christian, and which is interpreted for him in the vision of the *Comedy*. Thus Virgil in the *Divine Comedy* is the historical Virgil himself, but then again he is not; for the historical Virgil is only a *figura* of the fulfilled truth that the poem reveals, and this fulfillment is more real, more significant than the *figura*. With Dante, unlike modern poets, the more fully the figure is interpreted and the more closely it is integrated with the eternal plan of salvation, the more real it becomes. And for him, unlike the ancient poets of the underworld, who represented earthly life as real and the life after death as shadow, for him the other world is the true reality, while this world is only *umbra futurorum*—though indeed the *umbra* is the prefiguration of the transcendent reality and must recur fully in it.

For what has been said here of Cato and Virgil applies to the *Comedy* as a whole. It is wholly based on a figural conception. In my study of Dante as a poet of the earthly world (1929) I attempted to show that in the *Comedy* Dante undertook "to conceive the whole earthly historical world . . . as already subjected to God's final judgment and thus put in its proper place as decreed by the divine judgment, to represent it as a world already judged . . . in so doing, he does not destroy or weaken the earthly nature of his characters, but captures the fullest intensity of their individual earthly-historical being and identifies it with the ultimate state of things." At that time I lacked a solid historical grounding for this view, which is already to be found in Hegel and which is the basis of my interpretation of the *Divine Comedy*; it is suggested rather than formulated in the introductory chapters of the book. I believe that I have now found this historical grounding; it is precisely the figural interpretation of reality which, though in constant conflict with purely spiritualist and Neoplatonic tendencies, was the dominant view in the European Middle Ages: the idea that earthly life is thoroughly real, with the reality of the flesh into which the Logos entered, but that with all its reality it is only *umbra* and *figura* of the authentic, future, ultimate truth, the real reality that will unveil and preserve the *figura*. In this way the individual earthly event is not regarded as a definitive self-sufficient reality, nor as a link in a chain of development in which single events or combinations of events perpetually give rise to new events, but viewed primarily in immediate vertical connection with a divine order which encompasses it, which on some future day will itself be concrete reality; so that the earthly event is a prophecy or *figura* of a part of a wholly divine reality that will be enacted in the future. But this reality is not only future; it is always present in the eye of God and in the other world, which is to say that in transcendence the revealed and true reality is present at all times, or timelessly. Dante's work is an attempt to give a poetic and at the same time systematic picture of the world in this light. Divine grace comes to the help of a man menaced by earthly confusion and ruin—this is the framework of the vision. From early youth he had been favored by special grace, because he was destined for a special task; at an early age he had been privileged to see revelation incarnated in a living being, Beatrice—and here as so often figural structure and Neoplatonism are intertwined. In her lifetime she had, though covertly, favored him with a salutation of her eyes and mouth; and in dying she had distinguished him in an unspoken mysterious way. When he strays from the right path, the departed Beatrice, who for him was revelation incarnate, finds the only possible salvation for him; indirectly she is his guide and in Paradise directly; it is she who shows him the unveiled order, the truth of the earthly figures. What he sees and learns in the three realms is true, concrete reality, in which the earthly *figura* is contained and interpreted; by seeing the fulfilled truth while still alive, he himself is saved, while at the same time he is enabled to tell the world what he has seen and guide it to the right path.

Insight into the figural character of the *Comedy* does not offer a universal method by which to interpret every controversial passage; but we can derive certain principles of interpretation from it. We may be certain that every historical or mythical character occurring in the poem can only mean something closely connected with what Dante knew of his historical or mythical existence, and that the relation is one of fulfillment and figure; we must always be careful not to deny their earthly historical existence altogether, not to confine ourselves to an abstract, allegorical interpretation. This applies particularly to Beatrice. The romantic realism of the nineteenth century overemphasized the human Beatrice, tending to make the *Vita Nova* a kind of sentimental novel. Since then a reaction has set in; the new tendency is to do away with her entirely, to dissolve her in an assortment of increasingly subtle theological concepts. But actually there is no reality in such a choice. For Dante the literal meaning or historical reality of a figure stands in no contradiction to its profounder meaning, but precisely "figures" it; the historical reality is not annulled, but confirmed and fulfilled by the deeper meaning. The Beatrice of the *Vita Nova* is an earthly person; she really appeared to Dante, she really saluted him, really withheld her salutation later on, mocked him, mourned for a dead friend and for her father, and really died. Of course this reality can only be the reality of Dante's experience—for a poet forms and transforms the events of his life in his consciousness, and we can take account only of what lived in his consciousness and not of the outward reality. It should also be borne in mind that from the first day of her appearance the earthly Beatrice was for Dante a miracle sent from Heaven, an incarnation of divine truth. Thus the reality of her earthly person is not, as in the case of Virgil or Cato, derived from the facts of a historic tradition, but from Dante's own experience: this experience showed him the earthly Beatrice as a miracle. But an incarnation, a miracle are real happenings; miracles happen on earth, and incarnation is flesh. The strangeness of the medieval view of reality has prevented modern scholars from distinguishing between figuration and allegory and led them for the most part to perceive only the latter. Even so acute a theological critic as Mandonnet considers only two possibilities: either Beatrice is a mere allegory (and this is his opinion) or she is [the daughter of Folco Portinan], a notion that he ridicules. Quite aside from the misunderstanding of poetic reality that such a judgment shows, it is surprising to find so deep a chasm between reality and meaning. Is the *terrena Jerusalem* without historical reality because it is a *figura aeternae Jerusalem?*

In the *Vita Nova*, then, Beatrice is a living woman from the reality of Dante's experience—and in the *Comedy* she is no *intellectus separatus*, no angel, but a blessed human being who will rise again in the flesh at the Last Judgment. Actually there is no dogmatic concept that would wholly describe her; certain events in the *Vita Nova* would not fit into any allegory, and in regard to the *Comedy* there is the additional problem of drawing an exact distinction between her and various other persons of the *Paradiso*, such as the Apostle-Examiners and St. Bernard. Nor can the special character of her relation to Dante be fully understood in this way. Most of the older commentators interpreted Beatrice as theology; more recent ones have sought subtler formulations; but this has led to exaggeration and mistakes: even Mandonnet, who applies to Beatrice the extremely broad notion of *ordre surnaturel*, derived from the contrast with Virgil, comes up with hairsplitting subdivisions, makes mistakes, and forces his concepts. The role that Dante attributes to her is perfectly clear from her actions and the epithets attached to her. She is a figuration or incarnation of revelation (*Inf.*, 2, 76): *sola per cui l'umana spezie eccede ogni contento da quel ciel, che ha minor li cerchi sui* ("through whom alone mankind excels all that is contained within the heaven which has the smallest circles"); (*Purg.*, 6, 45): *che lume fia tra il vero e l'intelletto* ("who shall be a light between truth and intellect") which, out of love (*Inf.*, 2, 72), divine grace sends to man for his salvation, and which guides him to the *visio Dei*. Mandonnet forgets to say that she is precisely an incarnation of divine revelation and not revelation pure and simple, although he quotes the pertinent passages from the *Vita Nova* and from St. Thomas, and the above-mentioned invocation, *O Donna di virtù, sola per cui*, etc. One cannot address the "supernatural order" as such, one can only address its incarnate revelation, that part of the divine plan of salvation which precisely is the miracle whereby men are raised above other earthly creatures. Beatrice is incarnation, she is *figura* or *idolo Christi* (her eyes reflect her twofold nature, *Purg.*, 31, 126) and thus she is not exhausted by such explanations; her relation to Dante cannot fully be explained by dogmatic considerations. Our remarks are intended only to show that theological interpretation, while always useful and even indispensable, does not compel us to abandon the historical reality of Beatrice—on the contrary.

With this we close for the present our study of *figura*. Our purpose was to show how on the basis of its semantic development a word may grow into a historical situation and give rise to structures that will be effective for many centuries. The historical situation that drove St. Paul to preach among the Gentiles developed figural interpretation and prepared it for the influence it was to exert in late antiquity and the Middle Ages.

ERICH AUERBACH

St. Francis of Assisi in Dante's "Commedia"

Few passages in the *Paradiso* are as well-known and as generally admired as the eleventh canto; this is not surprising, for its subject is St. Francis of Assisi and the verse is exceptionally beautiful. Yet the admiration for this canto is not entirely self-explanatory. Francis was one of the most impressive figures of the Middle Ages. The whole of the thirteenth century, which covered Dante's youth, was as it were impregnated with his personality. No contemporary habit of life, voice, or behavior have reached us as clearly as his. His character stood out by virtue of its many contrasts. His piety, at once solitary and popular, his character, at once sweet and austere, his appearance, at once humble and striking, have remained unforgettable. Legend, poetry, painting, made him their own, and long after his death, every mendicant friar in the street seemed to carry in himself something of his master, and so to spread it thousandfold. His personality undoubtedly contributed much toward awakening and sharpening the sense of the originality and distinctness of the individual, just that sense whose great monument is Dante's *Commedia*. From the encounter, therefore, of Dante and St. Francis, that is to say, from the entrance of Francis into the *Comedy*, we should expect one of the highlights of concrete life painting in which the *Comedy* is so rich. In the already half legendary biography of Francis, Dante found ample material for the portrayal of such an encounter. It is the more strange that he did not let it take place at all.

Nearly all the characters in the *Comedy* appear in person. Dante finds them in the place God's justice has appointed for them, and there, direct encounter is developed by question and answer. With Francis of Assisi it is otherwise. True, Dante sees him, right at the end of the poem, sitting in his seat in the white rose among the blessed of the New Testament; but he does not speak to him, and in the other passages where he is mentioned, he does not appear himself; not even in the most fundamental, the most detailed of these passages, namely the eleventh canto of the *Paradiso*, where Francis does not speak himself; instead, others give an account of him. However surprising this may be, the form and manner of the account are even more so.

Dante and Beatrice are in the Sun Heaven, surrounded by a caroling band of blessed spirits who interrupt their dancing to make themselves known as Fathers of the Church and philosophers. One of them, St. Thomas Aquinas, names and characterizes himself and his companions, and then they begin the dance again. Dante, however, has not understood the meaning of some of Thomas's words: "I was a lamb of Dominic's flock, where one finds good pasture if one does not stray." For this line—*u' ben s'impingua, se no si vaneggia*—(and also for another passage about Solomon), Dante needs an explanation. Thomas, who, like all the blessed, enjoys direct vision of the eternal light so that nothing of Dante's thought can remain hidden from him, fulfills the unspoken desire for interpretation of his words. Once again song and dance are interrupted so that Thomas, assisted by Bonaventura, can make a commentary on his words. The commentary fills three cantos. In the first of them, the eleventh canto, Thomas tells the life of St. Francis, and adds to it a lament over the decline of his own, the Dominican order; in the twelfth, conversely, the Franciscan Bonaventura recounts Dominic's life and closes with a censure of the Franciscans; the thirteenth canto contains, again from Thomas's mouth, the commentary on the utterance of King Solomon already mentioned. From the two cantos about the mendicant orders, Dante and the reader learn that both orders were founded with the same purpose, that they complement each other, and that in both orders alike the life of the founder was equally perfect and the decadence of the followers equally detestable; that, therefore, in each of them men thrive if they follow the example of the founder and do not stray from it. Both cantos make a didactic commentary, closely built into the framework of Dante's interpretation of history, with sharp polemical passages directed not only against the two orders, but against the papacy and clergy in general. Francis's life also belongs to the commentary. Thus, it is part of a commentary, several hundred lines long, on a subordinate clause which occupies only one line, and which could certainly have been made clear if presented more briefly. The frame, then, is this: Thomas, the great Church teacher, comments copiously on one of his own sayings. Such a procedure is entirely in character with Thomas: but is it suitable for a presentation of the biography of St. Francis? According to our modern way of thinking, no. Through study of the medieval background we have learned to understand the medieval method of commentary. We know that it grew out of the peculiar system of contemporary teaching. We may have discovered also that from the foliage of the epiphytes of commentaries and paraphrases there blossoms sometimes an unlooked-for flower where the supporting tree, that is to say, the text, gives little promise of it; and very often the text is completely hidden by the commentary. Indeed, when we think of many an illuminated initial, of many a liturgical sequence, this phenomenon is not restricted to literature. But here, where Dante is telling the life of St. Francis, could he not have found a less academic, a less scholastic frame?

Furthermore, the biography that Thomas gives contains only a very small part of all the enchanting and overwhelmingly concrete details preserved by the Franciscan legend. The essentials indeed, the birth, the building-up of the work, the death, he tells according to tradition, but he gives nothing of the individual stories to enliven the picture. Even the essentials are given in a documentary way, in chronological order: birth, the vow of poverty, the founding of the order, the ratification by Pope Innocent, the second ratification by Honorius, the journey to the Saracens, the stigmatization, death. Even the wall paintings at Assisi tell much more, and they tell it much more gaily, more anecdotally—not to speak of the other literary treatments of the legend. And there is still something to add: In Dante, besides the outward frame of the commentary of which it is part, the biography has also an inner leitmotiv, and an allegorical one. The life of St. Francis is represented as a marriage with an allegorical female figure, the Lady Poverty. We know of course that this was one of the themes of the Franciscan legend; but was it necessary to make this theme the predominant one? Insofar as we are specialists in medieval art or literature, we have learned gradually and a little laboriously that for certain groups in medieval spirituality, allegory meant something more real than it does for us; in allegory people saw a concrete realization of thought, an enrichment of possibilities of expression. But this did not prevent one of its most ardent and discerning modern interpreters, Huizinga, from calling it, almost slightly contemptuously, "the rank weeds of the late antique hot-house." In spite of all our knowledge of its meaning, we can no longer spontaneously feel its poetry. And yet Dante, who makes so many people speak directly, gives us the most living figure of the period before his own, Francis of Assisi, wrapped in the drapery of an allegorical account. What almost all later poets have done, what he himself so often did, the art in which he was the first master, that of fashioning people through their own words and gestures in the most concrete and personal way, he has not done here. The Church teacher Thomas recounts the wedding of the Saint with Lady Poverty so that Dante may understand the meaning of the sentence that a man finds good pasture in Dominic's flock if he does not stray.

If we think of the famous allegorical poems of late antiquity and of the Middle Ages, of Claudian's or Prudentius's works, of Alain de Lille or Jean de Meun, there is surely little in common between them and the biography of Francis in the *Comedy*. These works call up whole armies of allegorical figures, describe their persons, their clothes, their dwellings, make them discuss and fight with each other. Paupertas does indeed appear in some of these works, but as a vice or as the companion of a vice. Dante here introduces one single allegorical figure, Poverty, and connects her with a historical, that is to say, a concrete, real personality. This is something entirely different; he draws the allegory into actual life, he connects it closely with historical fact. It is, to be sure, not Dante's discovery; he inherited it with the whole theme from the Franciscan tradition, where, from the beginning, the wedding with Poverty appears as typical of the Saint's attitude. Very soon after his death a treatise was written with the title *Sacrum Commercium Beati Francisci cum Domina Paupertate*, and echoes of the theme are found frequently, for example, in the poems of Jacopone da Todi. But it was not fully worked out; it was scattered in many didactic and isolated anecdotes. The *Sacrum Commercium* contains nothing biographical at all, but is essentially a doctrinal writing, in which Lady Poverty makes a long discourse. Equally, the representation in the Lower Church at Assisi, formerly ascribed to Giotto, shows the wedding as far removed from all concrete biography. Christ unites the Saint and haggard, old, ragged Poverty, while on either side several rows of angel choirs take part in the celebration. It has nothing direct to do with the actual life of the saint; this was the subject of another cycle of pictures. Dante, on the contrary, combines the two; he links the wedding-feast with the impressive, even shrill scene in the market place at Assisi, where Francis openly renounces his patrimony, and gives his father back his clothes. The renunciation of patrimony and clothes, which emerges everywhere else as the intrinsic event of the story, is not explicitly mentioned by Dante; it is woven into the allegorical marriage. Here Francis breaks free from his father for the sake of a woman, a woman nobody wants, whom everyone rejects as if she were death; before all eyes, before the eyes of the bishop, before the eyes of his father, he joins himself to her. Here both the particular and the universal meanings of the incident are at once brought more clearly into prominence than could be revealed through the bare renunciation of particular things. He rejects his father's goods and breaks free from his father not because he wants *not* to possess anything, but because he desires something else and strives to possess that. He does it for the sake of love, for the sake of a desire, which involuntarily wakens memories of other similar occasions when young men have left their families for the sake of evil women who have inflamed their desires. Shamelessly, in the sight of all, Francis casts in his lot with a woman scorned by all, and the reminiscences of bad women become more and more vivid as the theme is elaborated, as we shall see from closer study. It is therefore a strange marriage, repellent according to usual standards, a base union which is here celebrated, bound with strife against his own father, openly, shrilly, and for this very reason more full of significance than the giving back of the clothes, which evokes the contrast between abjectness and sanctity much less than the marriage with a despised woman. And here another memory awakens, of Him who once formerly celebrated another such wedding, of Him who married a despised, abandoned woman, poor rejected humanity, the daughter of Sion. He also, of his free will, gave away his inheritance to follow his love for the abandoned one. The conception that Francis revealed, in his life and destiny, certain correspondences with the life of Christ, the theme of imitation or conformity, has always been fostered lovingly by Franciscan tradition. Bonaventura's biography is dominated by this conception, which also appears in painting, first in the Lower Church of Assisi, where five incidents from the life of Christ are placed opposite five corresponding ones from the life of Francis. The conformity appears also in many particulars, such as the number of disciples, in the community life with them, in the various miracles, and above all, in the stigmatization. Dante did not work the theme out in detail, indeed in general he gives no details; but he consciously worked it into the mystical marriage, thus following it not in isolated occurrences but in the whole and in the fundamentals; although in a way that made it more directly clear to the medieval reader than to the modern.

The biography that Thomas of Aquinas here tells begins with a description of the topography of Assisi. "From this slope," Thomas then continues, "a sun came into the world, shining like the earthly sun when it is rising. Who speaks of this place should call it not Ascesi, but the Orient." This play on words can only serve to emphasize the comparison between Francis's birth and the rising sun; but *sol oriens, oriens ex alto*, is a very widespread medieval conception of Christ himself (following Luke 1:78 and several passages containing the symbol of light in John); this symbol is based on myths much older than Christianity, firmly rooted in the Mediterranean countries, especially in connection with a mystical marriage. For Dante, the birth of the Lord, the marriage of the Lamb, and the vision of Virgil's Fourth Eclogue, which was to him and his contemporaries a prophecy of Christ, were blended with the figure of the Sun-Child as the Saviour of the world for whom the mystical wedding is appointed. There is no doubt therefore that by the comparison with the rising sun, directly followed by the mystical marriage as the first confirmation of the sun-like power of the Saint, Dante wanted to sound the note of conformity to, or imitation of, Christ, and to work it out fully. The metaphor of the rising sun is an exceedingly joyful introduction to which the bitterness of the marriage, ugly and repulsive, stands out in effective contrast. The contrast has already been long prepared-for, and I do not believe by accident. The theme of the mystical marriage has indeed been introduced twice before, briefly, once in a very lovely, once in a solemn and sublime way, both times with all the enchanting beauty of which Dante is capable. The first time it appears as an image, in the simile of the carol of the blessed spirits as a peal of bells ringing to matins, at the end of Canto 10 (ll. 139–46):

> Indi come orologio, che ne chiami
> nell' ora che la sposa di Dio surge
> a mattinar lo sposo perchè l'ami,
> che l'una parte l'altra tira ed urge,
> tin tin sonando con sì dolce nota,
> che il ben disposto spirto d'amor turge;
> così vid'io la gloriosa rota
> moversi . . .

(Then as the horologue, that calleth us, what hour the spouse of God riseth to sing her matins to her spouse that he may love her, wherein one part drawing and thrusting other, giveth a chiming sound of so sweet note, that the well-ordered spirit with love swelleth; so did I see the glorious wheel revolve . . .)

(Temple Classics ed., pp. 125 f.)

Here the theme is indicated only by a simile, but it is made concrete by all its charming joyousness, by its *dolcezza*; here as in the following passage, the bridegroom is Christ, and the Church, that is to say, Christendom, is the bride. In the second place, just before the beginning of the *Vita Francisci*, it is more dramatic, more fundamental and more significant: it directly concerns the marriage on the Cross itself. At the beginning of his commentary speech, Thomas wants to elucidate for Dante the purpose of Providence. Two leaders, he says (namely, Francis and Dominic), were sent by Providence so that the Church could make her way to Christ with steps more sure and true; and this "so that" sentence runs (*Par.*, 11, 31–4):

> però che andasse ver lo suo diletto
> la sposa di colui, ch'ad alte grida
> disposò lei col sangue benedetto,
> in sè sicura ed anco a lui più fida . . .

(In order that the spouse of him, who with loud cries espoused her with the blessed blood, might go toward her delight, secure within herself and faithfuller to him . . .)

(Temple Classics ed., p. 133.)

This is no longer charming, it is solemn and exalted; the whole history of the world after Christ is, for Dante, enclosed in the image of the bride who goes to her Beloved. Here also the joyousness, the jubilant passion of the nuptials is very strong; true, the bitterness of the agony of that marriage on the Cross is indicated; with a loud cry, through the holy blood, it is consummated; but now "It is finished," and the triumph of Christ is accomplished.

The two passages, one lovely, one solemn-sublime, both full of nuptial joy, stand as two preannouncements, just as the sun-birth does, in sharp aesthetic contrast with the wedding for which they prepare the way. Shrilly, with the discord of the struggle against the father, with the hard rhyme-words *guerra* and *morte*, this celebration begins. And above all, the bride: she is neither named nor described, but she is such that no one will open the gates of desire to her—as little as to death (*la morte*). It seems to me absolutely necessary to interpret the opening of the gates of desire in the proper sense as a sexual act, and thus *porta* as the gateway to the feminine body. The other explanation preferred by many commentators, that the reference is to the door of the house, which denies entrance to poverty or death, can indeed be supported by many passages from various texts where it is said that neither to knocking death nor to knocking poverty will anyone open the door: it does not, however, fit the bridal context, and it does not sufficiently explain *porta del piacere*; furthermore, Dante would certainly have avoided such a strongly obtrusive possibility of a sexual explanation if he had not expressly intended it: it corresponds perfectly to the concrete impression of the bitterly repulsive that he here evokes in general. Thus, no one likes the woman that Francis has chosen, she is despised and shunned, for centuries she has waited in vain for a

lover—one of the old commentators, Jacopo della Lana, explicitly stresses
that she has never said no to anyone—but Francis, the sun rising from
Mount Subasio, openly unites himself to this woman whose name is still
not given, but whose portrayal must waken in every hearer the image of a
harlot, old, contemptible, hideous, but still thirsty for love. From now on
he loves her more from day to day. More than a thousand years ago she
was robbed of her first husband (Christ, although He is not named), and
since then she has lived scorned and abandoned until Francis appeared.
Nothing availed her, neither that she bestowed peaceful security on her
companion, the fisher Amiclates (according to Lucan), during a visit,
from Caesar; nor that, strong and courageous, she mounted the cross with
Christ, and, as Mary herself, remained at the foot of it. Now, of course, it
is clear who she is, and now Thomas gives her name: but the sublime and
heroic figure of Paupertas is still not free from a grotesque and bitter
aftertaste. That a woman should climb on the cross with Christ is in itself
rather a stage conception; still stranger is the application of the allegory to
the winning of the first disciple. However one may interpret the obscure
sentence vv. 76–8 syntactically, the general sense is quite clear: the
harmonious community of wedded love between Francesco and Povertà
rouses in others the deisre to take part in such happiness; first Bernard (of
Quintavalle) took his shoes off and began "to run after this peace, and
while he ran, he seemed to himself still to be too slow"; then Egidio and
Silvestro took their shoes off and followed the spouse, the young husband;
so much did the bride please them!

    To the grotesque and dreadful picture of sexual union with a
despised woman, who is called poverty or death and who manifests the
meaning of her name in her outward appearance, is here allied an image
that, to later aesthetic taste, would be improper to the point of being
intolerable: the pious, ecstatic adherence of the first disciples is presented
as a love-thirsty pursuit of the wife of another. In the Christian Middle
Ages, at the beginning of the fourteenth century, such images were just as
telling as they are today, but the form of the impression was different. The
corporeal, intense and plastic, found in erotic imagery: to run after a
woman, to be sexually united to her, was not felt as improper but as a
symbol of fervency. To later taste, of course, the combination of such
differing spheres, the mingling of what goes even as far as physical
indignity with the highest spiritual dignity, is hard to tolerate, and even
today when people tend much more to admire extreme mixtures of style in
modern art; yet in a generally honored poet like Dante such passages are
seldom understood in their full meaning. For the most part they are
neither noticed nor read twice. Of course, it would be even worse to read

into them an anarchical extremism as it exists now, and for very serious reasons; Dante is doubtless often "expressionistic" to the highest degree, but this expressionism grows out of a complex heritage; it knows what it wants to express and does so.

The model for a style in which the utmost grandeur is combined with the utmost degradation, according to this world, was the story of Christ, and this brings us back to our text. Francis, the imitator of Christ, now lives with his beloved and his companions, all of them girt with the cord of humility. He is also, like his beloved, allergic to outward appearance, and of mean descent; but this does not make him mean-spirited. Rather, like a king he reveals his "harsh intention," namely the foundation of the mendicant order, to the Pope; because he is, like Christ, the poorest and the most despised of the poor, and at the same time a king. And as in the first part of the *Vita* humility comes more to the fore, so, in the second part, which deals with the papal ratification, the journey to the Saracens, his stigmatization and death, his triumph and transfiguration come out more strongly. Royally he discloses his plan to the Pope, and obtains the ratification; the band of friars minor grows, following him whose life could better be sung in the glory of Heaven; the Holy Ghost crowns his work through Pope Honorius; and after he had in vain sought martyrdom among the heathen, he receives from Christ Himself, in his own country on the rugged slope between the Tiber and the Arno, the last seal that confirms his imitation: the stigmata. When it pleases God to reward him for his humility with death and eternal blessedness, he commends his beloved to the true love of his brethren who are his lawful heirs; and from her bosom, the bosom of Poverty, his glorious soul climbs upward to return to its kingdom; for the body he wishes no other bier than the very bosom of Poverty. The whole concludes in a strong rhythmical, rhetorical surge that leads on to the denunciation of the later Dominicans; Thomas challenges his listener, Dante, to measure the greatness of Francis against that of the other leader, Dominic, who founded the order to which Thomas himself belonged: *Pensa oramai qual fu colui . . .*

Beyond doubt Poverty is an allegory. Yet the concrete details of the life of poverty—as elsewhere the *Sacrum Commercium* lists them—would not have evoked so genuine a shudder as the description, briefly but impressively worked out here, of nuptials with an old, hideous, and despised woman. The bitterness, the physically and morally repellent disagreeableness of such a union shows the greatness of the saintly resolution with strong sensuous power; and it shows also the antithetical truth that only love is capable of realizing this resolution. In the *Sacrum Commercium* a feast is celebrated, during which it turns out successively that the brothers possess only half an earthenware vessel to wash their hands with, no cloth to dry them with, only water to wash the bread down with, only wild herbs to eat with the bread, no salt wherewith to salt the bitter herbs, no knife to clean them with or to cut the bread with. One cannot altogether suppress a certain disgust at this enumeration and description; they produce an effect of pedantry, paltriness, and self-consciousness. It is different immediately when one single dramatic act of voluntary poverty is related, such as is often found in the legends of the saints; for example, the scene in Greccio where he sees the brothers through the window, eating at an all too well-decorated table: he borrows the hat and staff of a beggar, goes loudly begging to the door, and, as a poor pilgrim, begs for admission and food; when the astounded brothers, who naturally recognize him, give him the desired plate, he sits with it in the ashes and says: *modo sedeo ut frater minor.* This is a scene that beautifully expresses the peculiar emotional effect of his behavior, but it still does not express the whole meaning of his life. To complete the picture, many similar anecdotes would have been necessary, each contributing a detail to the whole; the biographical and legendary tradition accomplished this, but there was no room for it in the *Commedia.* Moreover, this was not its task. The anecdotes of the legend were known to everyone; more than that, Francis of Assisi had been, on the whole, a clearly defined figure for a long time in the consciousness of all his contemporaries. Otherwise than with many less famous or more hotly debated characters appearing in the *Commedia,* Dante had here a firmly outlined pattern for his subject, and his task was to present this pattern so that it stood out in the larger context of Francis's significance. The reality of the saint's character had to be sustained not as the specific aim of the presentation, but as fitting into the order in which that character was placed by Providence; the personal reality of the saint had to be subordinated to his office, it had to shine forth from the office. It was for this reason that Dante did not describe a meeting in which the saint could reveal or express himself in an intimate way; instead he wrote a *Vita,* a saint's life. Dante could scarcely let the founders of both mendicant orders proclaim with their own lips the great significance that he, Dante, attaches to their efficacy. He presents it through the two Great Church teachers, Thomas and Bonaventura, both of them products of the orders. In both *Vitae* the character is subordinated to the office, or rather to the mission, to which they were called. With the cherubically wise Dominic, whose office was teaching and preaching, and whose character could not be compared with that of the seraphically ardent Francis in popularity, the individual biography receded even further, and in its place comes an abundance of images: the bridegroom of faith, the gardener of Christ, the vine-dresser in the vineyard, the champion of the sowing of Holy Scripture, the torrent over the fields of the heretic, the wheel on the Church's war-chariot. All these are symbols for the office. The *Vita Francisci* is much nearer to life, but it also is subordinated to the office; here there is only a single sustained image, that of the wedding with Poverty, which fixes the form of the life and at the same time ranges it under the banner of the office. The office is thus the decisive factor in the biography of Francis also, the realism of the life must be subordinate, and the allegory of Poverty serves just this purpose. It combines the saint's mission with the peculiar atmosphere of his personality, rendering the latter with the utmost intensity, but always under the banner of the office; just as Francis himself had revealed his personality. His strong and passionate personal realism never wandered at large (*vaneggiava*), but poured itself into his office. "Franzisce" said God to the saint in a German Passional, "take the bitter thing for the sweet, and spurn thyself that thou mayest acknowledge me." Take the bitter thing for the sweet . . . Is there indeed anything more bitter than union with such a woman? But Francis took it, as Dante shows, for a sweet thing. All bitter things are embraced in this union, all that could be construed as bitterness and self-contempt is contained in it, together with love that is stronger than all bitterness, sweet beyond all sweetness, and the avowal of Christ.

Yes, certainly Paupertas is an allegory; but she is not introduced, much less described, as such; we learn nothing about her appearance, nothing about her clothes, as is usual in allegories elsewhere; we do not even learn her name at first. To begin with, we hear only that Francis loves a woman in spite of the whole world, and that he unites himself to her; her appearance comes to us only indirectly, but so impressively that it is distinct, for all the world shuns her like death, and, abandoned and despised, she has waited a very long time for a lover.

She does not speak, either, as Poverty speaks in the *Sacrum Commercium*, or as the allegorical figures Want, Debt, Care, and Distress speak in the last act of the second part of Goethe's *Faust*; she is only the mute beloved of the Saint, bound to him much more tightly and truly even than Care to Faust. The didactic strain in the allegory thus penetrates our consciousness not as a didactic lesson but as a real happening. As Francis's wife, Poverty exists in concrete reality; but, because Christ was her first husband, her concrete reality becomes part of the great scheme of the world history, of the dogmatic plan. Paupertas links Francis with Christ, she establishes the role of Francis as the *imitator Christi*. Of the three motifs in our text that point toward the imitation—*Sol oriens*, mystical marriage, stigmatization—the second, the mystical marriage, is by so far the most important in this respect, that the two others and Francis's whole attitude are made to develop from it. As the second husband of Poverty he is the successor to or imitator of Christ.

Succession to or imitation of Christ is for all Christians a fixedly pointed goal as it appears from many passages in the New Testament. In the first century of the Church Militant it was shown through the blood testimony of the martyrs that the succession was to be accomplished not morally only in the observance of commandments and in imitation of virtues, but integrally through sufferings like or similar martyrdom. Again and again after this period the integral following of Christ, the imitation of his destiny, was striven for; so that even a hero's death in battle against unbelievers came to be felt as a form of succession. In twelfth century mysticism, apparently chiefly through Bernard of Clairvaux and his Cistercian followers, there developed an ecstatic feeling that sought to achieve an integral imitation of the Saviour through absorption in Christ's suffering, thus in an essentially contemplative way, one in which the inward experience of the Passion, *unio mystica passionalis*, was regarded as the highest stage of the contemplative absorption. So far Francis of Assisi is a continuer of the Cistercian passionate-mysticism, for in his nature also, indeed at its strongest in his nature, the experience of the Passion appears as *ultimo sigillo*; but the path to it is much more active and nearer to life. The succession is based in the first place not on contemplation, but on poverty and humility, on imitation of the poor and humble life of Christ. To the mystical spirituality of the succession, Francis gave a foundation resting directly on Scripture, directly practical and immediately based on life; the imitation of the practical poverty and humility of Christ. This concrete renewal of the integral succession is the reason why Francis was acknowledged by his contemporaries as worthy to receive the stigmata: no one else re-formed the idea of integral succession from the bottom as he did.

Now it becomes clear that Dante could present the reality of the saint's figure in no more simple or immediate way than through the mystical marriage with Poverty, the basis of his *imitatio Christi*. This fitted Francis into the scheme of world history to which, in Dante's view, he belonged: a scheme that in his period was still extremely alive. For the medieval period, and even late into the modern world, a significant occurrence or a significant figure was "significant" in the literary sense; it meant fulfillment of a plan, fulfillment of something foreordained, repeating confirmation of something in the past and prophesying something to come. In an earlier essay on "*figura*" I have tried to show how the so-called typological interpretation of the Old Testament, in which the events are construed as practical prophecies of the fulfillment in the New Testament, particularly the incarnation and the sacrificial death of Christ, created a new system of interpretation of history and actuality which dominated the Middle Ages and decisively influenced Dante; I must refer the reader to this essay and can here only indicate that the figurative interpretation establishes a relationship between two happenings, both of which are historical, in which each one becomes significant not only in itself but also for the other, and the other in turn emphasizes and completes the first. In the classical examples, the second is always the incarnation of Christ and the happenings connected with it, which led to the liberation and the rebirth of man; and the whole is a synthetic interpretation of the pre-Christian world history in view of the incarnation of Christ. Now the integral imitation with which we are dealing here in the mystical marriage of Francis with Poverty is as it were a recurring figure; it repeats certain characteristic themes of Christ's life, renews them and revivifies them for all to see, and at the same time renews the office of Christ as the good shepherd whom the herd must follow. *Io fui degli agni della santa greggia che Domenico mena per cammino*, says Thomas, and Francis is named as archimandrite. The figure and the imitation together make an image of the completed teleological view of history whose center is the incarnation of Christ; this creates the boundaries between the old and the new covenants; one remembers that the number of the blessed in both covenants, as they are presented in Dante's white rose in the Empyrean, will at the end of all days be exactly the same, and that on the side of the New Covenant, only a few seats were still unoccupied—the end of the world was not far off. But, among the saints of the New Covenant, Francis takes a special place in the white rose, opposite the great patriarchs of old, and just as these were precursors, so he, the stigmatized bridegroom of Poverty, is the most outstanding among the later followers of Christ, appointed to guide the herd along the right way, to support the Bride of Christ that she may hasten to her beloved with sure and true steps.

All these relationships were spontaneously recognizable to the medieval reader, for he lived in them; the presentations of forerunning and after-following repetitions were as familiar to him as the conception of historical development is to a modern reader; men thought of even the appearance of Antichrist as an exact, but delusive repetition of the appearance of Christ. We have lost the spontaneous understanding of this conception of history; we are obliged to reconstruct it through research. But it kindled Dante's inspiration, and we can still feel the glow of it; in spite of our antipathy to allegory, the living reality of the eleventh canto of the *Paradiso* grips us; a living reality that only lives here, in the verse of the poet.

R. E. KASKE

Dante's "DXV"

In Canto 32 of the *Purgatorio*, we are shown an allegorical survey of the fortunes of the Church Militant. The triumphal car of the heavenly procession (the Church) has been left by the Griffon (Christ) bound firmly to the great tree (lines 49–60). After the ascension of the Griffon (89), the car is assailed by a series of allegorical enemies representing major vicissitudes in the history of the Church: an eagle (112–7); a she-fox (118–23); a gift of feathers left in the car by the eagle on a second visit (124–9, 137–8); and a dragon (130–5). The result of these assaults is to turn the once triumphal chariot into a broken, feathered, seven-headed monster (136–47); and the end of *Purg.* 32 finds it possessed by 'una puttana sciolta' obviously recalling the *meretrix magna* of the Apocalypse, together with a ferocious giant introduced as her lover (148–60). It is with reference to these final outrages that Beatrice, in the following canto, delivers her prophecy concerning 'a Five Hundred, Ten, and Five' (or a *D*, *X*, and *V*), which has made an honest reputation as one of the most perverse cruxes in literary history:

> Know that the vessel the serpent broke was and is not, but let him that has the blame be assured that God's vengeance fears no sop. Not for all time shall the eagle be without heir that left its feathers on the car so that it became monster. . . .

The basis for this strange allusion can be found, I believe, in a well established medieval allegorization of a monogram that appears consistently in the liturgical books of Dante's time. Then as now, the Canon of

From *Traditio: Studies in Ancient and Medieval History, Thought and Religion*, vol. 17 (1961). Copyright © 1961 by Fordham University.

the Mass was immediately preceded by a short series of prayers called the Preface, beginning with the words 'It is truly meet and just, right and availing unto salvation, that we at all times and in all places give thanks to Thee, O holy Lord, Father almighty, everlasting God. . . .' In missals and sacramentaries from the ninth century through at least the early part of the fourteenth, this liturgical formula commonly begins with some form of the monogram **⊕** —composed of the initial letters of the opening words 'Vere dignum,' joined and embellished by the cross which results from an added horizontal stroke at their center. Though properly representing the two words 'Vere dignum,' the monogram is often substituted for various larger segments of the opening formula, down to '. . . eterne Deus'; on the other hand, it sometimes stands only for 'Vere' plus the initial d of 'dignum,' or for the word 'Vere' alone, or even for the single letter V. From the ninth century on, but particularly during the twelfth and the thirteenth, this picturesque but familiar character is a favorite subject for illumination. . . .

Among twelfth- and thirteenth-century liturgists, the monogram **⊕** is conventionally interpreted as a symbol of the mysterious union of natures in Christ—the V signifying His human nature, the D His divine. This explanation, apparently invented in the twelfth century by John Beleth, is repeated near the end of that century by Sicard of Cremona; in the latter part of the thirteenth, it is expanded by the great liturgist William Durandus. . . . A simpler version is incorporated into the *Mammotrectus*, a popular compendium written by an Italian Franciscan, John Marchesini of Reggio, not far from the year 1300. . . .

So far, then, the monogram **⊕** offers us the two end-letters of Dante's *DXV* in reverse order, along with a potentially interesting allegorical interpretation of them; but no central X. Various strong suggestions of an X do exist within the monogram, however, particularly in the vicinity of the juncture between the V and the D. Most simply and consistently, the vertical centerline of the **⊕** itself, with its curving forks at the top and bottom, bears an inevitable resemblance to medieval forms of X in which the point of juncture appears vertically elongated; and this structural likeness is sometimes greatly heightened by features of individual design. Occasionally, the horizontal arm of the central cross is modified into some semblance of an ornamental X. More complex and varied suggestions of a central X in the monogram are frequently created by its decorative detail. An especially provocative example is the geometrical design, where the number of possible X's, large and small, seems limited only by the responsiveness of the eye. More often, decorative branches, tendrils, or foliage within the two open spaces of the **⊕** take the form of a single large

X—sometimes luxuriantly curved—with its point of juncture apparently hidden behind that of the central cross. Smaller but more distinct decorative X's are particularly frequent at the top and/or bottom forks of the vertical center-line; they are also found at the center of the cross, and sometimes on its horizontal or vertical arms. I do not mean to insist, of course, that these decorative devices were necessarily intended as alphabetical X's by the men who drew them; my argument is that the poetic imagination of Dante, alive as it must have been to possible significances of design, would surely have had little difficulty in finding visual suggestions of an X at or near the center of the monogram ⊕ , particularly in highly ornamented examples. Some such analytic approach to decorative detail, indeed, could hardly have been altogether foreign to the informed reader of illuminated manuscripts—in which one or more of the opening words of a chapter are sometimes incorporated, letter by letter, into the detail of the large illuminated initial.

Besides these purely visual suggestions, the center of the monogram ⊕ contains at least two possible kinds of figurative X. The first is the cross which is a constant feature of the monogram, and which, as we have seen, is explained by medieval liturgists as the Cross of Christ. The inevitable connection between the Cross and the letter X is expressed, for example, by Isidore in the *Etymologiae*: "the letter X, which both signifies the Cross in a figurative sense, and designates the number ten." A second and more important figurative X is the pictorial representation of Christ Himself at the center of the monogram, which becomes especially popular in the twelfth and thirteenth centuries; one hardly needs to be reminded of the standard medieval designation χ$\bar{\varrho}$s or of its further abbreviation to a Greek χ, naturally associated with Latin X. This picture of Christ in the monogram is always strongly Apocalyptic—is, in fact, the conventional *Maiestas Domini* or picture of Christ in glory, familiar in illustrations of the Apocalypse and in portrayals of the Last Judgment generally. Besides appearing within the ⊕ itself, the *Maiestas Domini* becomes in a larger way the distinctive iconographical feature of the Preface in medieval missals and sacramentaries—sometimes accompanying the monogram independently, sometimes replacing it altogether, and sometimes partly absorbing it. . . .

I propose, then, that in Dante's *DXV* we are to recognize a symmetrical reversal of this monogrammatic 'VXD'; that the D and the V represent Christ's divine and human natures respectively, just as in the medieval allegorization of the monogram; and that the central X represents the person Christ as the meeting-point of these two natures—paralleling the significance of the cross at the center of the monogram, 'per quam

diuinis sociantur et vniuntur humana.' This interpretation of the X receives incidental support from the common association of the letter X
with the name 'Christ,' as well as from the corresponding position of the
Maiestas Domini—a picture of the person Christ—between the V and the
D of the monogram. If all this is so, it seems that the event prophesied by
Beatrice must surely be a future coming of Christ, the *Deus-homo*—whether
to be thought of as the traditional second coming, or in terms of some less
orthodox eschatology. Such an interpretation is in turn strongly supported
by the Apocalyptic character of the *Maiestas Domini* in the monogram,
particularly in view of the Apocalyptic imagery of the preceding canto;
and possibly also by the traditional prominence of the Cross (signified by
the cross within the monogram) at Christ's final coming, following a
standard exegesis of the 'signum Filii hominis in caelo' of Matt. 24.30. By
a rather striking coincidence, the V and D of the monogram correspond
also to the initial letters of the Italian words *Uomo (Vomo)* and *Dio*.

For Dante's reversal of the D and the V there are several plausible
explanations, probably more or less complementary. If, as I intend to
suggest presently, the full meaning of Dante's symbol embraces also the
numerical values of the three letters as components of a single larger
number, the order *D–X–V* would in fact be the only one possible. This
reversal does, however, contribute to the theological coherence of the
figure as well, by making the D of Christ's divine nature precede the V of
His human nature instead of vice versa. A subtler significance is perhaps
created by the position of the monogram ⊕ at the beginning of the
Preface of the Mass, 'in preconio saluatoris'—looking forward to a real
re-enactment of the sacrifice on the Cross, the completion of Christ's
historical first coming. If in these terms we can allow ourselves to conceive of this monogrammatic 'VXD' as an anticipation of the first coming,
with the precedence of V signifying the greater outward prominence of
Christ's humanity, Dante's reversal of the letters to *DXV* may be seen as a
dramatic 'preconium' of the divinity which will shine forth at Christ's
final coming. In any case, this symmetrical reversal of the three letters
seems much more in accord with Dante's usual practice than do the various
other rearrangements sometimes proposed—most notably, the transparently simple and imaginatively rather unrewarding change from *DXV* to
DVX, or 'Dux.'

But if this really is Dante's intended significance, why has he
chosen to introduce an already enigmatic figure by way of the further
numerical conundrum 'un cinquecento diece e cinque'? A superficial
though not altogether irrelevant answer might be that Beatrice's prophecy
is expressly called an 'enigma forte' (50); for a more precise explanation,

we must turn at this point to a somewhat anticipatory discussion of Dante's giant—who has been introduced along with the whore as a usurper of the car (32.151–60), and is to be killed with her by the *DXV* (33.44–5). According to a common medieval exegesis of Gen. 6.2,4, the giants of the Old Testament were double-natured, born of a union between the sons of God and the daughters of men. So pervasive is this idea, that by analogy with it Ps. 18.6, 'Exsultavit ut gigas ad currendam viam,' is from the time of Ambrose consistently interpreted as a prophetic reference to the fusion of the divine and human natures in Christ. With these familiar correspondences in mind, it would seem reasonable to see in Dante's giant a double-natured antithesis of Christ the *Deus-homo*—Himself represented not only in a future coming by the double-natured *DXV*, but also in His first coming by the double-natured Griffon of *Purg.* 29–32. One might also expect, however, to find some sort of connection between this giant and the imagery of the Apocalypse, surrounded as he is in the poem by Apocalyptic figures like the whore, the dragon, the monster-car with seven heads and ten horns, and finally the *DXV* Himself. Though there is no giant in the text of Apocalypse, one does appear with a good deal of consistency in medieval commentary on the famous Apoc. 13.17–8. . . . Among the many ingenious interpretations of this number 666, one of the most popular is that which explains it as the sum of the numerical values represented by the letters of the Greek word τειτάν, 'giant'—which, through an explicit parallel with the double-natured giant Christ, is in turn made to signify the Antichrist. . . . In the thirteenth and early fourteenth centuries, this exegetical commonplace is sometimes absorbed into the literature of eschatological controversy—appearing, for example, in treatises by William of St. Amour and John Quidort of Paris, and in a *quaestio* by Henry of Harclay.

My proposal, then, is that Dante's giant represents primarily the Antichrist, expressed in the Apocalypse through the number 666, the 'number of the beast'; that his antithesis in the *Purgatorio* is Christ, expressed through the number 515, the 'number' of the *DXV* or *Deus-homo*; and that Dante's numerical introduction of the *DXV* is, accordingly, a device for pointing up His antithetical relationship to this numerically begotten Antichrist. In addition, just as Dante's 515 reflects the monogram ☧ , so the 666 of the Apoc. 13.18 is often explained by commentators as a reflection of the monogram ✗ or ✗ —a traditional symbol of Christ, which will be unjustly appropriated by the Antichrist. It seems just possible also that Dante's awareness of the already evident parallelism between 666 and 515 may have been heightened by some knowledge of an early version of Apoc. 13.18, in which 666 is replaced by the number 616. This reading, strenuously denounced by Irenaeus, seems to have existed in the important early commentary of Tyconius, and reaches the later Middle Ages as part of a popular pseudo-Augustinian homiletic cycle sometimes attributed to Caesarius of Arles.

II

So far . . . this interpretation of Dante's *DXV* seems to me stronger in three fundamental ways than any of those offered previously: first, in its reliance on a traditional symbol of some potential profundity, whose currency within Dante's own time can be specifically and extensively documented; second, in the orderly precision with which the component parts of the monogram ✠ can be fitted to those of the *DXV*, with respect to both pattern and meaning; and third, in the distinct relationship that this interpretation establishes between the *DXV* and another figure in the immediate context, which in turn provides an intelligible reason for Dante's numerical introduction of the *DXV*. I am aware, of course, of the low fame of previous attempts to relate Beatrice's prophecy to the Second Coming, and of the resulting general assumption that the *DXV* must refer to a political or spiritual leader—an opinion that cannot be too lightly dismissed, in view of the enormous vogue enjoyed by such cryptic political prophecy in thirteenth- and fourteenth-century Italy, and of Dante's own idealistic hopes as expressed in the *De monarchia* and the political letters. It seems to me, however, that the total force of such evidence in itself is to show not that Dante's *DXV* *must* be interpreted with reference to a temporal leader, but only that it *may* be so interpreted if the interpretation proposed can be shown to be supported in detail by the prophecy and its context. Within the *Commedia*, the various clearly political 'prophecies' all deal with events apparently antedating their composition, and so are confined to a quite limited period of time besides revealing little of Dante's current attitude toward an actual political future. . . .

What remains, then, is to demonstrate an accord between this interpretation of the *DXV* and other crucial parts of the *Commedia*—a task that in one way or another will occupy all the rest of this study. . . . I do not intend, of course, to deny altogether the existence of 'political allegory' in the *Commedia*, particularly in passages like the usurpation of the ear by the giant and the whore (*Purg.* 32.148–60). It seems to me, however, that such allegory in literature, if it is to become much more than a series of arbitrary and imaginatively jejune equations, must by its very nature draw strongly on other more fundamental and universally significant meanings, already somehow implicit in the figures it is made to inhabit. . . .

I begin with the series of Apocalyptic figures culminating in Beatrice's prophecy itself. . . . In *Purg.* 32, the whore and the monster on which she sits represent a degradation and a partial unification of two previously distinct symbols for the Church—the *'bella donna'* and the triumphal car of the heavenly procession (*Purg.* 29ff.)—into the Apocalyptic image of the *mulierem sedentem super bestiam* (Apoc. 17.3). This coalescence seems clearly influenced by Joachistic exegesis of Apoc. 17, one of whose innovations was to conflate whore and beast into virtual unity; in the *Purgatorio*, however, the two figures seem to me to remain somewhat more distinct. . . .

I would interpret the *'puttana'* of the *Purgatorio* as signifying the corrupted Church insofar as its members have become estranged from *good*, the final cause of the human will—a significance implicit also in the pervasive figure of the *sponsa* (traditionally signifying also the individual Christian soul) and her estrangement from the divine *Sponsus*. The car, damaged and overgrown though apparently not basically transmuted, seems to signify rather the corrupted Church insofar as it has become crippled and disguised in its role as the vessel of *truth*, the final cause of the human intellect. . . . It is in accord with this distinction that the *DXV* will destroy the whore, but not, presumably, the car. . . .

With these proposed significances in mind, let us bypass the assailants of the car temporarily (*Purg.* 32.109–47) and proceed to the episode of the whore and the giant, which begins,

> Secure, like a fortress on a high mountain, appeared to me an ungirt harlot seated on it, looking about her with bold brows, and as if that she might not be taken from him I saw a giant standing beside her, and they kissed each other again and again.
>
> (32.148–53)

My interpretation of Dante's giant as the Antichrist has been introduced [previously]. Our first view of the giant, sitting upon the corrupted car, allegorizes one of the more prominent exploits of the Antichrist: He 'opposes, and is lifted up above all that is called God, or that is worshipped, so that he sits in the temple of God, showing himself as if he were God.'

The pertinent explanations are summarized, for example, by John Quidort:

> There have been others who have maintained that he will sit in the Church of God as if he were God, that is, the vicar of God. If, however,

one says more properly not *in templo Dei* but *in templum Dei* (for so it is in the Greek), and accordingly says, 'he will sit *in templum Dei*,' [the meaning is that he will sit] as though he and his followers *were* the temple of God, declaring that the rest of the faithful are therefore outside the Church. . . . Augustine likewise mentions these explanations [*City of God*, XX, 19], though they can also be satisfactorily expounded [so as to mean] that he will sit *in templum Dei*, that is, over the temple of God and the Church.

The giant's dalliance with the whore reflects another traditional interest of the Antichrist, based on Dan. 11.37. '. . . et erit in concupiscentiis feminarum.' The literal meaning of the verse is epitomized in the thirteenth-century *Compendium theologicae veritatis* once attributed to Albertus Magnus: 'Antichristus erit luxuriosus . . .'; its allegorical significance is expounded by William of St. Amour: he will desire the souls of men 'so that he may make them commit fornication with him against the Lord, seeking the adoration of a god from those who are pliant and unstable after the manner of women.' Dante's initial picture of the whore and the giant, then, is a composite of traditional images, juxtaposing the 'sitting' of the whore in Apoc. 17.3 and 18.7 with the 'sitting' of the Antichrist in 2 Thess. 2.4; debasing the once-triumphal car into a point of coalescence for the figures of the beast on which the whore sits and the Church on which the Antichrist sits; and combining the traditional lustfulness of the whore and of the Antichrist into a terrible parody of the Church as the bride of Christ. This last significance seems obviously pointed by the familiar pictorial representation of Christ and the Church as seated lovers. The concept of the Antichrist as lover of the whore is itself closely approximated by William of St. Amour in an exegesis of Apoc. 18.7: '*I sit as a queen, and I am no widow*, having as her mate Antichrist and the devil. . . .'

We are now confronted by the difficult passage that begins with the whore's casting her eye on Dante himself:

But because she turned on me her wanton and roving eye that savage lover beat her from head to foot; then, full of suspicion and fierce with rage, he loosed the monster and dragged it through the wood so far that he made the wood itself screen from me the harlot and the strange brute.

(32.154–60)

The restless eyes of the whore (150,154)—naturalistic accuracy apart—reflect a literal detail almost emblematic in its conventionality. In addition, they seem to carry an allegorical suggestion of spiritual instability, sharpened by the verbal correspondence between 'occhio . . . vagante' (154) and medieval interpretations of the *viros . . . vagos* of Judges 9.4 as followers of the Antichrist. The whore's casting her eye on Dante may include a superficial echo of the advances of Putiphar's wife to Joseph in Gen. 39.7, along with some of their interpretations; the central significance of the action, however, is surely dependent on Jer. 3.1–3:

> It is commonly said: If a man shall put away his wife, and she, going from him, shall marry another man, shall he return to her any more? will not that woman be polluted and defiled? You, however, have committed fornication with many lovers. Nevertheless return to Me (says the Lord), and I will receive you. Lift up your eyes in a straight gaze (*or* on high), and see where you have not prostrated yourself. . . . In you the forehead of a woman has become that of a whore. . . .

The great thirteenth-century Joachistic commentary on Jeremias (traditionally ascribed to Joachim himself) interprets these verses in a way that bears directly on the situation in the final part of *Purg.* 32:

> *Lift up*, from the mirror of dignity, *your eyes*, fastened upon the dregs of cupidity, *in a straight gaze*, of just contemplation, *and see*, blinded by the darkness of error [but now] illuminated by the faith of heavenly learning, *where now* [sic] *you have prostrated yourself*: the place of your prostitution and the act of your iniquity. The place is the world, situated in wickedness; this in which the Church is "prostrated" is earthly cupidity. . . .

At the beginning of the *Inferno* (1.16–8), the character Dante has lifted up his eyes 'in directum'; at the present moment in the *Purgatorio*, he represents the perfected human nature to which that act has ultimately led:

> from me. Free, upright and whole is thy will and it were a fault not to act on its bidding; therefore over thyself I crown and mitre thee.'
>
> (*Purg.* 27.140–2)

The whore—signifying not only the corrupted and deformed Church, but also its individual members, corrupted and deformed to varying degrees—recognizes in Dante the fulfillment of the command 'Leva oculos' and the potential perfection of her own nature, which at one volitional level she has no choice but to desire; her casting her eye on Dante is an initial motion toward reform, paralleling Dante's first raising his eyes to the summit (*Inf.* 1.16), but ending in a return 'per la selva' (*Purg.* 32.158) that recalls inevitably the 'selva oscura' from which Dante has escaped in the opening lines of the poem. Dante's own role in the allegory, then, is that of the elect who in the final time will remain free from domination by the Antichrist; and this role seems supported by an analogy between Dante as beholder and recorder of the Apocalyptic drama within the

Purgatorio, and John the Evangelist as beholder and recorder of the Apocalypse—an aspect much emphasized in medieval illustration of the Apocalypse, and pertinently glossed by William of St. Amour in connection with the fall of the *meretrix*: 'Now the damnation of the whore is shown to John, personifying the elect of that time. . . .'

This pattern of eschatological imagery is resumed in Beatrice's prophecy of the *DXV*. Her announcement that the car 'che 'l serpente ruppe / fu e non è' (33.35), with its obvious echo of the 'fuit et non est' applied to the beast in Apoc. 17.8, is ostensibly a sardonic comment on the corruption of the car from its earlier perfection, an idea that is clearly completed by the rest of the tercet (35–6). Traditional commentary on Apoc. 17.8, however, explains 'fuit et non est' as an allusion to the brevity of the Antichrist's rule and the quickness of his downfall, taking it to mean in effect, 'is, and shall not be.' Olivi, in a passage dependent on Joachim, applies the expression in a similar way to the combination of whore and beast which for him signifies the *ecclesia carnalis*. . . . In the light of this interpretation, and within the frame of reference suggested by my interpretations of the whore, the car, and the *DXV*, Beatrice's 'fu e non è' seems to carry overtones also of a future purification of the car, through its release from bondage by the promised extinction of the whore. In the following line (36), Beatrice's 'vendetta di Dio' is paralleled significantly by the eschatological 2 Thess. 1.8, and is of course a commonplace both in exegesis of the Apocalypse and in the literature of medieval eschatology generally. Her remark that this vengeance 'non teme suppe' is no doubt an immediate allusion to the sop by which a murderer could at one time escape justice in Florence, as explained by the early commentators. Its implicit theme of confusion between the ways of human and divine justice seems heightened, however, by a suggestion of symbolic meaning in the 'suppe' themselves—illustrated by the comment of Peter Lombard on Ps. 10(1).14: 'Thou seest, since Thou considerest labor and grief, that Thou mayest deliver them into Thy hands,' as an assurance that God will withhold His vengeance through fear. . . .

Beatrice's next lines include a reference to the eagle of *Purg.* 32, clearly representing the temporal power of Rome:

> God's vengeance fears no sop. Not for all time shall the eagle be without heir that left its feathers on the car so that it became monster and then prey; for I see assuredly, and therefore tell of it. . . .
>
> (33.37–9)

So far as I am aware, the prevailing tendency is to explain the *reda* here as someone who will inherit the eagle itself—that is, as a future temporal ruler. Surely, however, the subject under discussion at this point in the prophecy is not the eagle but the car. It is the car that has been the subject of the tercet immediately preceding (34–5); and here too it has been alluded to paraphrastically, in terms of the action performed on it by one of its allegorical assailants. Our reference to the eagle itself leads directly to the result of the gift upon the car (39)—a curiously incidental inclusion, if the two preceding lines (37–8) are really an allusion to the rulerless empire. And finally, the whore and the giant to be killed by the *DXV* (the direct prophecy of Whose advent begins with this tercet) are the usurpers not of the eagle but of the car. The whole immediate context, then, indicates that the *reda* is not someone who is to inherit the eagle, but rather someone who is to succeed the eagle in possession of the car. The resulting concept of the Church as one-time 'possession' of Rome is made plausible by the Joachistic commentary on Jer. 2. . . .

If this analysis is convincing, it will be difficult not to see in this tercet an allusion to the common eschatological belief that the final time will include the extinction of the Roman Empire, along with the rise of the Antichrist and the ultimate return of Christ to reclaim His Church. . . . That such traditions could be applied to the political situation in the early fourteenth century, and by sophisticated minds, is clearly demonstrated in a *quodlibet* of 1310 by Nicolas of Lyra, who at one point replies to an argument based on Jerome's statement that the fall of the Roman Empire will precede the coming of the Antichrist: 'But that observation of Jerome seems to work no less well for the opposing side, because the Roman Empire is now disappearing, as it seems, and does not survive except in name; for the Romans neither rule nor elect, and neither has [the emperor] any authority in Rome nor the Romans in the empire.'. . .

The prophecy of the *DXV* is immediately introduced by the astronomical explanation

> . . . for I see assuredly, and therefore tell of it, stars already near, to give us the time, secure from all check and hindrance.
>
> (33.40–2)

Whatever the allusion here, it is evidently the same as that inspired earlier in the *Purgatorio* by Dante's recollection of the *antica lupa*:

> which is bottomless! O heavens, by whose wheeling men seem to believe their conditions are changed here below, when will he come before whom she shall flee?
>
> (20.13–15)

In the two passages quoted, at any rate, this insistence on the role of the heavens may seem to point not toward a final advent of the

Deus-homo, but rather toward a temporal leader subject to the powers of nature and fortune. Let us begin by noticing, however, that in neither passage is the awaited arrival explicitly attributed to the power of the heavens; in *Purg.* 33 the stars are to give a *time in which* (41–3) the *DXV* will appear, while in *Purg.* 20 the reference could be simply to the final consummation of the celestial movement. In the latter passage, moreover, 'par che si creda' seems a curiously tentative reference to so generally acknowledged a fact as the influence of the heavens—a difficulty not wholly accounted for by *Purg.* 16.67ff., where the question is not whether the power of the heavens is to be credited, but what part of man's activities they affect.

Now in 1297, Arnold of Villanova composed the work which we know (in a revision of 1300) as the *Tractatus de tempore adventus Antichristi*, in which he defends the possibility of predicting the coming of the Antichrist through astronomical computation, offering the year 1366 as the product of his own research. The resulting controversy—including the inevitably related disputes about the second coming of Christ and the end of the world—seems to have flourished with particular vigor during the next fifteen years, involving among others John Quidort, Peter of Auvergne, Nicolas of Lyra, Guido Terrena, and Henry of Harclay. One prominent aspect of the problem is the implicit contradition between the astronomical theory that the world will endure through a complete annual revolution of the heaven of fixed stars, or 36,000 years; and the common eschatological belief that it will end in the seventh millennium from its creation—by medieval reckoning, already well underway in the fourteenth century. . . . Such a controversy must, at the very least, have established a topical connection between astronomical speculation and Christ's second coming, and so would provide a likely enough explanation for Dante's two astronomical references. The noncommittal 'par che si creda' (20.13) would then become understandable as a reference not to the acknowledged significance of the heavenly movements in general, but to their disputed significance in this particular respect. This interpretation, in turn, suggests a conceivable parallel between 'nel cui girar' (20.13) and 'per cui' (20.15), based on a traditional association of Christ's first and second comings with the revolution of the heavens. . . .

We find ourselves, at last, at the climactic killing of the whore and the giant by the *DXV*. The killing of the Antichrist by Christ is of course a commonplace in medieval eschatology, derived primarily from 2 Thess. 2.8: 'And then shall be revealed that iniquitous one, whom the Lord Jesus shall kill with the spirit of His mouth; and He shall destroy him with the brightness of His coming . . .' Its obvious parallel to the death of Dante's

giant seems heightened by its characteristic brevity and lack of circum-
stantial detail; and possibly also by its invariable location on Mount
Olivet, the spot from which Christ ascended into heaven (Acts 1.12)—
which, through its conventional significance as the Church, would correspond figuratively to the car on which the giant will presumably be killed.
Various similarities can be found between the fall of the Antichrist and
that of the *meretrix*, like the fact that each is emphasized by commentators
as a death both physical and spiritual. More important, William of St.
Amour's description of the Antichrist as mate of the *meretrix* is closely
followed by a passage which—despite a figurative echo of the 'widowing'
of the *meretrix* from Apoc. 18.7—seems clearly to imply a simultaneous
death of the pair like that foretold in the *Purgatorio*. . . .

Beatrice's announcement of the *DXV* has been accompanied by
the words 'messo di Dio' (33.44)—an expression generally familiar from
the New Testament, where it is approximated more than fifty times. . . .
William of St. Amour, applying this concept of *missio* to the second
coming in an exegesis of Apoc. 10.7, provides an extremely close parallel
to Dante's 'messo di Dio,' along with a meaningful play on the word
angelus and an echo of the well known 2 Thess. 2.8 with its reference to
the killing of rhe Antichrist:

> Will not the beginning of the trumpet of this seventh angel—that is, of
> Christ the Lord, because He, sent by the Father (A *Patre missus*), is by
> prerogative, as it were, called the Prince of angels, and the "Angel" of
> great counsel, and the Seventh, to Whom each trumpet of the other
> angels leads up, and He is a byword for perfection just as is the number
> seven—[will not this beginning] be brought to completion when He shall
> kill the man of iniquity with the spirit of His mouth?

And finally, the prophecy itself is followed by Beatrice's further
cryptic comment:

> And perhaps my dark tale, like Themis and the Sphinx, persuades thee
> less because, in their fashion, it clouds thy mind; but soon the facts shall
> be the Naiads that will solve this hard enigma without loss of flocks and
> corn.

>   (33.46–51)

A distinctive error in the medieval text of Ovid's *Metamorphoses* puts it
beyond question that these references to Themis, the Sphinx, and the
Naiades are derived primarily from the allusions in a brief passage (*Met.*
7.759–62) introducing the story of Laelaps, the dog of Cephalus (7.763–93):
how, after the death of the Sphinx, a second monster was sent to afflict
Thebes; how this monster was pursued by Laelaps; and how both animals

were turned into marble statues. In the *Ovide moralisé* (written not far from the possible dates of the *Purgatorio*, and in any case traditional in much of its content), the monster is interpreted as the beast of the Apocalypse, evidently with a suggestion of his usual significance as the Antichrist; the transformation of the two animals is attributed literally to Juppiter and allegorized as the intervention of God, Who when He sees the affliction of His people 'secours bon lor envoiera' (7.3672). Dante's recognition of such meanings in the *Metamorphoses* is shown, of course, by his own well known example of Orpheus in the *Convivio*. The story of Laelaps will meet us again in connection with the *Veltro*; for the moment, we need notice only that this allegorization of it contributes a further possible eschatological overtone to Beatrice's prophecy.

If this labored analysis has been essentially sound, it implies that Dante's eschatological allusion in these two cantos is more firmly grounded in the meaning of the Apocalypse and its surrounding tradition, and also is more consistent and purposeful, than has sometimes been supposed; and that an interpretation of the *DXV* as Christ in a future advent is less unlikely than we have been led to believe. With these observations in mind, let us glance backward to the series of assaults on the car in *Purg.* 32, preceding the appearance of the whore and the giant. So far as I know, the violent descent of the eagle (109–17) has been most often interpreted as signifying the early persecutions of the Church; the visit of the she-fox (118–23), as signifying the early heresies; the second descent of the eagle and the gift of feathers (124–6, 136–8), as signifying the donation of Constantine and its results; and the attack of the dragon (130–5), as signifying the schism either between West and East or between Christian and Mohammedan. These interpretations, developed in a general way by the early commentors, bear a tantalizing resemblance to the familiar eschatological pattern of the *status Ecclesie*, derived primarily from the opening of the seven seals in Apoc. 6–8. Though unanimity is not to be looked for, a kind of rough common denominator for the scheme in pre-Joachistic exegesis would identify the first *status* with the time of the Apostles, the second with that of the early presecutions, the third with that of the early heresies, the fourth with that of hypocrites or 'falsi fratres,' the sixth with that of the Antichrist, and the seventh with the time of peace after the death of the Antichrist; the fifth seems never to have developed a comparably distinct identity, and is represented by a miscellany of more or less individual interpretations. . . .

Let us turn at last from *Purg.* 32–3, to notice the relevance of this interpretation of the *DXV* for certain more distant parts of the *Commedia*. In *Purg.* 12 there is a passage of thirty-nine lines (25–63) describing the examples of pride that Dante and Vergil find sculptured in the stone over which they walk. The first four tercets of this passage (25–36) begin with the word 'Vedea,' the second four (37–48) with the exclamation 'O,' and the third four (49–60) with the word 'Mostrava'; the final tercet repeats the three as the initial words of its three lines:

> Vedea Troia in cenere e in caverne:
> o Iliòn, come te basso e vile
> mostrava il segno che lì si discerne!
> (12.61–3)

There seems little doubt that these repetitions are an acrostic, spelling out the word *VOM*—that is, *Uom*', or *Uomo*. . . . If this is true, then the removal of the *P* of pride from Dante's forehead by the angel later in the canto (97ff.) is a small inevitable analogy of the Redemption, which relieved mankind of at least the worst effects of the pride underlying Original Sin.

Now the whole account of these sculptures and their effect on Dante (16–75) is a passage of sombre and unrelieved meditation on the ravages of pride in a fallen humanity; as such, it contrasts unmistakably with the joy and renewal of spirit that attends the arrival of the angel and Dante's subsequent purification (77ff.). The new note is first struck in Vergil's speech announcing the approach of the angel—which, in terms of the analogy I have just proposed, would be a speech 'in preconio Saluatoris,' a looking forward to a 'Redemption':

> Lift up thy head! There is no more time to go thus absorbed. See there an angel who hastes to meet us. See how the sixth handmaid returns from the service of the day. Let thy looks and bearing be graced with reverence, that it may please him to direct us upwards. Remember that to-day never dawns again.
> (12.77–84)

If we examine this speech in the light of the foregoing acrostic, we find that its two complete tercets begin respectively with 'Vedi' (79) and 'Di' (82), whose initial *V* and *D* correspond to the two components of the monogram ☧ . In addition, 'Vedi' repeats the word 'Vedea' which in the first four tercets of the acrostic and in line 61 furnishes the initial of *Vom*' (*Uomo*); while 'Di,' if it is subjected to a process analogous with *Vom*' > *Uomo*, becomes *Di*' > *Dio*. The pattern is intensified by the obvious strong alliteration of *v* and *d* in the speech, particularly the 'venir verso . . . vedi . . . dal . . . del . . . di' of lines 80–1. I take the *VD* of these two tercets, then, as an extension of the acrostic *VOM*, signifying a coming 'Atonement' through its allusion to the monogram ☧ in the Preface of the

Mass, and meaningfully attached to a speech that bears a natural analogy to a heralding of the Redemption. This whole theme is supported also by Vergil's reference to approaching noon (80–1), itself a familiar figure of Christ, the Crucifixion, or the Redemption; and by the choice of Vergil himself as speaker of the 'prophecy.' The relation of lines 79–84 to the *DXV* is, I suppose, obvious.

Outside of Beatrice's prophecy itself, however, the clearest single piece of evidence for an eschatological interpretation of the *DXV* is probably her well known exclamation late in the *Paradiso*, concerning the heavenly city:

> See our city, how great is its circuit! See our seats so filled that few souls are now wanting there!
>
> (30.130–2)

So far as I can see, these lines must imply a comparatively small number of people who have yet to undergo death, and so also a comparatively short period of future earthly time. Any reasonable possibility of explaining them instead as a comment on the proportion of Christian mankind who attain salvation, seems eliminated by the cause-and-effect relationship between 'sì ripieni' and 'che poca gente . . . si disira,' as well as by the overall proportions of the *Commedia*; and to suggest that Dante's 'poca gente' may refer to a number small only according to some unexpressed criterion, and by other standards perhaps rather large, would surely be to ignore all considerations of emphasis as it is normally conceived to exist in the written word. In addition, the very currency of such eschatological prophecy in early fourteenth-century Italy makes it difficult to imagine how Dante could have erred into so clear a statement of so patently eschatological a concept in the process of trying to say something else. Within the fictional world of the *Commedia*, at least, this brief passage stands not only as a clear announcement of the impending end of time, but also (unless we are willing to take refuge in the facile assumption that 'Dante was inconsistent') as a contradiction of any other conceivable significance for the coming of the *DXV*.

Finally, if this whole lengthy defense has carried conviction, Beatrice's prophecy of the *DXV* falls symmetrically into place as the climactic 'revelation' in the *Purgatorio*, corresponding to the vision of Lucifer at the end of the *Inferno* and to that of the Trinity at the end of the *Paradiso*. As part of such a pattern, the prophecy of the *DXV* seems in every way more credible than the pageant of the Church in *Purg.* 29ff., which has sometimes been proposed. Like the two visions, it occupies the final canto of its *cantica*; like Lucifer and the Trinity themselves, the *DXV* is represented as 'triune'—God, man, and the person in Whom the two are joined. It is in keeping with the finality of heaven and hell that the 'trinity' of the *Inferno* is beheld as a static vision of completed and unchanging evil, and the Trinity of the *Paradiso* as a static vision of perfect and unchangeable good; by contrast, the *DXV* is not beheld, but is announced in a prophecy to be fulfilled in time. The reason, I would suggest, lies in the nature of Purgatory itself: a place of no final state, but of progressive repair for past evil and of hope for future beatitude. In traditional eschatology, it is the advent of the *DXV* (whether in precise chronological terms, or simply as the dominant symbol of the final days) that will set the boundary between time and eternity, abolish all change along with Purgatory itself, and divide mankind forever between the timeless kingdoms of 'triune' evil and Triune Good. Seen in this light, Beatrice's prophecy becomes the announcement of an ever-approaching final harmony and a message of hope to those righteous who still inhabit a world of change—on the ledges of Purgatory, or on earth as part of the struggling and bedevilled Church Militant.

FRANCIS X. NEWMAN

St. Augustine's Three Visions and the Structure of the "Commedia"

At the beginning of *Paradiso* Dante tells us how the poem will end:

> The glory of Him who moves all things penetrates the universe and shines in one part more and in another less. I was in the heaven that most receives His light and I saw things which he that descends from it has not the knowledge or the power to tell again. . . .
>
> *(Par.*, i,1–6)

The *Comedy* is the narrative of a journey through a universe whose parts are distinguished by the degree to which they "re-glow" with the divine Light. The end of the journey comes in a heaven which is filled with that light, and its climactic event is therefore an act of seeing, a vision which the pilgrim attains, but which the poet, "chi di là su discende," cannot describe.

The language of these opening lines of *Paradiso* points clearly to the source from which Dante drew the conception of a supreme vision about which it is impossible to speak: "I know a man in Christ: above fourteen years ago (whether in the body I know not, or out of the body, I know not: God knoweth), such a one caught up to the third heaven. And I know such a man (whether in the body, or out of the body, I know not: God knoweth): That he was caught up into paradise and heard secret

---

From *Modern Language Notes*, vol. 82 (1961). Copyright © 1967 by The Johns Hopkins University Press.

words which it is not given to man to utter." (II Corin. xii, 2–4) That the conclusion of the *Comedy* is modelled on St. Paul's flight to the third heaven would be evident enough even if Dante himself had not made the connection explicit in the letter to Can Grande, but the relevance of this fact to the structure of the poem has not been clearly recognized. Paul's account of his experience (the Middle Ages never doubted, incidentally, that the "man in Christ" was Paul himself) mentions a *third* heaven and in so doing it set a classic exegetical problem. There was no question of Paul's being in error; therefore what were the three heavens that he mentioned? There are a number of answers to the question in the commentaries, but the most influential was given by St. Augustine in the final book of his *De Genesi ad litteram*. What I wish to propose in the following pages is that the theory of vision advanced by Augustine in his exegesis of Paul's *raptus* eventually exercised a significant influence on the structure of Dante's *Comedy*.

To speak baldly of the "structure" of Dante's poem is, of course, to raise a virtually inexhaustible question, but I want to discuss only the most obvious of the multiple patterns of the poem: the division into three *cantiche*. The apportioning of the *Comedy* into *Inferno*, *Purgatorio*, and *Paradiso* constitutes the primary aspect of the "form of the treatise," a form given the poet by conventional eschatology. But eschatology merely provided the premise of the narrative; it did not tell Dante how to make the experience of each realm distinct for the pilgrim and thereby for the reader. Nothing is clearer about the *Comedy* than that Hell, Purgatory, and Heaven are more than places with different kinds of souls in them. Indeed, so striking is the difference between successive realms that we can describe the pilgrim's journey as a passage through three different kinds of experience. That is the essential argument of this essay.

While Dante differentiates the three kingdoms in many ways, the most pervasive pattern of distinction lies in his handling of the images of light throughout the poem. As the opening lines of *Paradiso* assert, the universe of the *Comedy* is one which "re-glows" with the light of God, here more, there less. And so Hell is a place of profound darkness (though the gloom is never absolute, for to be utterly without light in a poem where light is the sign of being could only signify annihilation). Purgatory, the middle kingdom, is alternately bright and dark, subject to the cycle of night and day. Heaven is filled with light, a brilliance that grows progressively more intense as the pilgrim approaches the Empyrean. The ultimate moment of the pilgrim's journey through the three realms is an explosion of illumination—Dante's word is *fulgore*—that is the vision of God unmediated. No reader of the *Comedy* needs to be told that progress toward

God in the poem is progress toward light, but a corollary fact is sometimes neglected: as light increases in intensity during the journey's course there is a corresponding and progressive dematerialization of the things which reflect or transmit that light. As he approaches the transcendent and incorporeal God, the objects of Dante's vision grow ever more translucent or, conversely, less corporeal. On the whole this double pattern of increasing brilliance and decreasing corporeality is a continuum, for the journey is a single journey, but it is also true that each of the three realms is essentially different as a place of vision, for the journey is three journeys. The *Comedy* depicts the journey of the pilgrim through a series of experiences which are meant to prepare him for a final centripetal moment of vision, but the separate *cantiche* are patterned in the same way. Each of the three major divisions of the action is arranged to lead the pilgrim to a climactic moment of seeing, so that in order to understand the structure of the poem we must perceive that it has three points of climax, three centripetal moments of vision, within the larger movement toward finality. The first two of these visions are not terminal, but point beyond themselves and require the pilgrim to journey further until he reaches the third and final vision which is an end in itself.

    Let us now turn to Augustine, where, I suggest, we find the ultimate, if not the proximate source of this pattern. *De Genesi ad litteram* is just what its title promises, but something else as well. The first eleven books of this commentary are a consecutive analysis of the opening chapters of Genesis, but the twelfth and last book is an explication of the single word *paradisus*. The problem Augustine frames for himself in Book XII is this: what did St. Paul mean when he spoke (in II Corin. 12:2–4) of being carried up into the *third* heaven? Are there three heavens and, if so, which of them is *paradisus*? He handles the question at length, but his solution can be briefly summarized. The three Pauline "heavens" are really figures for the three kinds of human vision, that is, the three fundamental modes of human awareness. The first of these is the *visio corporalis*, the literal sight of the eye or, more generally, knowledge by means of the external senses. The second is the *visio spiritualis* or *imaginativa*, knowledge by means of the imagination. In "spiritual" vision we do not see bodies themselves, but images that have corporeal shape without corporeal substance. Dreams, for example, are a sub-class of the *visio spiritualis*. The third and highest of the classes of vision is *intellectualis*, the direct cognition of realities such as God, the angels, *caritas*, etc., which have neither corporeal substance nor corporeal shape. Whatever man knows he knows in one of these three ways, but Augustine is particularly interested in how we know God. In this regard he asserts that man can know God by means of any of the three visions: Moses gazing on the burning bush "saw" God with corporeal sight; John in the Apocalyptic vision saw Him by means of the figures and images of *visio spiritualis*; and St. Paul's *raptus* is the great exemplar of the *visio intellectualis*. Only the last, however, is a direct intuition of God Himself; the others are indirect visions by means of bodies or images. While he speaks of three different visions, moreover, Augustine is also at pains to emphasize that vision is essentially a continuum, in which corporeal, spiritual, and intellectual vision are related in a hierarchical system. In normal human experience, that is to say, sensation is primary, but its data are transformed into and stored as the phantasms of imagination, and these in turn are the material from which are drawn the imageless ideas of intellectual vision.

The structure of the *De Genesi ad litteram* itself invites comment. In the first eleven books Augustine limits himself to the portion of the Genesis narrative that concludes with the expulsion of Adam and Eve from Paradise. The twelfth book, while it opens almost as if it were a philological treatise, is really a meditation on man's return to Paradise. Hence the choice of the Pauline rapture as the central text. As Augustine explores the text, the "questio paradisi," as he calls it, becomes a discussion of vision, for man's return to Paradise will not be a literal return to the garden of Genesis, but the vision of God in "the third heaven." To speak of Paradise is therefore necessarily to speak of vision, because Paradise *is* vision, and Paul's account of being carried up to the third heaven is the central Biblical paradigm of man's hoped-for destiny: the "intellectual" or unmediated vision of God.

The schema of visions that Augustine proposed in the *De Genesi ad litteram* was widely influential throughout the Middle Ages. . . . Exegetes found the triple vision particularly useful in the explication of Biblical visions, especially the Apocalypse and, of course, II Corinthians, xii, 2–4, but it also appears in a variety of other contexts (particularly in places where a tripartite division was a useful analytic tool). One appearance of the formula that is especially pertinent to the present discussion is in Honorius of Autun's *Scala coeli major*, where the sequence of three visions constitutes the structure of the work. The informing metaphor of the treatise is the *scala paradisi* which the true Christian ascends in order to come to the vision of God. As Honorius elaborates the allegory, the ladder to Paradise is composed of three sets of hierarchically arranged steps, corporeal, spiritual, and intellectual vision. By climbing this series of steps the Christian eventually reaches the third heaven of beatific vision. A similar instance of such structural use of the Augustinian formula may perhaps be found in the popular satire *Apocalypsis Goliae*. In this curious poem a bewildered narrator is granted a series of three visions: the first is a brief glimpse of a great crowd of pagan *auctores*, who represent the liberal and practical arts; the second is a parodic pseudo-Apocalypse; and the third is a burlesque version of Paul's elevation to the third heaven. Critics of the poem, who have complained of its incoherent structure, have failed to notice that the obvious clue to the arrangement of the narrative is the very common use of Augustine's doctrine of vision in the exegesis of the canonical Apocalypse. The apparently random set of three visions in the poem becomes coherent when we perceive that the satirist is mocking not only Apocalypse but the vision form itself. The vision of the pagan sages, representing the *artes*, is a parody of corporeal vision (knowledge derived from sense-data); the pseudo-Apocalypse and burlesque Pauline flight are parodies of conventional instances of spiritual and intellectual vision. The structure of the poem is thus precisely the kind of learned joke that "Golias" was so fond of.

The variety of instances that have been cited indicate the widespread currency of Augustine's schema. We can now return to the *Comedy*. The first *cantica* of the poem leads us through a realm that is emphatically corporeal throughout, a place of mud, ice, palpable air, running sores, stone sarcophagi, grappling hooks, leaden cloaks, etc. The almost tactile experience of reading *Inferno* is a commonplace of Dante criticism. Corporeality, however, is more than a matter of poetic texture in *Inferno*; it also is the key to the structure of Hell as a place. As Dante and Virgil descend further into the pit they move ever closer to that point in the universe which is the center of corporeal weight: "lo mezzo / al quale ogni gravezza si rauna" (*Inf.*, xxxii, 73–74), "il punto / al qual si traggon d'ogni parte i pesi" (*Inf.*, xxxiv, 110–111). In other words, Dante conceives the bottom of the pit of Hell as both cosmically peripheral (at the maximum distance from the source of all being) and cosmically central (a *mezzo* or attracting center for everything in the universe that is weighted). It is not patently anachronistic, given the association of the pit with *gravezza*, to say that the law of descent in the *Comedy* is the law of gravity. Indeed it is possible to understand *Inferno* as a poetic realization of what Augustine and Gregory called the *pondus* of evil, or the *gravitas* of the sinner. As Ciacco explains when Dante inquires after some fellow Florentines:

> They are among the blackest souls and different faults weigh them dow
> to the depth; if thou descend so far thou canst see them.
>
> (*Inf.*, vi, 85–87)

It is consistent with such a conception of the descent that the least culpable inhabitants of Hell, the trimmers and the lustful, are spun round and round in windy circles, while the worst sinners, the traitors, lie frozen and immobile in the lake of ice. All of this emphasis on corporeality in *Inferno* is not, as some classically-minded critics have asserted, merely a sign of Dante's medieval fascination with "Gothick" grotesquerie; it is rather the poetic means of displaying the essential meaning of Hell. To be in Hell is not to be in Heaven, not to be with God. By choosing Hell, the sinners reject the Creator for his creation and accept a contingent reality in place of true substantiality. In *Inferno* Dante presents this fact in realized action: the sinners condemn themselves to live forever in the kind of material world they were meant to transcend. To turn from God, then, in Dante's poetic universe, is to be afflicted with *gravezza* and to plunge downward into corporeality.

The plot of *Inferno* is thus a movement toward a center, and at the center the pilgrim discovers the meaning of the realm in a climactic and synoptic of vision. Regarding the action as a process of vision, we can say that the emphatically tactile imagery of *Inferno* is all preparative, a way of readying the pilgrim's eyes to see what they see at the bottom of the pit. This explains one particularly striking scene that might otherwise seem anomalous:

> . . . and while we were going towards the centre at which all gravity converges and I was shivering in the eternal chill, whether it was will or fate or chance I do not know, but, walking among the heads, I struck my foot hard in the face of one.
>
> (*Inf.*, xxxii, 73–78)

At the very moment when the poet announces the pilgrim's approach to the center of weight, he offers what amounts to a visual demonstration of that fact. The pilgrim not only stumbles over the protruding head of the traitor Bocca, but even seizes it and rips out handfuls of hair. This despite the fact that Bocca is only a shade, still to be joined with the body he left in the grave. Bocca's tangibility is neither an error on the poet's part nor a casual dramatic device; it is a metaphor, an identification of image and the moral condition which the image signifies. It is also an adumbration of and preparation for the concluding vision of *Inferno*, the encounter with a Satan whose condition is even more anomalous than that of the tangible shade. Before his fall Lucifer was the angel of light, created but incorporeal. Nevertheless, although he never had a body to lose to the grave or regain at the judgment, the Satan whom the pilgrim sees in Giudecca is in cosmological position the heaviest thing in the universe. Once utterly incorporeal, he is now the most corporeal of beings, having sunk to the center of the earth, where he remains, hairy, rime-encrusted, and forever fixed in place. At the end of Canto xxxiv Dante tells us that when

Satan fell he displaced the earth that formerly occupied the cave of Hell and in consequence thrust up the mountain of Purgatory. Now the name Lucifer is only a bitter parody, for the Satan Dante gives us is a fallen star, embedded like a frozen and blackened meteor in the bowels of the earth. Satan, in fact, *is* "lo punto / al quale si traggon d'ogni parte i pesi," a lodestone of evil who draws the sin-weighted souls downward.

In Dante's universe, then, the opposite of light is not darkness, but body: at one pole stands the "luce che da sè è vera" and at the other Lucifer, heaviest of all the inhabitants of Hell. It may be that Satan's corporeality explains the very shape that Dante gives him. To see how this is we must go back to the beginning. The *Comedy* opens with Dante, the confused pilgrim, wandering in a *selva oscura*. Landino may have been the first (though not the last) of the commentators to suggest the connection between this originating image and the use of the word *silva* as a philosophical term. In Chalcidius most notably, but also in Bernard Silvestris and others, *silva* is the customary translation of the Greek ὕλη: prime matter, the unformed chaotic stuff of which all corporeal beings are made. *Silva* itself is unintelligible; Chalcidius, in fact, says that our knowledge of it is "obscurus." If Dante intends the *selva oscura* to carry a philosophical resonance, it suggests the state of chaotic indirection in which the pilgrim finds himself at the outset, but it also suggests the character of the place through which he will move. Hell is *silvestris*: gloomy, rude, and corporeal. What the opening lines can mean, then, is that insofar as we, in *our* life, choose to turn from God we live in a world of corporeality and are ourselves corporeal. Read in this way, the opening of the *cantica* points toward its conclusion. The final canto of *Inferno* begins with an inverted allusion to the "Vexilla regis," the great liturgical hymn in praise of the wood of the cross. The allusion is not random, for Dante does show us a cross in the canto, not the "arbor decora et fulgida" of the "Vexilla regis," but its parody, the towering trunk and huge branching wings of Satan. He is the perversion of the *lignum vitae*, a sterile tree set upside-down in a frozen anti-paradise, and therefore an appropriate terminus for the journey that began in the *selva oscura*. If, as some have suggested, the *selva* is a philosophical pun, then the shape of Satan identifies him not only as anti-type of salvation, but also as the synoptic symbol of Hell's corporeality.

The confrontation with Satan is the ultimate exercise of the *visio corporalis* since Satan is the ultimate center of corporeality. But Augustine said that it is possible to see God in each of the three modes of vision and that is true even in *Inferno*. To look upon Satan is to look upon a body, but a body stamped with the sign of God. In his three heads we discern the Trinity, in his parody of the Cross we discern Christ. And so it is that the act of vision at the end of *Inferno* is not terminal, but leads inevitably beyond itself, just as Satan is himself a *scala* whom the pilgrims climb in order to ascend from Hell. Satan is a mock ruler, a parody figure, and, as with all parodies, to recognize him as such is at the same time to recognize what he apes. In seeing God's enemy and opposite, the pilgrim also sees God: as Augustine said we can see God even in corporeal vision.

The passage from Hell to Purgatory is an entry into the light and thereby into a realm which calls for a different kind of vision. The culminating action of *Purgatorio* is not a vision of *corporalia*, but of *spiritualia*, in Augustine's sense of the terms. We get a sense of this new pattern almost immediately, when the pilgrim encounters his old friend Casella:

> I saw one of them come forward with so much affection to embrace me that it moved me to do the same. O empty shades, except in semblance! Three times I clasped my hands behind him and as often brought them back to my breast.
>
> (*Purg.* ii, 76–81)

The episode is to be compared to the encounter with the quite tangible Bocca only a few cantos earlier. Casella, like all the inhabitants of Purgatory, is a shade without a shadow, empty save in appearance. Since he is nothing but "aspetto," Casella is aptly described by Augustine's formula for *spiritualia*: corporeal form without corporeal substance. Dante was obviously concerned with the reader's conception of the shades who populate Purgatory, since he devotes a long passage in Canto xxv to Statius's explanation of their nature. The passage is worth pausing over, for it is a significant clue to the character of Purgatorial vision.

After describing how the vegetative and sensitive souls of man are generated, Statius explains that the rational soul, created directly by God, absorbs these lower souls to itself, and the result is the single, undivided human soul. After the moment of death this soul is assigned to a place in one of the kingdoms of the afterlife. Therefore, though deprived of its proper body, the soul still exists *in a place* and as a result of this localization acquires a kind of new body:

> As soon as space envelops it there the formative virtue radiates round about, in form and measure as in living members; and as the air, when it is full of rain, becomes adorned with various colours through another's beams that are reflected in it, so the neighbouring air sets itself into that form which the soul that stopped there stamps upon it by its power. . . .
>
> (*Purg.* xxv, 88–96)

Statius's language throughout his discourse is heavily scholastic, but his meaning in these lines, the heart of his speech, is elusive. It is customary to summarize what Statius says in the words "aerial body," but this phrase, though accurate enough, is still ambiguous. For example, Etienne Gilson in a very recent discussion understands "aerial body" as meaning a body *made of* air. . . . It seems to me, however, that the text itself gives a different reading. Statius says that just as rays of light, reflected by moist air, adorn that air with the splendor of the rainbow, so the souls impress on the environing air a shape which conforms to the "informative virtue" they still possess. Unless Statius is careless in his simile, what the analogy of the rainbow means is that the shades are images created by reflections in air. The *ombre*, in other words, are not made *of* air, any more than the rainbow is made *of* vapor. Such an interpretation is reinforced by returning to the two similes that Virgil uses before turning the discussion over to Statius. To understand what the shades are, he says, Dante ought to consider two things: first, how the body of Meleagar wasted when the wood was consumed by the fire and, second, how his own image in a mirror moves when he moves. Meleagar was not made of wood, nor Dante of glass: the point is that these are images, reflections. When Dante confronts the shade, say, of Casella, what he is seeing is the image of the body Casella once bore, reflected in the air: corporeal form without corporeal substance. Bocca and Casella are separated by only a few cantos in the poem, yet the pilgrim's encounter with each one is sharply different; the difference is that between *corporalia* and *spiritualia*.

Perhaps we need not debate over the merits of "by" versus "of" so scholastically; the important point is that the shades are somehow like reflections, empty except in "aspetto." The importance of the point lies in the fact that it draws our attention to the characteristic pattern of vision experience that Dante has in Purgatory. To put it as directly as possible: the dominant note in Dante's experiences as a seer in Purgatory is the perception of images. For example, it is only in Purgatory that Dante dreams. The Middle Ages had many theories about dreams, but the theorists were virtually unanimous in assigning dreams to the faculty of imagination. As we noticed above, Augustine made dreaming a species of the *visio spiritualis*, because in dreams we apprehend neither physical bodies nor incorporeal ideas, but images of bodies. While at night in Purgatory Dante dreams, during the day he undergoes a similar form of experience (also unique to the realm)—instruction by means of the various "whips" and "reins" appropriate to each ledge. The inhabitants of Purgatory are taught the nature of their sins by contemplating historical instances of the vice itself and its opposing virtue. Though drawn from

Biblical and secular history, there is no sense that these events are witnessed by the pilgrims as actual occurrences. They are *exempla,* the visual or auditory re-presentation of events for didactic purposes.

> . . . from its long interdict appeared before us so truly graven there in a gracious attitude that it did not seem a silent image.
>
> (*Purg.* x, 37–39)

This is Dante's reaction to the first of the "whips": the sculpture is so realistic that he almost believes it is not an "imagine." In successive ledges the mode of representation changes to visions, voices, and recitations by the sinners themselves, but always the "whips" and "reins" are historical images of virtue and vice.

All of the pilgrim's experiences with the shades, dreams, and *exempla* on the mountain comprise a distinctly novel kind of apprehension for him, which constitutes a preparation for the culminating moment of Purgatorial vision. *Inferno* concludes with the vision of God in a body; *Purgatorio* with the vision of God in an image. The setting for this climactic vision is appropriate: a gigantic allegorical pageant of imaginary shapes. If the climax of *Paradiso* recalls the Pauline *raptus,* the masque which concludes *Purgatorio* recalls Apocalypse in its imaginative splendor. In the course of the procession Dante is given to see such incorporeal realities as the theological and cardinal virtues, not as they are in themselves, but as beautiful ladies dressed in symbolically colored clothes. The Bible appears in the shape of thirty-one old men and Christ in the form of the griffon, a figure that with centaurs, golden houses and other such composites, was a perennial medieval example of a creature existing in imagination alone. It is in the midst of this profusion of imaginary shapes that Dante has his second vision of God. As in *Inferno* the vision has two aspects, but presented here in two separate stages. The first is the vision of Christ: Dante sees in Beatrice's eyes the reflection of the Griffon:

> . . . even like the sun in a mirror the two-fold beast shone within them, now with the one, now with the other nature. Think, reader, if I marvelled when I saw the thing still in itself and in its image changing.
>
> (*Purg.* xxxi, 121–126)

The mystery of the incarnation appears to Dante as a shifting *idolo* reflected in Beatrice's eyes as the sun is in a mirror. The second stage of the climactic vision comes when Beatrice turns her face directly to Dante and unveils her smile:

> '. . . of thy grace do us the grace to unveil thy mouth to him, that he may discern the second beauty, which thou concealest.'

O splendour of living light eternal, who has ever grown so pale under Parnassus' shade or drunk so deep of its well that he would not seem to have a mind disabled, trying to render thee as thou appearedst there, heaven with its harmonies overhanging thee, when in the free air thou didst disclose thyself?

(*Purg.* xxxi, 136–145)

In describing the revelation of the second "bellezza" Dante uses images of veils rather than mirrors: standing before a man who has lived beneath the shade (of Parnassus), Beatrice "dis-veils" and stands revealed under no other shadow but the sky. But the veil and the mirror are really synonymous, as we can discern in the word that Dante uses to describe what he sees when the veil is removed—*isplendor*. The customary gloss on the word is from the *Convivio*: "Ma però che qui è fatta menzione di luce e di splendore, a perfetto intendimento mostrerò differenza di questi vocabuli, secondo che Avicenna sente. Dico che l'usanza de'filosofi è di chiamare 'luce' lo lume, in quanto esso è nel suo fontale principio; di chiamare 'raggio,' in quanto esso è per lo mezzo, dal principio al primo corpo dove si termina; di chiamare 'splendore,' in quanto esso è in altra parte alluminata ripercosso." When, therefore, Dante turns his gaze to the brilliance of Beatrice's smile what he sees is not the living and eternal Light "nel suo fontale principio," but the splendor of that light "in altra parte alluminata ripercosso." That is to say that Beatrice unveils, but is *herself* a veil and a mirror, through whom Dante perceives the Light of the Godhead. The figure of Beatrice is the highest of the *ombre* that occupy the eyes of the pilgrim in *Purgatorio*.

The concluding moment of centripetal vision in *Purgatorio*, then, is the vision of God by means of images and the vehicle is the corporeal form of Beatrice. . . . Purgatory is the realm in which the pilgrim begins to see the heavenly Light, but his eyes are not yet ready to look upon it directly. He still requires media to shield him from its full brilliance. In Paradise Dante will see God face to face; here in Purgatory he still sees *per speculum in aenigmate*: through a glass and in a sign.

Images are neither wholly corporeal nor wholly incorporeal, as Augustine said. *Spiritualia* are intermediate entities, not only epistemologically, but also ontologically. Dante's emphasis on the image in *Purgatorio* is thus perfectly suited to the transitional character of the realm. Even the physical design of the place, an immense mountain whose massive base tapers to a peak, is symbolic of the fact that Purgatory mediates between the shadowed corporeality of Hell and the lucid incorporeality of Heaven. The design is the precise reverse of that of Hell: there the descent is into an ever-narrowing cave toward a point where the souls are buried in matter; here as the pilgrim climbs, the mountain itself—quite literally— grows less corporeal at each stage. And so does the pilgrim. At the base of the mountain his step is weighted and the climb hard. With the removal of the first *P*, however, the pilgrim feels lighter, as if some "cosa greve" (*Purg.* xii, 118) has been lifted from him, the reverse of the system of Hell. He grows still lighter as he climbs until, when he has passed through the refining fire of the last ledge, he feels himself ready to transcend gravity completely: "ad ogni passo poi / al volo mi sentìa crescer le penne" (*Purg.* xxvii, 122–123). As the angel of the first cornice said, flight is man's true destiny ("o gente umana, per volar su nata," (*Purg.* xii, 95) and it is the function of Purgatory to cleanse the sinner from the encumbering sin that holds him back. To be cleansed is to be freed of the *pondus* that weighs down the souls in Hell, so that "mondi e lievi" (*Purg.* xi, 35) the saved may ascend to the stars. Therefore when Dante reaches the peak of Mount Purgatory he is at the nexus of the corporeal and incorporeal worlds, the appropriate locale for the *visio spiritualis* that takes place there. The vision of God is not in a body nor direct, but as reflected by and through the veil of Beatrice's corporeal form.

When Dante passes from Purgatory to Paradise he enters a world that is light-filled throughout, but even here there is progression toward a moment of climactic brilliance. Though movement upward is as swift as that of light itself, Dante nonetheless consumes thirty-three cantos of poetic time in reaching the summit point, and we should be aware of the enormity of his narrative problem. He was writing a poem made of finite words and images about a realm that transcends time and space, a narrative of the human actions of a "transhumanized" actor. Dante's solution to this narrative problem is simple in conception though astonishingly complex in execution. Throughout the poem the core of the narrative has been the gradual purification and strengthening of the pilgrim's power of vision, but in *Paradiso* Dante makes the very possibility of narrative depend on the capacities of his eyes. At the start of his flight, and, in fact, until its very conclusion, the pilgrim is still seeing (that is, knowing) with a mind conditioned to corporeal forms. For this reason, although the inhabitants of Paradise are properly incorporeal, they are given a perceptible shape of light—now not *ombre*, but *luci*—in order that the pilgrim may be prepared gradually for the final truly incorporeal vision. Beatrice explains the procedure in Canto iv when she tells Dante that the saved souls have their true home in the Empyrean but appear in the various spheres in order that the pilgrim may be instructed:

> These have shown themselves here, not that this sphere is allotted to
> them, but in sign of the heavenly rank that is least exalted. It is

necessary to speak thus to your faculty, since only from sense perception does it grasp that which it then makes fit for the intellect.

(*Par.* iv, 37–42)

The souls function as signs ("per far segno") adapted to the capacities of a knower whose faculties are still sense-oriented and not yet ready for an act of intellectual intuition, a mode of instruction Beatrice compares to the anthropomorphic techniques of Scripture, which attributes hands and feet to a transcendent God. The arrangement of Paradise, then, as a place to be seen, is the result of an act of divine benevolence which adapts the process of illumination to Dante's limitations. Beatrice reminds Dante of this near the end of the journey as they enter the Empyrean. They come upon a river of light ("lume in forma di rivera" *Par.* xxx, 61) whose banks are lined with flowers and whose waters scintillate with living sparks. The river is grace, the flowers the souls of the saved, and the sparks angels. Beatrice explains:

> The river and the topazes that pass into it and out and the laughter of the flowers are shadowy forecasts of their truth; not that these things are imperfect in themselves, but the defect is in thyself, that thy vision is not yet so exalted.

(*Par.* xxx, 76–81)

Her language reveals the paradoxical nature of Paradisal imagery: even these brilliant forms, which are themselves lights, are "umbriferi prefazii," shadows and prefaces—shadows *because* they are prefaces. Throughout *Paradiso* lights are shadows, reflections of the true Light. After Dante bathes in the river these light-shadows undergo a visual metamorphosis. He compares the change to the way the mask worn by someone at a festival might be dropped in order to reveal the masquer's true identity. So the "sembianza" of the river of light vanishes to reveal a greater festival.

> . . . the flowers and the sparks changed for me into a greater festival, so that I saw both the courts of heaven made plain.

(*Par.* xxx, 94–96)

Dante's metaphor here is compressed and suggestive. The masked revellers at a festival are gay partly because of the *personae* that their masks allow them to adopt. The putting off of the masks is a sign that the festival and its rejoicing are ended. Dante tells us, however, that it is different in the kingdom of Heaven; there *unmasking* is our joy, and the true face of reality is more intoxicating (cf. 1. 67) than its shadow. But Dante's image of the two festivals further alerts us to the fact that the pilgrim has still not come to the vision of the fully revealed light. Even though the heavenly courts are now "manifeste," the greater festival still involves a kind of masking. The souls and the angels are transformed from the flowers and sparks of the river into a single flower and swarm of bees. Dante does not dispense with images; he simply exchanges one image for a new and more transparently revealing one. The rose of souls itself rests on a compound of reflected lights and each face in it is a reflector that transmits the Light of "another" (xxxi, 48).

Dante's vision of the river and its metamorphosis in Canto xxx is a helpful guide to the understanding of the way the poet makes us experience the pilgrim's progress through Paradise. The climax of *Purgatorio* depicts an encounter with dazzling brilliance, yet Dante manages to convince us at every stage of the way through Paradise that the pilgrim is apprehending an even more intense level of illumination. The essential difference between the objects of vision in Purgatory and in Paradiso is that in the middle kingdom the "shadowy prefaces" are images of bodies, while in Paradise the shadows are lights, as Beatrice points out. The method of *Paradiso*, then, is to have the Light *veiled by lights*. So it is that Dante can begin *Paradiso* at the brilliant peak where *Purgatorio* ended and trace the pilgrim's encounter with a series of always more brilliant lights which are nonetheless only semblances and shadows of God's transcendent reality. The climactic shadow-light in *Paradiso* is the Mystic Rose, and the highest glory of the Rose is Mary,

> Look now on the face that most resembles Christ, for only its brightness can fit thee to see Christ.
>
> (*Par.* xxxii, 85–87)

In this pilgrimage of the eye, not even the vision of Mary can be an end in itself, but is given to Dante as the highest human similitude of divinity. The pilgrim looks on the Mother of Christ as on everything he sees: to prepare himself to see God, for she is "di Dio tanto sembiante" (*Par.* xxxii, 93).

It is only at the very end of his journey that Dante's eyes are ready for the vision of God without semblances, the *visio intellectualis* that tradition associated with St. Paul. As in the other two realms the climactic vision takes place in an appropriate environment, the Empyrean or heaven of "pura luce: / luce intellettüal (*Par.* xxx, 39–40). It is here that Dante is finally allowed to look upon the "alta luce che da sè è vera" (*Par.* xxxiii, 54). We should notice how carefully Dante depicts this supreme confrontation. When Mary turns her eyes toward God and Bernard commands the pilgrim to imitate her example, the poet does not immediately narrate the moment of *visio intellectualis*. Dante the pilgrim, even here, is not yet beyond the vision of images. As his eyes begin to penetrate the *raggio* of divine Light he first sees a series of figures: the Book which is the unity of many leaves (an image of the transcendence of substance and accident in God), the three-in-one circle of light (an image of the Trinity), and the union of the human shape with the circle of the Son (an image of the Incarnation). He has still not reached the direct intuition of God as He is, but he has come at last to the end of the preparative vision. The point to be recognized about this final series of semblances is that they are all symbols of mysteries which transcend merely human under-standing. The human mind can construct analogies of these facts, it can reason out the necessity of their existence, but it cannot understand them as they are in themselves so long as it still operates within the categories of space and time. The simplicity of God, the Trinity, the Incarnation are, in Augustine's word, *intellectualia*—realities which are utterly beyond space and time. The moment when the pilgrim confronts this vision is a crucial one and the poet pauses to describe his reaction:

> Like the geometer who sets all his mind to the squaring of the circle and for all his thinking does not discover the principle he needs, such was I at that strange sight.
>
> (*Par.* xxxiii, 133–136)

The simile is exact. The intellectual fact that the pilgrim is seeking to apprehend evades the measuring of the mind. The geometer may manipu-late images of square and circle and may cover sheets with his calcula-tions, but none of this will allow him to *see*, to apprehend intuitively, the square circle itself. The simile warns us that we cannot see God by thinking about Him; rather God must reveal Himself to us by raising us to a transhumanized mode of knowledge. It is grace that lifts us beyond thinking to the intellectual vision of God.

It is while Dante, in the fashion of the geometer, struggles to know, that the moment of grace comes:

> . . . but my own wings were not sufficient for that, had not my mind been smitten by a flash wherein came its wish.
>
> (*Par.* xxxiii, 139–141)

His own wings are too weak to lift him up to the final height, but the Light descends from above with the suddenness and intensity of a light-ning bolt. This is the moment of *visio intellectualis*: a *fulgore*, an enveloping explosion, a blow to the mind. The image of the lightning flash conveys the sense of an experience of light—that is, of intellectual reality—so encompassing that the mind cannot contain it; it contains the mind.

Dante fills the final canto of *Paradiso* with confessions of his inability to render the final vision of God in words. These professions are not mere instances of the *topos* of authorial modesty, but acknowledgments of the Pauline injunction that it is not licit for man to describe what he sees in the "third heaven." The concluding lines of the poem, we should realize, do not violate the Pauline prohibition. Even though everything that has gone before has only been preface to the moment of supreme vision, Dante nevertheless refrains from describing that final vision. He tells us *that* he saw, but he does not tell us *what* he saw. He simply says that to look on God directly is to be overwhelmed as by lightning. Here *alta fantasia*, the expressive power of images, fails, because the experience of God in the *visio intellectualis* is utterly beyond similitudes. All the poet can do is what Dante does in the poem's final lines: suggest the effect of the vision on his will (and by implication on his subsequent actions) and then end his poem.

These notes on the structure of vision in the *Comedy* have been necessarily schematic, and I have avoided attendant problems in the interest of bringing a view of the narrative's framework into clear relief. When Dante chose to write a poem about how we, in our life, can discover God, he chose as his essential narrative action the act of seeing. The classical model, reflected in the choice of Virgil as guide, is not the voyage of Odysseus, but the underworld tour of Aeneas, for the most significant thing about the journey is not what the pilgrim *does*, but what he *sees*. The mark of progress in the journey is therefore the growth of the pilgrim's power of vision, the education of his eyes. This growth in visionary capacity is continuous, but it is also divided into three stages that correspond to the three realms of the afterlife through which the pilgrim passes. At the climactic point in each realm the pilgrim experiences a moment of epiphany which is a vision of God (both as Christ and as the Godhead). In Hell Dante sees God in a body; in Purgatory in an image; in Paradise in Himself. The first two epiphanies are indirect, representing the knowledge of God by means of something other than Himself; only the third vision is direct and intuitive.

In ordering his poem in this way, I suggest, Dante was responding to the tradition of commentary that flowed from Augustine's *De Genesi ad litteram XII*. While the classical prototype for the pilgrim of the *Comedy* is Aeneas, the Biblical prototype is Paul, concerning whose vision of the "third heaven" Augustine's is the conventional medieval exegesis. Augustine proposed the sequence of three visions, corporeal, spiritual, and intellectual, as the solution to a specific exegetical problem, but he also asserted their universality as the essential modes by which man can know God. What I have tried to show is that this Augustinian pattern gives us a very direct clue to the structure of the *Comedy* as an act of vision. Dante begins in a dark wood, apprehending reality as a chaos of materiality, obscurely without meaning; in the subsequent action he passes from the condition of seeing reality as a corporeal mass to seeing it as incorporeal substance. The *Comedy* is therefore the narrative of an act of total vision which penetrates through the apparent substantiality of this world of time and space to the God who transcends time and space and is "true of Himself." The Augustinian tradition provided Dante with the essential clue to how such an act of total vision might be structured.

MARGUERITE MILLS CHIARENZA

The Imageless Vision and Dante's "Paradiso"

In interpreting St. Paul's claim to have been rapt to the third heaven, St. Augustine developed a theory of knowledge which influenced the entire Middle Ages. For St. Augustine the problem was to define the third heaven and this involved discovering what was meant by the other two as well. He concluded that the three heavens are to be taken in a spiritual sense and represent three modes of vision. Briefly, the first mode is *visio corporalis*, knowledge through the senses of material objects; the second, *visio spiritualis*, is knowledge through the imagination in which, as in dreams, the senses are inactive but forms of physical objects are the means of representation; the third and highest, *visio intellectualis*, is intuition of spiritual substances *facie ad faciem*, without direct or indirect participation of the senses. Both spiritual and intellectual vision are immaterial but while intellectual vision is emphatically direct, spiritual vision is mediated by images.

Francis X. Newman, to whom I refer the reader for a fuller discussion of St. Augustine's doctrine, has suggested most convincingly that the Augustinian modes of vision are a governing principle in Dante's imagery, that each of the *cantiche* tends toward a vision of God in one of the Augustinian modes and that the imagery of each reflects this tendency. Lucifer, the most corporeal object in the universe, parodies God in *Inferno*; the reflected image of the griffon in the *Purgatorio* is Dante's spiritual vision of Christ and, finally, in the *Paradiso* Dante sees God

From *Dante Studies*, vol. 90 (1972). Copyright © 1972 by State University of New York Press in cooperation with the State University of New York at Binghamton.

directly. Newman's suggestion is of particular significance for the *Paradiso* where Dante makes the unique claim to have followed in St. Paul's footsteps and to have seen God face to face. And yet, except for the last cantos, Newman seems hesitant in his application of the concept of intellectual vision to the *Paradiso*:

> At the start of his flight, and, in fact, until its very conclusion, the pilgrim is still seeing (that is, knowing) with a mind conditioned to corporeal forms. For this reason, although the inhabitants of Paradise are properly incorporeal, they are given a perceptible shape of light—now not *ombre*, but *luci*—in order that the pilgrim may be prepared gradually for the final truly incorporeal vision.

Intellectual vision is by its very nature incongruent with poetry, for it is the denial of that of which poetry is made, images, and perhaps this is what leads Newman to imply that such an experience does not occur until the end of the voyage. However, what Dante claims in the *Paradiso*, to have seen God and lived, is as inconceivable as representing or mediating that which is by definition unmediated. Therefore, I would like to go further than Newman and suggest that the basic position of the poet in the *Paradiso* is revealed by his struggle to express a vision which was imageless from the start.

The *Paradiso* is possibly the greatest paradox in the history of poetry and it is small wonder that we are often distressed by a certain ambiguity found in the descriptions of its poetics. Nonetheless, if certain basic problems are clarified it is easier to arrive at some degree of precise statement. The two aspects of the *Paradiso* which lead to most confusion are, I think, the hierarchy represented there and the fact that the pilgrim's ultimate vision is of God. Both of these can lead the critic to distinguish stages in such a way as to imply that the poetics proper to the *Paradiso* are to be found only in the last cantos. If too much emphasis is placed on the division of the *cantica* in preparatory vision in the heavens and final vision in the Empyrean and if this division is then extended to the poetics of the *Paradiso*, the end of the poem becomes the true *Paradiso* and we are left with some thirty cantos which are not the *Purgatorio* and are not the *Paradiso*. To avoid this we must stress the declared superhuman quality of vision in these cantos and do away with the definitions, such as *per speculum* or *in aenigmate*, which make of it nothing more than a rarefied version of human experience.

The division of the *Paradiso* in vision in the heavens and vision in the Empyrean is partially false. Clearly, the vision of God's face is to be distinguished from all other vision. But this vision transcends the poem, it does not end it. In the last verses Dante tells us that he did penetrate

God's face and he tells us something of the effect it had on him, but he also tells us that this experience is lost to him as a man in whom memory fails and as a poet in whom *fantasia* fails—indeed failed already in the moment that vision was granted him. These last verses, not all of the Empyrean, are perhaps to be distinguished in that they represent the little that can be said of the ultimate vision. But all other vision in Paradise ends in the sum total of its parts, leaving only the mystery of God's nature to be known. What the poet can say of God's face is possible only because all conceivable vision has been exhausted. Vision in heaven is universal vision of truth which becomes a totality only when its separateness is transcended. This transcending of separateness is foreshadowed in the Empyrean but becomes a reality only as the pilgrim turns to God's face and, just before all experience, superhuman as well as human, is left behind, sees the unity implicit in the nature of truth, only to transcend even that unity in the vision of the Trinity and the Incarnation.

> In its depth I saw that it contained, bound by love in one volume, that which is scattered in leaves through the universe.
>
> (*Par.* XXXIII, 85–87)

This image not only clarifies the content of Dante's vision but also, because he uses the book as his metaphor, it is a clue to his poetics as well. God's face is not the universe but in it is contained the universe in its truest form. In Medieval doctrine every creature has its truest existence in the mind of God, although its natural existence is external. . . . St. Augustine compares the difference between the natural existence of creatures and their existence in God to the difference between night and day and tells us that knowledge of a creature in itself compares to knowledge of it in God in the same way that no knowledge at all compares to knowledge in the creature. . . . Dante's *terzina* is inspired by the doctrine of the double existence of creation, separate in the universe and unified in its Creator's conception. The unity of creation in God's mind is the pilgrim's final vision of the universe and represents the point at which the poem begins to be transcended. The pilgrim sees again all that he has hitherto seen, in its truest form. Dante tells us that he saw a repetition of his entire vision but does not describe it, for he has only human tools and to describe it would be literally a repetition. However, the image is far from being simply a statement of the whereabouts of the universe's conception, precisely because Dante chooses the book as his metaphor. When the universe is transcended, what was separate becomes unified just as all the pages when bound become the book. Dante does not represent the vision of always greater things ending in a thing greater still but the vision of all things followed and transcended by the vision of their unity. Vision of unity and totality are not a part of the poem but a result of it. The mind, the pilgrim's and the reader's, absorbs totality in its separate parts but is destined to transcend that separation. This principle is true of the poem also. The pilgrim does not see the last page of the book in God's face, he sees the book bound together, for when the poem is complete it is no longer a sequence but a unity. The reader transcends the pages to retain in his mind the poem, which was conceived by the author before it was written and is now transcended by him much the same as creation is conceived and transcended by God.

As the pilgrim turns to God's face all that is left to be seen of the universe is its unity. If vision until this moment is of spiritual substances, such as souls, and is defective only in its lack of unity, then it is intellectual in the Augustinian sense. It is direct intuition of spiritual substances even though not yet intuition of them in God. The notion that the highest form of vision is only to be found in the Empyrean seems, however, to be supported by the hierarchy represented throughout the heavens. Because of this some discussion of hierarchy will be necessary if we are to maintain that St. Augustine's highest mode of vision is the mode of all of the *Paradiso.*

Hierarchy, whose incongruous presence in the *Paradiso* is the source of some equivocation, is itself presented as an equivocation. It is presented, in fact, as an artificial structure which does not exist outside of the momentary need for it. The saints descend to various spheres which dramatize their place in a harmonious world of beatitude where the greater and the lesser are equally perfected, where qualitative difference does not diminish quantitative completeness, for "ogni dove in cielo è paradiso" and each position is unlimited. They stage this hierarchy because the pilgrim is not ready for a vision of totality. He must see the parts in order to see the whole. Because this hierarchy is not temporal in nature, time is so underplayed in the *Paradiso* that there is no way of accurately measuring it. The various entities must all appear to the pilgrim to give him the whole vision but their ordering is not a sequential phenomenon. They do not have to follow one another in taking their place, they simply must all be there. The poem, on the other hand, is constrained in a sequential form and, if it is to be read, verse must follow verse. In fact, while the pilgrim is speeding through the heavens at a velocity inconceivable to the human mind, time for the poet, the length of the third *cantica,* is the same as it was in the other two. This consideration leads us to confront the new relation between the pilgrim and the poet.

In the *Inferno* and the *Purgatorio* the poet's struggle is secondary to the pilgrim's and the danger is essentially in the voyage. In the *Paradiso* it is the poet who struggles while the pilgrim is safe. This is because the pilgrim was in possession of transhuman powers while the poet, who has returned to the human, is not. The pilgrim transcended time in Paradise, which from the start of his flight approached deletion. Human categories of perception were left behind with Purgatory. His vision was essentially "in un ponto solo," which *punto* substituted and annulled a kind of paraphrase which led up to it. The poet, however, must work exclusively with human categories and make the paraphrase take the place of the essential vision, that is, spend thirty three cantos telling us that he approached the vision which he uses only a few verses to tell us he has forgotten. The pilgrim should not be seen as one who is passing from one stage to another in order to acquire his highest faculties but as one in whom these faculties are already activated and who is growing, through the accumulation of vision, not toward a new kind of vision but toward the supreme object of vision. If this growth appears to occur in stages it is because the poet is representing it. Whatever the pilgrim's limitations, which made certain concessions from heaven necessary, the poet's are far greater and his concessions to the reader greatly exceed those of heaven to him. We must not attribute all of the characteristics of the representation to the vision itself but must remember that what we read is twice medi-ated, first through memory for the poet and then through words for the reader. This mediation must not be confused with any mediation in the experience itself. My purpose is (1) to show that Dante denies mediation in the experience and (2) to illustrate partially how he copes with its necessity in the poem.

Just as Dante gives us a hierarchy but at the same time undercuts its value by denying its independent reality, so he makes the limitations to which he (who has returned to the human) is subject work in his favor. These limitations are memory and words. From the start he tells us that the vision is no longer accessible to him and that memory must take its place. If intellectual vision—unmediated, imageless knowledge of spiritual substances—is the subject of the *Paradiso* and memory which, like the imagination, functions through images is the source, then we should expect to find universal infidelity in the representation. . . . Dante is counting on us to know that memory will introduce images where there were no images. He tells us that we are reading only what his memory could retain:

> I was in the heaven that most receives His light and I saw things which
> he that descends from it has not the knowledge or the power to tell

again; for our intellect, drawing near to its desire, sinks so deep that memory cannot follow it. Nevertheless, so much of the holy kingdom as I was able to treasure in my mind shall now be matter of my song.

(*Par.* I, 4–12)

Thus, we are warned to look beyond what we are offered. Dante warns us and reminds us constantly of the limitations of the source, because if these limitations are forgotten, it will lose its truthfulness as a source.

What we have said of memory can also be said of words. Their insufficiency is declared from the beginning:

The passing beyond humanity cannot be set forth in words; let the example suffice, therefore, for him to whom grace reserves the experience.

(*Par.* I, 70–72)

Indeed words are one step further removed from the experience than memory itself. The poet can only communicate through verbal reference to experience derived from the senses, the denial of intellectual vision. Again, Hugh of St. Cher tells us, in terms very like Dante's, what happens when an attempt is made to communicate intellectual vision. He compares it to trying to describe the taste of wine to one who has never tasted it and can only refer the description to something else which he has tasted. . . . As with memory, Dante uses the obviousness of the insufficiency of his means to his advantage, and creates his most revolutionary technique, that of using words and images not merely to point beyond themselves but to point against themselves as well.

As I will show, Dante tells us that his vision was intellectual throughout the journey in Paradise and, therefore, to acquire such vision is not a goal of the pilgrim. The representation of such vision is, however, a goal for the poet. He is human and must cope gradually with the elimination of mediatory images and will completely do away with them only when he is silent. Vision of God by a man in the flesh is parallel to the paradox of a poet attempting through images, which are incorporeal only in that they have no corporeal—or spiritual—substance but which are based on reference to the senses, to represent that which is by definition spiritually substantial and void of any reference to the senses. And yet Dante's imagery in the *Paradiso* is developed in two directions which tend precisely toward the fulfillment of the two attributes of intellectual vision, incorporeality and substantiality.

Light metaphysics is not the subject of this discussion, but since light plays a role in the representation of intellectual vision it will be necessary to make a few remarks, however general, on its function in the *Paradiso*. The pilgrim sees everything in Paradise in the form of light which is gradually intensified to the point of blindness. Light has the unique attribute of being the source of all vision though itself shapeless and invisible outside the objects it illuminates. In the *Paradiso*, however, it does not illuminate objects but shines forth from subjects. These are lights themselves, not shining on objects but reflecting their own vision. Everything in the *Paradiso* is a reflecting light and it is this light which Dante uses to represent substances, which light is not a passive reflection of an external source but an active reflection of internal vision. The souls are not represented as inferior versions of something else but as spiritual centers of energy and truths in themselves. In fact, the pilgrim does not see God indirectly in the souls but beatitude directly. The souls are, of course, dependent on God for their vision and their beatitude but this dependence in no way diminishes their substantiality, for God is reflected by the entire universe which could not exist without Him. For the souls not to reflect God would be to cease to exist.

The reflecting light characteristic of the *Paradiso* represents sub-stantiality in Dante's imagery. To represent substantiality is a challenge for a poet, but for him to attempt to represent the other essential quality of intellectual vision—absence of reference to experience derived from the senses—is more than a challenge, it is a contradiction in terms. It means, in effect, to represent through images that which is by definition incom-patible with images. Nevertheless, this is a theme of Dante's imagery already evident in the pilgrim's first encounter with the inhabitants of the heavens.

> As through smooth and transparent glass, or through limpid and still water not so deep that the bottom is lost, the outlines of our faces return so faint that a pearl on a white brow does not come less quickly to our eyes, many such faces I saw, eager to speak. . . .
>
> (*Par*. III, 10–17)

These souls are compared to mirrors but, immediately, the traditional mirror, that of Narcissus, is negated:

> . . . at which I ran into the opposite error to that which kindled love between the man and the spring.
>
> (18–19)

Most interesting is the way in which these images stress immateriality in their very reference to material objects. They are calculated to suggest incorporeality, even imperceptibility. Their visibility is described only through their near invisibility: reflections not in a mirror but in glass or shallow water so clear as to offer virtually no reflection at all; a pearl whose color so blends into the forehead on which it is worn that it cannot even be seen at first glance. Dante tells the reader what he saw in terms of visual experience in which the eye fails. I will return to this passage to show how directly it introduces the concept of intellectual vision, but first I would like to illustrate briefly, through a few other images, how what is already present here at the beginning is developed in the rest of the *Paradiso.*

When the pilgrim enters the heaven of Mars the souls arrange themselves in the pattern of the cross. Dante's images at this point (*Par.* XIV, 91ff.) are extremely complex and deserve a fuller analysis. For our present purpose, we should notice that now Dante does not describe the lights in terms of their individual visibility but only of the collective shape they form. It is as if, on the one hand, only the cross not the souls were visible; on the other hand, there is no material cross to be seen but only the souls in the shape of the cross. That of which the cross is formed is not described, all that we are told is that it is formed. We are given a shape formed of shapeless parts. Neither the cross nor the souls are directly more visible than light itself; what the pilgrim sees is the meaning which the souls wish to show him, the "venerabil segno" (v.101). That this cross is not a material shape but the spiritual shape it signifies, is reinforced by the fact that as the pilgrim looks at it, he no longer sees it but the mystery from which it is inseparable:

> Here my memory defeats my skill, for that cross so flamed forth Christ
> that I can find for it no fit comparison. . . .
>
> (103–105)

The spiritual value of his vision is further enhanced by his use immediately afterward of the metaphor, not so metaphorical for Dante, of the cross in each man's life:

> . . . but he that takes up his cross and follows Christ shall yet forgive me
> for what I leave untold. . . .
>
> (106–107)

The same can be said of the souls in the heaven of Jupiter who form the sign of the eagle (XVIII, 74ff.), but here Dante has progressed one step further beyond the material form. The eagle is the final shape in a series of metamorphic images which remain visible only until they have been comprehended. Furthermore, these images represent letters, shapes indeed but as inseparable from their collective meaning as they are individually meaningless. This inseparability is all the more evident because the letters are not seen together but one by one so that when their meaning is read they have already disappeared leaving only their message, a verse from the Bible, whose author is God. When they have disappeared, their meaning, now in the form of the symbolic eagle, emerges, and again Dante could say he saw no eagle but only the meaning of justice shining forth from the formless souls of the just.

The cross and the eagle are images taken from the middle cantos of the *Paradiso* and show an obvious development from the first images of the *cantica*. Turning to the last canto of the poem and necessarily skipping countless other equally significant images, we find the famous image with which Dante ends his series of "anti-images":

> Like the geometer who sets all his mind to the squaring of the circle and for all his thinking does not discover the principle he needs, such was I at that strange sight.
>
> (XXXIII, 133–135)

The squaring of the circle crowns a series of abstract geometrical shapes describing the mystery of God's nature and is the one shape in the universe which can be defined but cannot be seen. We, like Hugh of St. Cher's *caecus natus*, can "say much of it because we have heard much about it," but we have no experience of it.

There are, then, stages in the development of Dante's imagery in the *Paradiso*. Three of them are those mentioned, in which we find, first, concrete shapes which can barely be perceived, then shapes in which symbolic meaning overshadows concrete form, and at last purely conceptual shape not found in the material universe. These stages lead the poet to the point at which he can go no further but must end his poem in order that it become literally imageless. This does not mean that the pilgrim's vision was not imageless from the start. His vision was peripheral at the beginning as he tended toward "un punto solo" at the spiritual center of the universe. But that it was peripheral does not mean that it was not direct spiritual intuition. In describing the impenetrable depth of God's mind Dante uses an image which becomes very eloquent if we remember that the souls in the moon, the first encountered in Paradise, were compared to shallow water in which the bottom is still visible:

> Therefore the sight that is granted to your world penetrates within the Eternal Justice as the eye into the sea; for though from the shore it sees the bottom, in the open sea it does not, and yet the bottom is there but the depth conceals it.
>
> (*Par.* XIX, 58–63)

The difference between the pilgrim and the man whose faculties have not been elevated beyond the human is that the pilgrim approaches the spiritual creatures of the "gran mar dell'essere" without ever losing sight of the sea's bottom.

All of this might seem pure speculation if Dante did not make it explicit from the start, from that first encounter with the souls in the moon to which I must now return. In the moon the pilgrim is faced with a vision which seems designed to discourage the senses. The human mind knows incorporeality through spiritual and therefore unsubstantial vision. So incorporeal is the pilgrim's vision that, since his mind is still conditioned to human experience, he falls into the error of thinking it also unsubstantial and turns away looking for what he has taken to be an image. Beatrice corrects him with the words: "These are real beings that thou seest." Surely, by "real beings" Beatrice does not mean corporeal substances, for she is speaking of souls, not bodies. She means spiritual substances. But it is not through Beatrice's words, unequivocable as they are, that we first realize the nature of what the pilgrim sees, it is through the image with which Dante describes the pilgrim's error:

> . . . at which I ran into the opposite error to that which kindled love between the man and the spring.
>
> (III, 18–19)

The allusion is of course to the myth of Narcissus.

Twice already Hugh of St. Cher's discussion of intellectual vision has seemed relevant to Dante's poetic position in the *Paradiso*. It is perhaps most revealing with regard to the image of Narcissus which appears in Hugh's text as the image of the man, perhaps a philosopher or a mystic, who is so carried away with the flight of his imagination that he thinks he has transcended the senses altogether and does not realize that his vision is still mediated by images. Hugh is discussing the difference between spiritual and intellectual vision and poses the problem whether any man could so abstract himself from the senses as to see God as St. Paul did. The answer is that he could not, but he might think he had. . . . When Dante describes his error as the opposite of Narcissus' there can be no doubt that his Narcissus is the same as Hugh of St. Cher's, the man who mistakes an abstraction of the imagination for direct intuition or, what is the same, spiritual vision for intellectual vision. The pilgrim, who has been prepared on all levels of human experience, but only of human experience, when confronted with incorporeal vision assumes that it is also unsubstantial. His error is indeed the opposite of that of Narcissus for, while Narcissus mistook spiritual vision for intellectual vision, he mistakes intellectual vision for spiritual vision. While Narcissus failed to turn away from an image which he thought was substance, the pilgrim turns away from substance thinking it an image.

It is worthwhile comparing this episode to that of Casella in the *Purgatorio*:

> I saw one of them come forward with so much affection to embrace me
> that it moved me to do the same. O empty shades, except in semblance!
> Three times I clasped my hands behind him and as often brought them
> back to my breast. Wonder, I think, was painted in my looks. . . .
>
> (*Purg.* II, 76–82)

Like the souls in the moon, Casella is the first soul the pilgrim meets in the new realm. Newman has pointed out that the encounter with Casella represents a kind of introduction of the pilgrim to spiritual vision, for the pilgrim, who has just come from the realm of corporeal vision, does not realize at first that Casella is but an "ombra vana fuor che nell'aspetto," almost a technical definition of an image. In the *Paradiso* the situation is similar, for the pilgrim has just arrived from Purgatory and again misjudges his new vision which is again described in terms which seem almost a definition, "vere sustanze."

There is a further relation between the episode of Casella and its counterpart in the *Paradiso* for, while the pilgrim's error in the *Paradiso* is described as the opposite of Narcissus' error, with Casella it is strikingly reminiscent of the myth as it appeared in the classics. Like the classical Narcissus the pilgrim sees an image which appears to be a man and, like Narcissus, he attempts to embrace it. His error is identical to the one Ovid described: "corpus putat esse quod umbra est." Had the pilgrim, or Narcissus, turned away from the image before him, there would have been no error. Perhaps the pilgrim's very caution in the *Paradiso* ("sovra il ver lo piè non fida" v. 27), which causes him to turn from the souls, is a manifestation of his fear, when confronted with what does not even appear to have corporeal substance, of falling into his previous error. Yet, in the *Purgatorio*, the poet avoids any direct allusion to the myth of Narcissus. Had Dante's Narcissus been simply the one found in Ovid the image would have been appropriate to the *Purgatorio*. But this Narcissus has undergone a transformation in a tradition which treated him as the man who fails to turn away from an inferior experience toward the truth, a truth which has long since ceased to be the truth of the senses. As Narcissus appears in Hugh of St. Cher's version his error is clearly that of mistaking an image for spiritual, not corporeal substance and such an error has little to do with the passage from corporeal to spiritual vision.

The encounter with the souls in the moon is clearly an introduction of the concept of intellectual vision. And yet there is one aspect of it which, on the surface at least, seems to go against such an interpretation, encouraging the reader to suppose the pilgrim is not yet ready for a truly incorporeal experience. This is the presence of faces in the description of the souls. In no other part of the *Paradiso* do souls bear any resemblance to the human form. This corporeality is mitigated by the fact that only faces, not bodies proper, are present and by the fact that they are barely visible. However, in speaking of outlines ("postille"), Dante is using terms inapplicable to spiritual substance. . . .

Of course, as we have had occasion to say, the poet deals in images and shows us only conceptually what he can have no hope of showing us directly. Still, the form of the human face, in this instance, cannot be understood merely as a necessary imperfection in the representation. It could if there were no emphasis on it, but it is the key image of the passage. Dante compares what he saw, a group of faces, to the reflection of faces in water or glass, and he speaks of a pearl worn on the forehead. The image of Narcissus is the image of a reflected face. Finally, the pilgrim's error consists, dramatically, in his turning his face away from the vision.

Dante's vision could be purely incorporeal but, if it were not direct it would not be intellectual. The whole passage is intended to introduce into the poem the experience of direct spiritual intuition and the image of the face is no exception. It represents the dramatization of the Pauline phrase which was commonplace in describing the directness of intellectual vision, "facie ad faciem," and which was inseparable from its association with the phrase that described all other vision, "per speculum in aenigmate." Everything in the episode works to replace the mirror by the face. In fact, the pilgrim does not yet understand the nature of his vision and consequently puts himself in such a position as to reject it. With the help of Beatrice he corrects his error so that he can then receive the vision granted him. In order to see face to face he must turn face to face.

Somehow the pilgrim's error and its correction do not seem vital to his development. Surely, once granted his vision, he should be able to recognize it. But sometimes the pilgrim must show the reader the pitfalls to be avoided by himself failing to avoid them. If recognition should be fairly simple for the pilgrim, it is not simple for the reader. On the one hand, the reader sees what might be described as images of images; on the other hand, he finds the concept of images strongly denied. Different from the pilgrim, no matter how much the images tend to negate their nature as images, the reader will have them before him for the entire duration of the poem. Because of this it is necessary that he understand from the beginning that they were not there for the pilgrim, that the vision the poet describes was imageless. Dante could have followed St. Paul and resorted to silence, for of such things "it is not lawful for men to speak" and a poet cannot speak without images. Instead of this he chose to testify to his experience despite the fact that he could only offer an "essemplo," an imperfect rendering and a substitute for the experience itself. From the beginning of the *Paradiso* he confesses that it will be but an "ombra del beato regno," a shadow, a reflection, even an image. Yet from the very first heaven he shows us, through the pilgrim's initial error, that, though we shall see only images, he saw only substances. If he can make us accept this, then perhaps we will accept the climax of his claimed vision, substantial knowledge of God.

JOHN FRECCERO

Medusa: The Letter and the Spirit

Several times in the course of his poem, Dante insists that his verses be read allegorically, but nowhere is his insistence more peremptory or more baffling than in Canto IX of the *Inferno*, after Virgil covers the pilgrim's eyes to protect him from the sight of the Medusa:

> Ye that are of good understanding, note the teaching that is hidden under the veil of the strange lines.
>
> (*Inferno*, IX, 61–63)

These lines have always represented something of a scandal in the interpretation of Dante's allegory, primarily because they seem to fail in their didactic intent: in fact, the *dottrina* referred to here remains as veiled to us as it was to the poet's contemporaries. More than that, however, the *dottrina*, whatever it is, seems scarcely worth the effort. The verses suggest a personification allegory—Medusa as moral abstraction—very different from the theological allegory that, since the work of Charles Singleton, we have taken to be uniquely dantesque. The allegory of the episode would seem to be no different from the "allegory of poets," described in the *Convivio* as a *menzogna* hiding a moral truth, so that we are tempted to conclude either that Dante's allegory, though obscure, is no different from that of other poets, or that this first explicit reference to it in the poem is somehow atypical of the rest of the allegory.

My purpose in this paper will be to suggest that neither of these

---

From *Yearbook of Italian Studies* (1972). Copyright © 1972 by *Yearbook of Italian Studies*.

alternatives is correct and that this passage, when properly understood, can provide us with a model for understanding Dante's allegory through-out the poem. I hope to show that the allegory is essentially theological and, far from being of purely antiquarian interest, a bizarre exegetical theory irrelevant to poetic practice, is actually indistinguishable from the poem's narrative structure. Christian allegory, I will argue, is identical with the phenomenology of confession, for both involve a comprehen-sion of the self in history within a retrospective literary structure.

Perhaps the principal difficulty with the address to the reader in the episode of the Medusa has arisen from our tendency to read it as though it were dramatically unrelated to its context, a generic recall to a moral code exterior to the text. In fact, however, this passage, like all of the addresses to the reader, is exterior to the fiction, but central to the text. The authorial voice is at once the creation of the journey and its creator, an *alter Dantes* who knows, but does not as yet exist, dialectically related to the pilgrim, who exists but does not as yet know. The addresses to the reader create the author as much as they create his audience; they are as the paradigm of the entire narrative, ensuring the presence of the goal at each step along the way. It is Dante's fiction that the author's existence precedes that of the poem, as though the experience had been concluded before the poem were begun. In reality, however, the experi-ence of the pilgrim and the creation of the authorial voice take place at the same time, in the writing of the poem. The progress of the pilgrim and the addresses to the reader are dramatic representations of the dialectic that is the process of the poem. Journey's end, the vision of the incarna-tion, is at the same time the incarnation of the story, when pilgrim and author, being and knowing, become one.

In precisely the same way that the pilgrim and the authorial voice are dialectically related to each other, the dramatic action involving the Medusa is related to the address to the reader immediately following it. This is suggested by a certain inverse symmetry: the *covering* of the pilgrim's eyes calls forth a command to *uncover* and see ("mirate") the doctrine hidden beneath the verses, as if the command were consequent to the action rather than simply the interruption that it is usually taken to be. As readers of the poem, we ordinarily assume that the dramatic action is stopped from time to time for an authorial gloss, as if the poet were arbitrarily intruding upon a re-run of his own past in order to guide us in our interpretation. Here, however, the symmetry between the action and the gloss suggests a more intimate, even *necessary*, relationship. The antithetical actions (covering/uncovering) suggest that we look for antithetical objects (Medusa/*dottrina*) in two analogous or parallel realms:

the progress of the pilgrim and the progress of the poem. The threat of the Medusa lends a certain moral force to the command to *see* beneath the strange verses, just as the address to the reader lends to the Medusa a certain hermeneutic resonance. It is *because* the pilgrim averted his eyes from the Medusa that there is a truth to be seen beneath the veil; because seeing it is a way of understanding a text, however, the implication seems to be that the Medusa is an interpretive as well as a moral threat. In other words, the aversion from the Medusa and the *conversion* to the text are related temporally, as the *before* and *after* of the same poetic event. Between those two moments, there extends the experience of the pilgrim, who has himself seen the *dottrina* and has returned as poet to reveal it to us.

A passage in the *Purgatorio* lends considerable weight to our suggestion that petrification is an interpretive as well as a moral threat and that the act of interpretation depends on a moral condition. At the end of the second *cantica*, on the occasion of Dante's own revelation, Beatrice chides him for his *Vani pensieri* and for the delight he has taken in them:

> I see thee turned to stone in thy mind and, being petrified, darkened, so that the light of my speech dazzles thee.
>
> (*Purg.*, XXXIII, 73–75)

If we apply this imagery to the episode of Canto IX, then it is clear that petrification can mean the inability to see the light of truth in an interpretive glance. Thus, the threat of the Medusa may in a sense be a danger to be averted by the reader as well as the pilgrim: an "intelletto sano," as Dante tells us in the *Convivio*, is a mind that is not obscured by ignorance or *malizia*, a mind that is not petrified.

The dialectic of blindness and vision, aversion and conversion in the interpretation of the text, is central to biblical hermeneutics and is discussed by St. Paul with the figure of the veil. The use of the word "velame" in Dante's verses would seem to be an allusion to the Pauline tradition. To speak of a truth hidden beneath a veil was of course a banality in Dante's day, as it is in ours, but its familiarity derived from its biblical origin, where the veil was literally a covering for the radiant face of Moses and figuratively the relationship of the Old Testament to the New. Paul, in II Corinthians, extends his discussion of the "letter that kills" and of the "Spirit that gives life" by blending the words of Jeremiah about God writing his law in the hearts of his people with those of Ezekiel about the people of God having hearts of flesh instead of hearts of stone. In St. Paul's New Testament perspective, the hearts of stone become the inscribed tablets of the Law of Moses, contrasted with the inscribed hearts of the faithful. He then discusses the meaning of the veil:

> Having therefore such hope, we show great boldness. We do not act as Moses did, who used to put a veil over his face that the Israelites might not observe the glory of his countenance, which was to pass away. But their minds were darkened (*obtusi sunt sensus eorum*); for to this day, when the Old Testament is read to them, the selfsame veil remains, not being lifted (*non revelatum*) to disclose the Christ in whom it is made void. Yes, down to this very day, when Moses is read, the veil covers their hearts; but when they turn in repentance to God, the veil shall be taken away (*Cum autem conversus fuerit ad Dominum, auferetur velamen*).
> (II Cor. iii. 12–16)

Paul here contrasts the Letter of the Old Testament, written on tablets of stone, with the Spirit of the New, Who is Christ, the "unveiling," or *re-velation*. The significance of the letter is in its final term, Christ, Who was present all along, but revealed as the Spirit only at the end, the conversion of the Old Testament to the New. Understanding the truth is not then a question of critical intelligence applied here and there, but rather of a retrospective illumination by faith from the standpoint of the ending, a conversion. In the original Greek, the term used to describe the darkening of the minds of the Jews, petrification, is rendered in the Vulgate as *obtusio*, but the sense of the hardness remains alive in the exegetical tradition, where the condition is glossed as *duritia cordis*.

After the Revelation, the inability to see beneath the veil is attributable to the "God of this world," who strikes the unbeliever sense-less. It is this God, which later tradition was to identify with the devil, that provides a generic biblical meaning for the Medusa:

> But if our gospel also is veiled, it is veiled only to those who are perishing. In their case, the God of this world has blinded their unbe-lieving minds, that they should not see the light . . . while we look not at the things that are seen, but at the things that are not seen. For the things that are seen are temporal, but the things that are not seen are eternal.
> (II Cor. iv. 3 ff.)

The familiar dialectic of blindness and vision, as old as Sophocles, as-sumes a special poignancy in the life of Paul, who was at successive moments blind: first to the truth of Christ and then, on the road to Damascus, to the things of this world. Conversion is for him, much as it was for Plato, a turning away from the false light of temporal things, seen with the eyes of the body, to the light of eternity, seen with the eyes of

the soul. Above all, blindness and vision are in the Pauline text metaphors for interpretation, the obtuse reading of faithless literalists transformed, by unveiling, into a reading of the same text in a new light.

I should like to propose that the episode of the Medusa is an
application of this dialectic to both the pilgrim and the reader. The
"before" and the "after" of the conversion experience are rendered se-
quentially and dramatically by the threat to the pilgrim, on one hand, and
the authorial voice on the other. Between the aversion from a temporal
threat and the conversion to the Christian truth, the *dottrina*, there is the
Christ event in the experience of the pilgrim, the moment that marks the
coming together of pilgrim and poet. From that ideal moment, Dante
fulfills the role of a Virgil to the reader, sufficient to the task of averting
his pupil's glance from the "God of this World," the temptation of
temporalia, yet not sufficient for the task of *re-velation*. The threat to the
pilgrim, petrification, seems to correspond to the various conditions of
unbelief suggested by the Pauline text: blindness, hardness of heart,
darkening of the mind, senselessness; while vision (presumably accomplished by the pilgrim/author and now proffered to the reader) corresponds to the eternity of "things that are not seen." Literalists are blind to
spiritual truth precisely because they see temporal things, while the things
of this world are invisible to those who see the Spirit within. The Christ
event in history, as described by St. Paul, is applied to the *now* of the
pilgrim's journey in his meeting with Beatrice and is left as testament to
the reader, who is exhorted to follow in his own way. En route, however,
both must avert their glance from the God of this world.

Whatever the merit of this dramatic outline, it still leaves us in the
realm of poetic fiction. Several difficulties immediately present themselves
which can be resolved only by exploring more deeply the relationship
between the Pauline text and the verses of Canto IX. In the first place,
the Pauline dialectic is built upon the fundamental opposition of two
terms which are a unity in the Bible: the Letter and the Spirit, figuratively
translated into visual terms by the opposition "veil"/"face of Moses"
(Christ). Dante's use of the word "velame" also suggests a translation into
visual terms of the interpretive act required of the reader at this point;
what is not as yet clear is the sense in which the threat of the Medusa is in
Dante's text, as petrification is in Paul's, the corresponding threat of the
"Letter that kills." In other words, how is the face of Medusa the opposite
of the face of Moses? Secondly, once the opposition between the threat of
the Medusa and the *dottrina* is established, there remains the problem of
their relationship, for Letter and Spirit, though opposed, are still one, as
the Old Testament, written on tablets of stone or engraved on the stony

hearts of unbelievers, is still one with its New Testament interpretation, written upon the "fleshly tablets of the heart" (II Cor. iii. 3). The same is true of the figure of the veil: it is under the same veil, perceived by believers and unbelievers alike, that the Truth is hidden. Paul attributes interpretive blindness to the "God of this world," but in Dante's text it is the diabolic threat itself that must somehow lead beyond itself. In what sense might it be said that the threat of the Medusa masks a *dottrina* that is nowhere to be found on the printed page? The resolution of both of these difficulties will become clear when we decide which, precisely, are the *versi strani* referred to in the text.

Our response must begin with some interpretive and historical remarks about the Medusa herself. To begin with, her story in antiquity seems a perfect counterpart to the story of the veiling of Moses' face. Dante was doubtless aware of the false etymology of her name concocted by the mythographers. . . . To see her was death; in order to protect himself from this threat, Perseus required the shield of Minerva, just as we, according to the allegorization of Albertus Magnus, require the shield of wisdom to protect us. . . . On the other hand, the face of Moses is a figure for the glory of Christ, *illuminatio Evangelii gloriae Christi* (II Cor. iv. 4), requiring nothing less than a conversion in order to be unveiled (*revelatio*). It remained for Dante to associate the two stories, recasting the Pauline dialectic of blindness and vision into the figure of the Medusa (corresponding to St. Paul's "God of this world") and contrasting it with the admonition, immediately following, to gaze at the truth beneath the veil. The two stories serve as excellent dramatizations of the two moments of conversion: aversion from the self and the things of this world, conversion to God. Separating those two moments there extends the whole of the journey.

A closer look at the tradition surrounding the Medusa suggests a more than dramatic aptness in the choice of this figure for the representation of a diabolic threat. The most startling thing about traditional efforts to discuss this episode is that they have missed what to a modern reader is most obvious: whatever the horror the Medusa represents to the male imagination, it is in some sense a female horror. In mythology, the Medusa was said to be powerless against women, for it was her feminine *beauty* that constituted the mortal threat to her admirers. From the ancient *Physiologus* through the mythographers to Boccaccio, the Medusa represented a sensual fascination, a *pulchritudo* so excessive that it turned men to stone. In Dante's text, there seems to be a survival of the theme of fascination, for it would be difficult to imagine why Virgil does not trust the pilgrim's ability to shield his own eyes if the image were not an entrapment.

Fascination, in this context, suggests above all the sensual fascination celebrated in the literature of love. Whatever the significance of the Medusa motif to Freud and Ferenczy, we are dealing here with a highly self-conscious poetry and a kind of love poetry at that. It happens that there is an explicit reference in the text that helps to identify the subject matter as specifically erotic and literary, rather than abstractly moral. When the Furies scream out for the Medusa, they recall the assault of Theseus: "Mal non vengiammo in Teseo l'assalto" (IX. 54). This would seem to be an allusion to Theseus' descent into the Underworld with his friend Pirithoüs, a disastrous enterprise from which he, unlike his hapless companion, was rescued by Hercules, but the point is that the descent had for its objective the abduction of Persephone; it was therefore an erotic, not to say sexual, assault.

The presence of the theme here is not merely anecdotal; Dante is himself in a sense searching for a prelapsarian Persephone, an erotic innocence which he recaptures, at one remove, in his encounter with Matelda at the top of the Mountain of Purgatory:

> Thou makest me recall where and what was Proserpine at the time her
> mother lost her and she the spring.
>
> (*Purg.*, XXVIII, 49–51)

These two references to Persephone in the poem, the first implied and the second clearly stated, suggest that the figure of the Medusa is somehow coordinate to that of Matelda. Whatever else she may represent, the pastoral landscape and the erotic feelings of the pilgrim would seem to indicate the recapture, or near recapture, of a pastoral (and therefore *poetic*) innocence, a return to Eden after a long askesis. For the moment, it might be argued that the Medusa represents precisely the impediment to such a recapture; her association with Persephone goes back to the *Odyssey*, where Odysseus in the Underworld fears that Persephone will send the gorgon to prevent him from leaving. Whatever Dante's sources for making the same association, the point seems to be that, short of Eden, there is no erotic—or *poetic*—innocence.

A generation later, Geoffrey Chaucer was to use the Furies in a way that is quite consistent with my hypothesis about the passage in Canto IX. The invocation of *Troilus and Creseyde*, that bookish tale of woe, addresses the Furies, rather than the Muses, as the proper inspirers of the dark passion that is the subject of the romance. Indeed, the insistence on the Furies would seem to foreshadow the "anti-romance" quality of Chaucer's poem, deliberate undercutting of a genre that had been the poet's own. The *Troilus* is in many ways a palinodic auto-critique: the language with which it begins, with its address to "Thesiphone . . . cruwel Furie sorrowyng," may even be an allusion to the passage under discussion here, as well as to Statius. At any rate, it would seem to support our hypothesis: the threat of the Medusa proffered by the Furies represents, in the pilgrim's askesis, a sensual fascination and potential entrapment, precluding all further progress.

Of all the texts that one might adduce in order to support the hypothesis, however, one seems to me to give to the Medusa a specificity that is lacking in most moralizing interpretations: the *Roman de la Rose*. A passage from that work will establish the sense in which Dante's Medusa exists as a dark counter-statement to the celebration of a poetic eros for which the *Roman* was the quintessential type. It offers us a precise, if inverted, parallel of the action in Canto IX, an illusion, in Dante's view, of which the Medusa is the disillusioning reality. At the ending of Jean de Meung's poem, as the lover is about to besiege the castle, an image is presented to him from a tower, a sculptured image far surpassing in beauty the image of Pygmalion, fired by Venus' arrow. Of interest to us is that in some versions of the poem that might have been available to Dante, the image is contrasted for some fifty lines with the image of the Medusa. . . . With what seems to be an interminable series of oppositions, the passage goes on to provide us with an extraordinary parallel to the drama of Canto IX, an ironically optimistic view of the power of Eros, of which Dante's Medusa seems the dark and reversed counter-image. The presence of mock-epic machinery in this erotomachia is matched by the pointedly non-Christian fortifications of Dante's infernal city. The Medusa does not appear in the *Roman*, any more than it does in the *Inferno*, but exists only as an antitype to Venus' idol. Dante's Medusa, on the other hand, *is* Venus' idol, stripped of its charm and seen, or almost seen, under the aspect of death. Recent study suggests that, as a youth, Dante had written a poetic paraphrase of the *Roman*; it should be remarked that this episode constitutes Dante's final judgment on the dark eros celebrated in that work.

The figure of the Medusa would seem to be a perfect vehicle for conveying this kind of retrospective judgment because it seems to be inherently diachronic, stressing historicity and change: before and after, then and now, the beauty of the lady changed to ugliness, fascination turned to horror. In ancient mythology, she was said to be a kind of Siren and in this temporal respect she would seem to resemble Dante's Siren, the stinking hag of the *Purgatorio* whom the pilgrim, under the influence of song, takes to be a ravishing beauty.

It is for this temporal dimension of meaning that a simple abstraction of personification allegory seems least able to account, for the temporality is derived, not from the gap that separates the poetic statement from some abstract moral code, but rather from the temporality of the beholder. I should like to suggest that the temporality we sense in the threat of the Medusa is a representation of the temporality of retrospection, of a danger narrowly averted, of a former illusion seen for what it is. Such a temporality is the essence of the descent into Hell, the past seen under the aspect of death. The traditional threat on all such journeys is the threat of nostalgia, a retrospective glance that evades the imperative to accept an authentically temporal destiny. Moreover, the threat is not merely of petrification, but also of *no return*. . . . The Gospel of Luke (xvii. 32) warns of such a danger with an Old Testament figure that seems peculiarly appropriate here: "Remember Lot's wife."

The threat of the past faces St. Augustine just before his conversion, when his former mistresses seem to appear behind him, tempting him to turn and look at them, *respicere*, as they pluck at his fleshly garment. In the medieval allegorization of the journey of Orpheus to the Underworld, a similar significance is given to the irreparable loss of Eurydice. According to Guillaume de Conches, Orpheus' descent represents the sage's effort to find himself, his Eurydice, and he is defeated by his nostalgia for his own former sin. At this point in his descent, the pilgrim faces a similar temptation: the Furies, a traditional representation of guilt and remorse, urge him to confront what is, in effect, his own past as poet. Dante did not have to read the *Roman de la Rose* in order to learn of a lady who turned her lovers to stone, for he had in fact celebrated such a lady in his *Rime Petrose*, the stony rhymes, written for the mysterious *Donna Pietra*.

The *Rime Petrose*, the dazzling virtuoso pieces of Dante's youth, celebrate a violent passion for the "Stony Lady" whose hardness turns the poet, her lover, into a man of stone. In the survey of the progress of Dante's love and of his poetry from the *Vita Nuova* to the *Commedia*, the *Rime Petrose* constitute a surd element, radically fragmentary, Contini has called them, finding no place clearly identifiable in the poet's development. At one point in the *Purgatorio* when Beatrice castigates the pilgrim for his infidelity, she accuses him of a love for "vanità," a "pargoletta," or little girl, using precisely the same word that the poet had used somewhat disparagingly of his *Donna Pietra* in one of the *rime*. The recall in the *Purgatorio* of this word has given rise to endless speculation about the identity of the woman whom Dante noted with the code-name of "Donna

Pietra." Critics have been right, I think, to wish to see biography in the poem, but they have been incorrect to imagine that the words of the poem were simply vehicles for communicating true confessions. We have learned from Contini that the biography of a poet, as poet, is his poetry, and it is in a quite literal sense that the *Rime Petrose* are present and relevant here. In the same poem that has given rise to speculation about the "pargoletta," there appear some verses of potentially greater significance. They describe a wintry scene in which the despairing lover seems to have lost his beloved forever. They should be compared with the *versi strani* of Canto IX:

Versan le vene le fummifere acque
per li vapor che la terra ha nel
         [ventre
che d'abisso li tira suso in *alto;*
onde cammino al bel giorno mi
         [piacque
che ora è fatto rivo, e sarà mentre
che durerà del verno il grande
         [assalto
la terra fa un suol che par di
         [smalto
e l'acqua morta si converte in
         [vetro . . .
  (*Rime* 43 (C), 53ff.)

Con l'unghie si fendea ciascuna il
         [petto
Battiensi a palme e gridavan sì
         [alto
Ch'i'mi strinsi al poeta per sospetto,
'Venga Medusa, si 'l farem di
         [smalto,'
Dicevan tutte riguardando in giuso:
'Mal non vengiammo in Teseo
         l'assalto.'
    (*Inferno* IX, 49ff.)

    The veins pour forth smoking waters because of the vapors the earth has in her belly, who draws them up from the abyss;
    therefore the path that on a fair day pleased me has now become a river and will be one as long as the great assault of winter lasts;
    it turns the ground into a surface like enamel, and the standing water changes to glass because of the cold that locks it. . . .

    Each was rending her breast with her nails; they smote themselves with their palms and cried so loud that I pressed close to the Poet for fear.
    'Let Medusa come and we will turn him to stone,' they all cried, looking down; 'we avenged ill the assault of Theseus.'

The description of a world without love, matching the poet's winter of the soul, contains exactly the rhyme words from Dante's description of the Medusa, sibilants that might qualify as *versi strani* in the address to the reader. Thus, in a passage which threatens petrification, is recalled, in a reified, concrete way, precisely the poem that described such a reification at the hands of a kind of Medusa. The words themselves reflect each other in such a way that they constitute a short-circuit across the temporal distance that separates the two moments of poetic history, a block that threatens to make further progress impossible. For the reader, the parallel threat is to refuse to see the allegory through the letter, to ignore the double-focus of the *versi strani*. The appearance of a recall to the *Rime Petrose* is an invitation to the reader to measure the distance that separates the *now* of the poet from the *then* of his *persona*; in the fiction of the poem, the Medusa is, like the lady of stone, no historic character at all, but the poet's own creation. Its threat is the threat of idolatry. In terms of mythological *exempla*, petrification by the Medusa is the real consequence of Pygmalion's folly.

The point is worth stressing. Ever since Augustine, the Middle Ages insisted upon the link between Eros and language, between the reaching out in desire for what mortals can never possess and the reaching out of language toward the significance of silence. To refuse to see in human desire an incompleteness that urges the soul on to transcendence is to remain within the realm of creatures, worshipping them as only the Creator was to be worshipped. Similarly, to refuse to see language and poetry as continual askesis, pointing beyond themselves, is to remain within the letter, treating it as an absolute devoid of the Spirit which gives meaning to human discourse. The subject matter of love-poetry is *poetry*, as much as it is love, and the reification of love is at the same time a reification of the words that celebrate it.

The search for the self which is the quest of the poet can only be accomplished through the mediation of the imagination, the Narcissus image which is at once an image of the self and all that the self is not. For a medieval poet steeped in the Augustinian tradition, the search for the self in the mirror of creatures, the beloved, ends with a false image of the self which is either rejected in favor of God, the light which casts the reflection, or accepted as a true image, an image which is totally other. Seeing the self in otherness and accepting the vision as true reduces the spirit to something totally alienated from itself, like a rock or a tree, totally deprived of consciousness. Like language itself, the image can only represent by pointing beyond itself, by beckoning the beholder to pierce through it to its ultimate significance. Idolatry in this context is a refusal to go beyond, a self-petrification.

Virgil is the mediator between Dante's former dark passion and verbal virtuosity on one hand and the restless striving of the pilgrim on the other, at least until his guidance gives way to the guidance of Beatrice. It may seem strange to think of Virgil at all in the context of love poetry, except insofar as every poet is a poet of desire. Yet Virgil's

portrait of Aeneas was a portrait of passion overcome. At the opening of
the fifth book, as Aeneas sails away from Carthage, he looks back at its
burning walls and leaves Dido forever behind him. The chaotic force of
folle amore—mad passion—was epitomized for Dante by the figure of Dido
and of Cupid, who sat in her lap. Further, it is under the sign of Dido
that Paolo and Francesca bewail their adulterous love in Hell. In the
struggle between individual desire and providential destiny, Virgil's Aeneas
is the man who renounces self in the name of his mission. Perhaps it is for
this reason that he helps the pilgrim avert his glance, until Beatrice shows
the way to a reconciliation of human love with the Divine plan. Just as
the historic Virgil, in Dante's reading, had pointed the way out of the
erotic impasse toward *lo bello stilo*, so in the poem, it is Virgil who helps
him to avoid the pitfall facing all poets of love. It is perhaps in this sense,
specifically, that his help was spurned by Guido Cavalcanti (*Inf.* X. 63). In
any case, Dante's encounter with Beatrice is the moment at which the
poem transcends the Virgilian view of human love. Dante marks his
beloved's return with the words "conosco i segni dell'antica fiamma" (*Purg.*
XXX. 48), echoing the despairing words of Dido, while the angels sing
"Manibus o date lilia plenis," echoing the funereal gesture of Anchises in
the Underworld, but transforming the purple lilies of mourning into the
white lilies of the Resurrection. At that point, Virgil definitively disap-
pears, when death, before which even he and his Rome had to bow, gives
way to transcendent love (*Canticum Cant.* viii. 6).

There is some evidence that our suggested reading of the Medusa
episode may have been anticipated by a near contemporary of the poet, or
at least that the problematic was recognized and radically transformed by
him. I refer of course to Petrarca, whose very name was for him an
occasion for stony puns. In the course of his *Canzoniere*, he provides us
with a definitive gloss on Dante's Medusa. Like Pygmalion, Petrarca falls
in love with his own creation and is in turn created by her: the pun
Lauro/Laura points to this self-contained process which is the essence of
his creation. He creates with his poetry the Lady Laura who in turn
creates his reputation as poet laureate. She is therefore not a mediatrix,
pointing beyond herself, but is rather enclosed within the confines of his
own being as poet, which is to say, the poem. This is precisely what
Petrarch acknowledges when he confesses in his final prayer to the sin of
idolatry, adoration of the work of his own hands. Speaking of Laura no
longer as the infinitely beloved, he calls her a Medusa: "Medusa e l'error
mio m'han fatto un sasso." For all of his tears of repentance, however,
there seems to be a consolation for a more secular age. Petrarca's enduring
fame as the weeping lover seems to suggest that, if he was turned to stone

because of idolatry, at least a stone lasts forever. If it is devoid of the spirit linking it to reality and to the life of the poet, it is nevertheless immune to the ravages of time, a monumental portrait of the artist. In the same poem, he sees the problem of reification and idolatry as inherent in all poetry, including that of his illustrious predecessor. This, I take it, is the point of his address to the Virgin as the only true mediatrix and "bringer-of-blessings": *vera beatrice*, where the absence of capitalization drives the point home more forcefully. For Petrarca, precursor of Romanticism, there can be no middle ground, not even that occupied by Dante.

We are now in a position to answer some of the fundamental questions concerning Dante's allegory raised by the episode of the Medusa. Doubtless, the Pauline "God of this world" provides us with an appropriate and abstract moral meaning in the dramatization that might lead us to classify it as an example of the allegory of poets. At the same time, however, we have seen that the passage is charged with the temporality of the poet's own career, the Dante who *is*, looking back at the Dante who was, through the medium of words. This retrospective illumination is the very essence of Biblical allegory, what Dante called the "allegory of theologians." The Christ event was the end term of an historical process, the "fullness of time," from the perspective of which the history of the world might be read and judged according to a meaning which perhaps even the participants in that history could not perceive. The "then" and "now," the Old Testament and the New, were at once the continuity and discontinuity of universal history, the Letter and the Spirit respectively of God's revelation. Christian autobiography is the application of this diachronism to one's own life for the purpose of witness, "confession," of the continual unfolding of the Word.

Both confession and Christian allegory have their roots in the mystery of language. As language is unfolded along a syntagmatic axis, governed at each moment of its articulation by a paradigm present in the mind of the speaker and made manifest at the ending of the sentence, so the authorial voice in the text is as the paradigm of the entire narrative, of which the evolution of the pilgrim is, as it were, the syntax. When this dialectic is translated into dramatic terms that purport to be autobiographical, we are presented with a narrative which seems to demand both continuity and discontinuity: an organic continuity, so that it may make a claim to authenticity, yet with the definitive detachment of the author who makes a claim to finality. For the pilgrim and the author to be one and the same requires nothing short of death and resurrection: death, so that the story may be definitive and final; resurrection, so that it may be told. This narrative translation of the dialectic of language may in turn be translated into theological terms: Conversion, the burial of the Old Man and the birth of the New, the essence of Pauline allegory. Christ, the ending of the story, is simply the manifestation of its subject, paradoxically present as the paradigm, the Logos, from the beginning. The final manifestation of the paradigm is the presence of the Logos made flesh. Just as history required an Archimedean point from which Christians could judge it to have been concluded, so the literature of confession would seem to require an Archimedean point outside of itself from which its truth can be measured, a point that is at once a beginning and an end, an Alpha and an Omega. "Conversion" was the name that Christians applied to such a moment in history and in the soul. In this sense, Biblical allegory, conversion and narrative all share the same linguistic nature.

When St. Paul refers to the relationship of the Old Testament to the New, he is in fact applying this linguistic metaphor to the Christ event, the Spirit inseparable from the letter of the Bible whereby It is made manifest. Without the Letter, the Spirit is the eternal Logos, with no point of tangency to history, God's intentionality without relation to man. Without the Spirit, the Letter is utterly devoid of significance, as dead as the mute stones upon which it was written. God's utterance to man is the Word incarnate.

Paul goes on to suggest that the Word of God interprets the hearts of men, the stony tablets turning to stone the hearts of unbelievers, while the Spirit writes upon the fleshly tablets of the faithful. So too, in Dante's text, it is the power of the Letter to enthrall the beholder that makes of it a Medusa, an expression of desire that turns back to entrap its subject in an immobility which is the very opposite of the dynamism of language and of desire. To see beyond it, however, is to see in the spiritual sense, to transform the Eros of the Medusa into the transcendent Eros of Caritas. This is Dante's whole achievement as a love poet: a refusal of the poetics of reification, sensual and verbal, for the poetics of "translation," as scribe of the Spirit which is written on "the fleshly tablets of the heart": "I am one who, when love breathes in me, take note, and in that manner which he dictates within go on to set it forth" (*Purg.* XXIV. 52). The Book of Memory has as its Author God Himself. In this sense, Dante's poem is neither a copy nor an imitation of the Bible. It *is* the allegory of theologians in his own life.

Nonetheless, the passage from the events of Dante's life to the words and images he uses to signify them is one that we cannot make. This is why it is impossible to guess at the identity of the *Donna Pietra*, just as it is impossible to see in the Medusa some event of the poet's life. We must be content with words on words, the double focus on a poetic expression, beyond which it would take an act of faith equal to Dante's to go, beyond which indeed, there is no Dante we can ever know.

The address to the reader is thus not a stage direction, but an exhortation to conversion, a command to await the celestial messenger so that we, like the pilgrim, may "trapassare dentro." Beneath the veil of Moses, we behold the light of the Gospel; beneath the veil of Dante's verses, the *dottrina* is derived from that light or it is nothing at all.

ROBERT M. DURLING

Seneca, Plato, and the Microcosm

The first of Dante's *rime petrose* ["stony rhymes"], "Io son venuto al punto de la rota" ["I have come to that point on the wheel"], concerns the relation between the speaker and the rest of nature. At one level the poem is readily classifiable as exhibiting a familiar topos that goes back at least as far as Virgil's description of the contrast between the peace of night and the turmoil of the despairing Dido. In medieval lyric poetry the persistence of love in winter is, with the renewal of love in the springtime, one of the topics of exordium, and Dante's poem has affinities with the famous *carmen buranum* "De ramis cadunt folia," as well as with a whole series of poems by the "miglior fabbro" Arnaut Daniel. Some of the structural peculiarities of Dante's poem have been identified. It has been observed that there is a parallelism among the stanzas; that from stanza to stanza there is a descent along the ladder of creation; that there is both contrast and correspondence within individual stanzas; and that the last two stanzas are more complex than the preceding ones. It is clear that Dante's poem is unique in the insistence with which the parallels are carried out; in other cases the comparison of the lover with nature either occupies only part of the poem (this is true of Arnaut's experiments) or else is not developed systematically (as in "De ramis cadunt folia").

The poem is far more elaborately constructed than has been pointed out, however, and it is perhaps a more important moment in Dante's

---

From *Dante Studies*, vol. 93 (1975). Copyright © 1975 by *Dante Studies*.

development than has been realized. With few exceptions, in fact, discussions of this and the other *petrose* have tended to emphasize their technical virtuosity at the expense of their thematic seriousness; they emphasize the lexical "violence," and emphasize an imbalance or lack of dialectic. I think this traditional view needs a considerable degree of qualification, and I am going to argue that "Io son venuto" represents the emergence in Dante's poetry of what will become major structural principles of the *Commedia*. For "Io son venuto" is constructed as a *microcosm*. That is, it is based on: 1) an elaborate parallelism between the cycles governing the cosmos and the cycles governing the life of the self; 2) a system of correspondences between the realms of nature and the parts of the human body. Furthermore, I believe there is sufficient evidence to suggest that the astronomical position described in the first stanza of "Io son venuto" was thought of by Dante as significantly related to the position of the planets at the time of his birth, and that this idea is integral to the theme of the poem—the relation of tension between the speaker and the rest of the reality, the paradoxical concomitance of embeddedness in nature and superiority to it. This will, of course, be one of the major themes of the *Commedia*, where it is also inseparably connected with the question of the influence of the heavens.

I

It is not my purpose in this paper to identify the direct sources of Dante's conception of the macrocosmic-microcosmic relation. No doubt the most important ultimate sources include Plato's *Timaeus* (as translated and commented by Calcidius), and Macrobius' commentary on the *Somnium Scipionis*; but variants of the Platonic and neo-Platonic doctrines appear in literally countless texts available to him. However, in citing these and other texts my intention will be not so much to identify Dante's sources as to exemplify the traditions on which he was drawing. That human life is organically related to the cosmos both because, like the rest of nature, men are profoundly affected by the macrocosmic cycles (such as the annual cycle of the seasons) and because the endogenous cycles of human life are microcosmic imitations of the macrocosmic cycles, is an idea common to virtually all the traditions of ancient thought, including the Aristotelian. In a brilliant series of articles, John Freccero has demonstrated that the Platonic conception, combined with Aristotelian notions of absolute directions in space, lies behind the path of Dante the pilgrim through the three realms of the *Commedia*. For it is a continuously *spiral* path and it leads to a culmination, at the end of the poem, where in the vision of God the revolutions of the soul of the pilgrim are reconciled with the two revolutions of the cosmos, subjective and objective.

But the Platonic tradition is not the only one behind Dante's use of the idea of the microcosm. Another extremely important one is Stoic. Because the presence of Seneca is particularly strong in "Io son venuto" I would like to devote a few pages to an analysis of one of his most interesting productions, Book III of the *Naturales Quaestiones*. This work is commonly cited as a source of the scientific lore in "Io son venuto" and "Amor, tu vedi ben che questa donna" ["love, you see perfectly well that this lady"]. What needs emphasis is that it is a particularly interesting example of a *literary structure* based on the correlations among macrocosmic and microcosmic cycles and may well have furnished Dante some important structural ideas.

The *Naturales Quaestiones* are fragmentary. In the Proem to Book II Seneca announces the intention of treating all fields of natural science, but in fact the seven books that have come down to us (in questionable order and individually fragmentary in some cases) treat only meteorology (I. Meteors; II. Air; III. Terrestrial Waters; IV. Clouds and Hail; V. Winds; VI. Earthquakes; VII. Comets). Of all these Book III has by far the most elaborate structure. The subject of the book is the cyclical movement of water: what is the origin of fountains and rivers? why are some fountains sweet, some salt? some hot, some cold and so forth? Seneca's explanations are often quite erroneous, such as his refutation of the feeding of underground springs by rain: rain never penetrates, he says, more than ten feet into the ground. The rising of fountains and the flowing of great rivers are rather to be thought of as a circulation of fluids whereby ocean feeds rivers by underground cavities analogous to the veins in a human body. . . . Thus are explained not only the cyclical interchange between ocean and rivers, but also the varying nature of springs: those whose pressure varies (xvi), those which are alternately full and dry (xvi), those which are poisonous (xxv), hot, heavy (xxiv); for, like the human body, the earth has its quartan and tertian fevers, its distempers, all governed by cyclical process. An ultimately basic cycle is that of the interchange of the elements one into the other and back. . . .

Why,[Seneca] asks Lucilius, to whom he is dedicating the entire work, has he, Seneca, begun a work of such magnitude so late in his life? Here already at the beginning of the book is introduced the theme of the inevitable *end of the cycle of a human life*, immediately enlarged to include the contemplation of the downfall of noble houses and of all the empires of the past, according to the same inexorable natural process.

Like other Stoics, Seneca believed that life on earth was periodically destroyed and recreated in a ceaseless cycle of *alternae vices*. He cites the astrologer Berossus' doctrine that the process is governed by the stars: when all the planets come to conjunction in Cancer, the sign of the summer solstice, life on earth is destroyed by fire (*ekpyrosis*); when they all come to conjunction in Capricorn, the sign of the winter solstice, the destruction comes by water (*cataclysmos*, a washing clean). The book ends with a powerfully imagined fantasy of the terrific flood which will destroy all humankind in one day, analogous to the ending of an individual human life. Unending rains will pour down and the abyss will give up its waters so that the ocean will rise to cover the earth (xxvii–xxx).

Thus Book III of the *Naturales Quaestiones* adroitly connects a very large range of kinds of natural cycle with the central theme of terrestrial waters. They are, in descending order of length: 1. The great year, defined by the return of all heavenly bodies to their original positions (the period of the recurrence of all planets in Capricorn); 2. The period of recurrent destruction (i.e., the lifespan of the human race and half of the great year); 3. The lifespans of empires; 4. The lifespans of dynasties and families; 5. The span of an individual human life; 6. The lifespan of a fish; 7. Annual cycles: the seasons, the growth and diminution of the Nile, etc.; 8. Cycles of indeterminate length: the circulation of waters, the mutual conversion of elements, the diseases of the earth, the diseases of the human body, 9. Shorter cycles: alternation of night and day, circulation of fluids in the human body, the digestive cycle, respiration.

In addition to these cycles in history and nature, one must note the self-consciousness with which we are invited to see *the book itself* as cyclical, signaled at the outset where Seneca discusses the paradox of his beginning a long undertaking in old age. The book thus *begins* with the juxtaposition of an ending and a beginning; it posits nature as eternal and looks *back* toward completed cycles of history in the past. Then, at the end of the book, we look forward toward the universal cataclysm; but, after Seneca has described the destruction of humanity, he concludes with the reminder that the cycle of human life will begin again under the influence of the heavenly bodies, innocent, as always, in its first beginnings.

Within this overarching structure of 30 chapters are arranged the topics announced in Chatper ii; by a set of gradations we are led to the explicit statement *in Chapter xv* of the analogy between the earth and the human body. By the cyclical logic of analogical reasoning itself, alternating between the macrocosmic and the microcosmic, Seneca makes an apparently casual transition to a "digression" (*in Chapter xviii*) that attacks the corruption of Rome as exemplified by the cruel gourmets who have fish brought to the table to expire under their eyes and watch with enjoyment the spectacular color changes of the dying mullet, an *inversion* of the situation of the end of the book where all men are drowned which, it must be remembered, is itself an *inversion* of destruction by fire and is produced by astrological inversion (conjunction in Capricorn vs. conjunction in Cancer). After the centerpieces (the developed analogy with the body and the digression) we revert to the rhythm of special topics treated successively, until the last one—the nature of *self-purifying* springs—leads, again with apparent casualness, to the concluding cataclysm.

In a characteristically Stoic—and first-century-A.D. manneristic—way, then, Seneca's discussion of terrestrial waters is designed to liberate the spirit from its narrow concerns and perturbations by elevating it to the contemplation of the sublime spectacle of the inevitability of natural process. In the Stoic ascent it is especially the fear of death that must be conquered, and although this intention is only made explicit elsewhere in the *Naturales Quaestiones*, it clearly underlies the cyclical arrangement of Book III: the mind must realistically face the prospect of the extinction of individuals, families, empires, even the whole human race, and, by accepting and imitating the sublime inevitability of nature, gain the untroubled constancy of the sage. The artistic form of the book is a kind of Stoic enactment of the Platonic imitation of the heavens.

II

As we shall see, the most important points of connection between *Naturales Quaestiones* III and "Io son venuto al punto de la rota" are: 1) the theme of the relation between cosmic cycles and the life-cycle of the speaker; 2) the acting-out of cyclical recurrences and parallels as a principle of structure; 3) the idea of astrological inversion; 4) the parallel between the human body and the earth. The concomitance of all these points of connection makes it likely that Dante studied Seneca's text with some care. Leaving the analogy with the human body for later, I turn first to the theme of the cosmic cycles and begin with Renucci's observation that the successive stanzas of the poem describe winter in the different realms of nature, arranged in descending order: 1. the heavens; 2. the air; 3. birds and animals; 4. plants; 5. earth and water. The stanzas are rigorously parallel. Each consists of three groups of *three lines* each (I shall call them *a,b,c*) devoted to the description of winter, and a fourth group of *four lines* (I shall call it *d*) devoted to the state of the lover, and the respective parts are parallel to each other from stanza to stanza—formally

(=metrically), syntactically, and in terms of content. It is not merely that in each case nine lines go to the description of winter; rather, each stanza describes or alludes to one or more *cycles* characteristic of the level of nature with which the stanza is concerned. Thus:

1. a.   the annual cycle of the sun;
    b,c.   the periods of Venus and Saturn.
2. a,b,c. the generation of wind and the cycle of precipitation.
3. a.   the seasonal migration of certain birds;
    b,c.   seasonal apathy of other birds and animals.
4. a.   seasonal deciduousness of plants;
    b.   evergreens;
    c.   seasonal cycle of generation of plants (flowers).
5. a,b,c. the cyclical movement of waters.

In each stanza, furthermore, there is a complex but clearly discernible pattern in the arrangement of the cycles:

1. a. Night rises; sun sets.   b. Venus remote and veiled.   c. Saturn influential.
2. a. The wind rises,   b. approaches and clouds   c. rain and snow fall.
                                  the sky;
3. a. Migratory birds have   b. non-migratory birds are   c. other animals are
      departed;   silent;   apathetic.
4. a. Deciduous foliage has   b. non-deciduous foliage   c. flowers are dead.
      fallen;   remains;
5. a. Earth pours forth   b. the road is flooded;   c. the ground and the
      waters;   waters freeze.

To take parts *a* first, in 1.a the motion described is both a rising and a setting; thereafter rising predominates, 4.a being the only case which represents falling. In parts *b*, the emphasis is in each case on immobility. The motion is downward in 2.c, 3.c, and 4.c; in 1.c and 5.c the emphasis is on the increasing immobility of things in the freezing cold.

Thus, although Dante has very skillfully avoided a monotonous identity of pattern, the description of winter in each stanza follows a similar one: a. upward motion; b. motionlessness or ineffectiveness *above*; c. descent. The pattern is that of a half-cycle, if we think of the complete circle as a whole cycle. What we have here is closely related to Dante's conception of the "arc of life," which, as Bruno Nardi has demonstrated, depends on the idea of the alternate presence of the sun above the horizon and its nightly disappearance. Of course, it can hardly escape notice that—just as the successive stanzas concern progressively lower realms of nature—so both the high point of each stanza and the final low point are lower and lower as we move through the poem. Starting with the heavens, our eye moves in a descending series of half-circles, and in fact what is implied is a *descending spiral*. The pattern is an imitation of the gradually descending daily path of the sun across the heavens as it approaches the winter solstice: each day it rises a little later and a little further to the south, crosses the meridian a little lower in the sky, and sets a little earlier and farther to the south.

In describing the effects of winter in successively lower realms, the poem is of course following out the idea of the pouring down into the sublunary of the influence of the heavenly bodies. The planet that is most closely associated with the winter solstice is Saturn. At the solstice the sun enters Capricorn, the house of Saturn; the feast of Saturn, as Macrobius points out, directly precedes the winter solstice. The influence of Saturn (which may be either favorable of unfavorable, depending on circumstances) is particularly strengthened when it is in the ascendant in the east (as in "Io son venuto"), and stanzas 2–5 refer to events in the sublunary sphere that are not only associated with winter but were thought to occur in winter because of their association with Saturn. Saturn-Kronos, the eldest of the gods, is the father and destroyer of all earthly beings. He both benignly presides over the sowing of crops and the reproduction of animals and determines their senescence and death. As the coldest and slowest of the planets he is associated with earth and water; he governs rain (being particularly likely to cause rain when on the cusp between two signs) and floods.

So far we have not considered the function in each stanza of part *d*, where the state of the lover is correlated with that of nature. The full picture can only emerge when we consider the governing body-metaphor. But at this point we can make the following observation: in each stanza part *d* juxtaposes the state of the lover to the situation in nature in a way that is both syntactically parallel from stanza to stanza and also integrally related to the preceding description of nature. The governing theme is readily identifiable as the paradoxical combination in human experience of embeddedness in nature with independence from it.

"Io son venuto" juxtaposes the relative fixity of the two human beings with the changing seasons. There are, of course, larger cycles of human life involved—the *arco de la vita* in a stricter sense. Leaving aside until later the question of the astrological influences that may be affecting the lover's passion or the lady's indifference, at one level of meaning of the poem the lover's retaining in winter his warmth of passion is related to an implicit comparison of the lady with the sun: since she is quite young, her beauty is in its "dolce tempo novello," like the sun in spring. The clear implication of the poem (it recurs also in "Al poco giorno e al gran cerchio d'ombra") is that the lady is only approaching or has only just reached the season of her life to which love is appropriate. Presumably the refusal of love imagined in the *congedo* would involve the lady's refusal of the season of love in both cycles, that of the year and that of her life.

The cold stony cruelty of the lady is represented in all the *petrose* as unnatural to her youth and beauty. Her sun-like beauty governs the poet's love for her, but her stony coldness itself comes under the aegis of the cold planet of the element earth. Thus, the idea of the *donna pietra* brings the entire sequence of the *rime petrose* under the sign of Saturn. In embodying cold instead of the warmth that is natural to her youth, the lady represents one of the most important instances of the idea of seasonal (and astrological) *inversion* in the poem, which is closest to being made explicit in the *congedo*, where the situation of the body of the poem is imagined as reversed: instead of cold influence, love now rains down from all the heavens. This is the other half of the full cycle, of course: and the effect on the lover is again reversal, if the lady is still cold, he will freeze *in spite of* the influence of the rest of nature.

In the body of the poem, however, the protagonists are fixed in their attitudes and juxtaposed against the cyclical inevitability of the seasons. At the solstice all things come to frozen immobility in a way that seems to mirror the paired impasse between the two human beings. The rigidity of winter itself, however, is only temporary; further rotation of the heavenly wheel will eventually produce spring. And, as a matter of fact, as Dante knew, it is in Sagittarius and Capricorn that the sun seems to move fastest along its path in the ecliptic. The tension between process and immobility is thus a major principle in the poem; in so far as it can be imagined as a kind of incantatory magic, "Io son venuto," by acting out symbolically the approach to solstice, the descending part of the cycle, seeks to produce in the soul of the lady the solstice of her rejection, to be followed by a turn toward springtime. Thus "Io son venuto" must be seen as representing the first half of a pattern of descent followed by ascent—catabasis followed by anabasis—that will be more fully worked out in "Così nel mio parlar voglio esser aspro."

The congedo's being in so many respects a recapitulation of the motion of the entire poem (with the seasonal reversal) makes it possible to see with particular clarity how Dante has constructed *the poem itself* as an enactment of a cycle. For that Dante defined the form of the canzone as a sequence of melodic units is well known. What needs emphasis is that the form of the canzone, in which a fixed stanza form is repeated over and over again with different words, is a kind of cycle. In Aristotle's terminology, it is one of the kind in which "what recurs" is not "numerically the same" but rather "is the same only in species." This kind of cycle is characteristic of sublunary things—cyclical combinations and recombinations of the elements; Aristotle calls it a "rectilinear sequence," since it combines straight line motion and circularity. In these terms a canzone *is* a spiral in a fairly strict sense of the term, and that Dante was aware of this way of thinking about it can hardly be doubted, considering how thoroughly it permeates "Io son venuto" and the other *petrose*—especially the two sestinas.

III

It is time now to turn to the presence in the poem of the detailed parallelism between the realms of nature and the parts of the human body. Actually, what is involved is less a correlation of parts than a correlation of the macro- and microcosmic cycles, a static correlation of parts, as in Seneca's *Naturales Quaestiones* III, or indeed in Plato's *Timaeus*. For if according to Plato the spherical shape of the human head mirrors the shape of the cosmos as a whole (which, as Olerud acutely remarked, is imagined as being essentially an enormous head), that is because the head must house the revolutions of the soul:

> First, then, the gods, imitating the spherical shape of the universe, enclosed the two divine courses in a spherical body, that, namely, which we now term the head, being the most divine part of us and the lord of all that is in us; to this the gods, when they put together the body, gave the other members to be servants, considering that it must partake of every sort of motion.

The eyes, the organs of the highest sense, are analogous to heavenly lights, for vision results from the emission of rays of light from the eyes:

> And of the organs they first contrived the eyes to give light, and the principle according to which they were inserted was as follows. So much of fire as would not burn, but gave a gentle light, they formed into a substance akin to the light of everyday life, and the pure fire which is within us and related thereto they made to flow through the eyes in a stream . . . When the light of day surrounds the stream of vision, then like falls upon like, and they coalesce, and one body is formed by natural affinity in the line of vision . . . But when night comes and the external and kindred fire departs, then the stream of vision is cut off, for going forth to an unlike element it is changed and extinguished.
>
> (45b–e)

Thus vision is cyclical, both in the alternation of day and night and also—more importantly—as a rhythm of influx and efflux. In this respect it is related to bodily cycles in general. For the circular motions of the soul are set in a body made up of the four elements, whose cycles initially disrupt it. The lesser gods,

> in imitation of their own creator . . . borrowed portions of fire and earth and water and air from the world, which were hereafter to be restored—these they took and welded them together . . . and fastening the courses of the immortal soul in a body which was *in a state of perpetual influx and efflux.* Now these courses, detained as in a vast river, neither overcame nor were overcome, but were hurrying and hurried to and fro, so that the whole animal was moved . . . For great as was *the advancing and retiring flood which provided nourishment,* the affections produced by external contact caused still greater tumult—when the body of anyone met and came into collision with some external fire or with the solid earth or the gliding waters, or was caught in the tempest borne on the air—and the motions produced by any of these impulses were carried through the body to the soul.

(42e–43c; italics added)

. . . [Dante] is drawing on the *Timaeus* tradition, and there is a broad similarity of outline [to Bernard's system of correspondences.] Stanza 1, on the heavens, corresponds to the head; the microcosmic rhythm mentioned is the preservation in the memory of the image of the lady (the *petra*) drawn in through the eyes:

> . . . and nonetheless my mind casts off not one of the thoughts of love
> that burden me, mind harder than stone to hold fast an image of stone.

Stanza 2, on the air, explicitly brings in the analogy between atmospheric phenomena and weeping:

> . . . and then it resolves itself and falls in white flakes of cold snow and
> in harmful rain, and the air becomes all grieving and weeps. . . .

Stanza 3, on birds and animals, clearly corresponds to the heart. Here, as we have already noticed, there occurs the principal implicit reference to *fire* in the poem. Unlike Bernard—and the Platonic tradition in general—Dante does not identify the liver as the seat of sexual passion, but rather the heart, the seat of spirit:

> . . . and all animals that are happy by nature are released from loving,
> for the cold extinguishes their spirit: and mine bears more love. . . .

This is the central stanza of the poem and is clearly designed to stand as an axis of its symmetries. In terms of Bernard's system of correlations, Dante has simplified his and made it more schematic: with the animals we share motion and appetition because of the fiery spirit that resides in the heart; with plants we share the power of growth and nourishment. When in the fourth stanza, then, the analogy is drawn with plants, the emphasis is on the power of life; the evergreens are correlated with the possibility of immortality:

> . . . and his cruel thorn Love for all that does not draw from my heart,
> for I am certain to bear it ever while I am alive, though I should live forever.

As can readily be seen, the three central stanzas of the poem are grouped closely together; in the second and fourth stanzas the analogy of the poem with the body is more elusive than in the sharply focused first, third, and fifth stanzas. The fifth stanza in fact is the most explicit of the five:

> The veins pour forth smoking waters because of the vapors the earth has in her belly, who draws them up from the abyss;
> therefore the path that on a fair day pleased me has now become a river and will be one as long as the great assault of winter lasts;
> it turns the ground into a surface like enamel, and the standing water changes to glass because of the cold that locks it in from without: and I in my war have not turned back one step for all that, nor do I wish to; for if the suffering is sweet, the death must surpass every other sweet.

Here there is an explicit parallel between the *veins* of the human body and springs, and between the interior of the earth and the human belly. It is actually one of the keys to the whole poem. Far from being a mere decorative trope, it governs the motion of the entire stanza. For the "death of love" referred to in the last line can be no other than orgasm, so that the parallel with the emissions of the belly of the earth is striking. As we have seen, Bernard Silvestris used the metaphor of flooding to refer to seminal emission and associates it with a metaphor of astral influence; according to the physiology of the *Timaeus* adopted by Bernard, the seed flows down the spinal column from the brain. In the *Commedia* Dante adopts the view that semen is distilled heart's blood (*Purgatorio* XXV, 37–45), just as in "Io son venuto" he locates the seat of passion in the heart, not the liver. How detailed the sexual physiology is here is open to question, of course, but there is no question that the idea of petrifaction which is developed in the stanza is to be referred to the idea of tumescence; Dante is drawing on a common interpretation of the myth of Medusa.

As can be seen from the last stanza, the body-metaphor does not function merely in terms of a static correlation. Rather, as we have already seen, the macrocosmic cycles represented in each stanza are related to the bodily—and emotional—cycles of human life. Stanza 1 is related to the cycle of sight: taking in an image which then becomes a burden. Stanza 2 is related to the cycle of respiration, though how heavily we should allow the translation of external into emotional weather to impinge is open to argument. Stanza 3 explicitly refers to locomotion, but perhaps more important is the mention of the utterance of sound; unlike the birds, who have fallen silent, the poet is still singing, and it may be noted that this implication is conveyed in part *b* of the stanza, the second of the three groups of three lines referring to the outside world (the central group, then, in the central stanza). Singing, as related to love, is of course a bringing forth of what is in the heart. In literary terms, it goes back naturally also to previous hearing or reading. Stanza 4, to continue this catalog of cycles, explicitly mentions the life-span of the poet, and by implication, in distinguishing between deciduous and evergreen trees, suggests the distinction between flesh (deciduous) and soul (evergreen). Stanza 5, finally, alludes to the human cycles of ingestion and excretion, and to the death of love as the final stage in the cyclical process that began with the visual taking-in of the image of the lady.

The mention of the death of love at the end of stanza 5 brings in the idea that the species may be preserved at the expense of the individual life; at the end of stanza 5, then, and at the end of the poem as a whole, there is brought in the possibility of the death of the lover. "Io son venuto" announces in its first line that its subject is the involvement of the lover in the cycles of the cosmos and of his own body. Critics seem not to have much questioned the fact that although the wheel Dante mentions is certainly the zodiac, he refers to it in an unusual way. He says that *he* has reached a point on the wheel where the horizon gives birth at sunset to the twinned heavens:

> I have come to that point on the wheel when the horizon gives birth at
> sunset to the twinned heaven . . .

Now "the twinned heaven" presumably refers to the sign—or constellation—Gemini, Dante's natal sign. That Dante identifies the time of year by the sign in which or near which night is rising (rather than the sign in which the sun is) is one of the clues to the astrological significance of the passage, for it depends on a situation which is *inverted*. By describing the rising of Gemini with the words "gives birth" Dante was in any case describing one of the macrocosmic cycles—the alternation of day and night—with a term proper to one of the microcosmic cycles—gestation and parturition. In fact, at one level—the vehicle of two metaphors or tropes—the poem begins with allusion to birth and ends with allusion to death; at another level, it *ends* with a reference to orgasm, the *beginning* of the cycle of gestation and parturition, and *begins* with birth, the *end* of the process, in a line which refers to Dante's own natal sign.

The trope of birth in line 3 is rich in significances and one of the most important of them is its connection with the fact that love is represented in virtually every stanza of the poem as being a burden which the lover cannot throw off:

. . . and nonetheless my mind casts off not one of
the thoughts of love that burden me, my mind . . .

and Love . . . does not abandon me . . .

and my [spirit] bears more love . . .

and his cruel thorn Love for all that does not draw from my heart, for I
am certain to bear it ever while I am alive, though I should live forever.

Just as "Io son venuto" describes a descending spiral in the cosmos, then, so also it describes one in the body. As the influence of the heavenly bodies, especially the predominance of Saturn, affects the rest of nature, so the influence of the mind flows down to the rest of the body, and the mind of the lover is as dominated by the influence of Saturn (planet and lady). Whether the poem actually offers evidence that Dante thought of himself as of Saturnine—i.e., melancholy—temperament may be doubted, but there is no doubt that it is filled with references to the lore of the influence of the cold planet on the mind and on the body. In the poem as a whole the paradoxical combination of cold and fire and the hardness and tenacity of the mind are major instances. In the important last stanza the references to flood, earth, water, air trapped under ground, all form a complex of ideas inseparably bound up with the microcosmic theory of melancholic sexuality and the influence of Saturn. For the slow steadiness of Saturn was supposed to influence the strong vital spirits of the melancholic, who were thought to be particularly subject to lust because of the element of air combined with blood in the sperm, like the impetus of the underground waters mixed with vapor which Dante derives from Seneca.

In terms of the annual cycle of seasons and the analogy between the year and a human life, the poem describes the point of solstitial lowness. But for the microcosmic level the solstice may result in death; the little flood caused by the combined influence of Saturn, Mars, and Capricorn might become a cataclysmic flood analogous to the universal one Seneca describes. Thus the themes of solstitial inversion, tension against the season, the unnaturalness of a lady stony in youth, the analogy of the year and the life-cycle—all these are parallel to the idea of death as an inversion of birth. And if Saturn is preeminently a god of inversions, this is the most fundamental one he governs. As Manilius points out, his *locus* is the *imum coeli* because he has been cast down from his former eminence. All the systems of inversion in "Io son venuto" can be referred to and summed up to what seems to be a governing idea: that the astrological situation described in the poem is some kind of *inversion of the situation at Dante's birth*. Here it is sufficient to note that the moment is conceived as one of intense negativity in which the lover is pitted against the season, against the unnaturally stony lady, against his own stars as possibly lethal, against the negativity inherently a function of his own nature, which is shown in "Così nel mio parlar voglio esser aspro" as not only obsessive but also self-destructive: it offers him the sword that killed Dido (suicide).

But the destructiveness of the situation is not the whole story. Winter is only a phase of the year. The seasons will continue to turn. What the lover must do is ride out the negative phase in relation to the cosmos, the lady, his own body. And here we must take account of the fact that Saturn has another altogether different dimension of meaning in which, as the planet of theory, of contemplation, of study, of science, of astronomy itself, he is obviously to be seen as the patron of microcosmic poetics.

IV

The earlier part of this century saw many efforts to give the *rime petrose* allegorical significance. Most of them were capricious and unfounded, vitiated by the assumption that the erotic theme could be treated as a mere integument of "philosophical" content. In his excellent discussion of the history of opinion about the poems, Enrico Fenzi rightly warns also against the assumption of an *ex post facto* unity in the career of Dante, or of a unity in or with the fragmentary *Convivio*. We may simply be confronted with a plurality of interests and developments in Dante. This is salutary counsel. Fenzi's conclusion, however, that "non c'è nulla che autorizzi una lettura allegorica" of the *petrose* was, as I hope this paper has amply demonstrated, premature. Today there is a much broader and more accurate notion of Dante's allegorical habits of mind than earlier in the century. More accurate techniques of analysis and more inclusive lore do not *reduce* or *restrict* the meanings of poems, they add dimensions. The problematic of erotic passion cannot be eliminated from the *petrose*; rather it must be taken seriously as a human and poetic theme central to all of Dante's output as a poet.

To see allegorical dimensions of meaning in the *petrose*, however, does not mean that one may impose upon them from outside some theological scheme of judgment they do not invoke. "Io son venuto al punto de la rota" celebrates the negative phase of a passionate love, but there is nothing about it that justifies a theological view. Dante is not talking about a love that is damnable or sinful or demonic. Rather, he is representing the negative phase of this experience as a *natural* event, as similar in countless ways to other natural cycles that govern human existence, and specifically his own. The poem expresses not guilt but the fiery determination of the speaker to outlast the negative phase, to make the best of it, to conquer. This is one source of the enormous compressed power of this and the other *petrose*. And here the speaker as lover and the speaker as poet coalesce. The greatness of the *petrose* lies in the triumphant assertion of a new poetics. In their effort to include cosmological-scientific, microcosmic, even medical analysis with an uncompromising triumph over negativity in the external world and in the self, the *petrose* represent a major step forward toward the *integration* of poetic themes and technique. They herald a relation between craft and inspiration that is the reverse of fragmentary, for it demands a total account of the poet's individuality within the macrocosm, an interpenetration of all levels of meaning.

The question of the interpretation of the opening lines, then, should first be approached in relation to the poem itself:

I have come to that point on the wheel when the horizon gives birth at sunset to *the twinned heaven*

Does "the twinned heaven" have double meaning? How can it not have double meaning, since *twins* are by definition *double*? We do not have to appeal to the *Commedia* for substantiation of the importance for Dante of the theme of *doubleness*—doubleness of natures, doubleness of semiology, it is here in this poem. At the level of macrocosmic-microcosmic correspondences, there are two heavens in the poem, the cosmos and the human head. But in fact the very terminology of this opening is fraught with Dantean significance. . . .

The question of the relation of the *rime petrose*, and in particular of "Io son venuto" to the *Commedia*, . . . is far more interesting and complex than seems to have been recognized. In this concluding section I can do little more than give a broad outline of some of its dimensions.

1. There are many passages in the *Commedia* that allude to—or must be connected with—the *petrose*, and they are by no means confined to the *Inferno*. One of the most important of these is in *Paradiso* XXII, when Dante enters the sphere of the fixed stars:

> So may I sometime return, reader, to that devout triumph for which I often bewail my sins and beat my breast, thou hadst not drawn out and thrust in thy finger in the fire before I saw the sign that follows the Bull and was within it.
>
>   O glorious stars, O light pregnant with mighty power from which I acknowledge all my genius, whatever it be, with you was born and with you hidden he that is the father of each mortal life when I first tasted the Tuscan air; and after, when grace was granted me to enter into the high wheel that bears you round, your region was assigned to me. To you my soul now sighs devoutly that it may gain strength for the hard task that draws it to itself.

(vv. 106–123)

This passage is the principal source of our knowledge that Dante thought of himself as born under Gemini, and [there are] words and phrases that are connected with "Io son venuto": one of the many instances of *histeron-proteron* in the *Paradiso*; *indirect* identification of the sign Gemini; the metaphors of pregnancy and birth applied to heavenly bodies; and Dante's coming to a point on the wheel. It is practically inconceivable that Dante wrote this passage without intending the allusions. Similarly, when Dante tells us at the beginning of *Paradiso* XIII, in the sphere of the sun, that to imagine the 24 theologians circling around him we should imagine the Septentrion added to the fifteen brightest stars, he knows (whether he expects us to remember or not) that, according to Ptolemy and Alfraganus, Castor, then the brightest star in the constellation Gemini, is one of the fifteen.

The point would seem to be that Dante's knowledge or guess about his own natal horoscope impinges on the *sacro poema* more than we have hitherto taken account of, and indeed that is what one might expect, given the amount of attention the general theme receives in the *Paradiso*. It would mean that the astrological dimension of the poem needs to be explored more rigorously than it has been: as Dante moves up through the heavenly spheres his forward motion brings him closer and closer to his *origins* as well as to his *destination* (they perhaps become indistinguishable, as for Cacciaguida).

2. In its subject matter the *Commedia* represents the spiral path, first descending and then ascending, of Dante the pilgrim. Its subject matter includes also the cyclical motion of the heavenly bodies and their

influence in human affairs. The *form* of the *Commedia* is also a spiral. Whether or not "Io son venuto" is the first canzone in which Dante became fully aware of the possibilities of spiral form is less important than the fact that it initiated a series of self-conscious experiments in spiral form, including "retrogradatio cruciata." The form of the *Commedia* is spiral in two main senses: 1. Stanza-form. *a. Terza rima* forms a repeated pattern analogous to stanzas; as each sequence of three comes to a close another beginning has been superimposed. *b.* Cantos are analogous to stanzas. 2. The entire poem is a system of cyclical recurrences according to numerical principles; the parallel disposition of the three realms is an example of spiral content—spiral form gives us the pattern in which cantos that are numbered correspondingly allude to each other. Thus in *Inferno* XIX, *Purgatorio* XIX, and *Paradiso* XIX, the poem—by referring to itself— describes an ascending, more and more inclusive, spiral. The system of parallels goes forward in parallel in each *cantica*, axially out from the centers, eschatologically from end to beginning. Multiples answer each other (as *Inferno* VI, *Purgatorio* VI, *Paradiso* VI, *Paradiso* XVIII). Contiguous systems are both parallel and chiastic (as in *Paradiso* X–XIV or XIV–XVIII). These harmonies of form are an enactment of the *Timaeus* principle whereby human art imitates the heavens and orders the human soul by imposing harmonious motions upon it.

3. The *Commedia* develops in particularly rich ways the microcosmic idea of the parallels between the human body and other realms. In this respect also "Io son venuto" is a kind of microcosm of the *Commedia*. Here I can hardly do more than give a summary outline of one realm, Hell.

Some years ago Charles Singleton pointed out the existence, in *Inferno* XII–XIII, of what he called a "semantic field" involving many references to the breast and to the connection of the breast to the idea of *double nature:* We see Chiron first when he is looking at his breast; Virgil stands before Chiron's breast "where the two natures are joined" (XII, 84; cf. line 97). In the Malebolge we see a marked increase in references to the lower body: the soothsayers' tears flow between their buttocks; the simonists' legs protrude from their baptismal holes. Actually all Hell is a kind of great projection of the human body. We begin at the head—perhaps in the rear ventricle with Limbo, since the rear ventricle is the seat of memory; we pass the devouring gullet among the gluttons, the spleen with the sullen. Within the city, we reach the river of blood, the heart's forest, and what should be a fountain or reservoir of life but instead is an arid and sterile plain. Then we descend to the Malebolge, whose concentric circles correspond to the labyrinth of the intestines. Hell is divided, and Dante

130 • ROBERT M. DURLING

requires transportation, at points roughly corresponding to the major divisions of the human body. Flegias carries Dante across what corresponds to the division between head and breast; Geryon across the diaphragm. Anteo and the other giants are in location corresponding to the genitals: they are like grotesque rebellious penises. Cocito, finally, corresponds to the large intestine or to the anus, and there we find the infernal Saturn immobile in the floods frozen solid by his cold emanations, devouring his children.

Dante's spiral through Hell is a reenactment—in much greater detail, with much greater complexity, and in a different register (the infernal as opposed to the natural)—of the solstitial and microcosmic sequence that governs "Io son venuto." There are many correspondences between the five stanzas of the first of the *petrose* and the realms of Hell: a sky—the hemisphere of light in Limbo—as memory (stanza 1); wind and storm as erotic passion, related to mouth and eyes, cries and weeping (Canto V, stanza 2); the correlation of animal souls and plant souls with the powers of the human soul (Canto XIII, stanzas 3 and 4); the breast, especially the heart, as seat of *fire* (Cantos XII and XV–XVI, stanza 3). Cocito and the descent thereto, finally, have a clear correspondence with stanza 5.

Dante's Hell is an inverted parody of the body of Christ, the Church. It is Babylon, the body of Satan. This is a familiar idea in theology. . . . The body of Satan is upside down: functions are misdistributed and perverted: in the intestine-like Malebolge we find those who corrupt and sever the bond of love that should unit the body politic—instead of the healthy currency of faith and mutual trust, their perversion of *digestion* produces alloys, hydroptic humors, pitch. In the head we find those who "subject reason to desire," who misuse eyes and mouth—as a matter of fact the head, face, eyes, and mouth are the only parts of the body explicitly mentioned in the meeting with Paolo and Francesca. This is obviously appropriate to Dante's analysis of incontinence as involving systematic self-deception.

After Virgil carries Dante down Satan's side, turns laboriously around, and climbs up out of Hell (at a point corresponding to the anus, as Norman O. Brown pointed out years ago), they are in a position to see Satan from a truer perspective—as upside down. In terms of the overall pattern of Hell as a body of which Satan is the head, it can now be seen not only as upside down but also as inside out, or imploded: it is as if Satan had been flayed and his skin stretched up over his head to envelop all his children. (Perhaps this is the point of the reference to Marsyas in *Paradiso* I, 20–21). The simonists, finally, have a punishment that is strikingly similar in appearance to Satan's—they protrude feet first from holes in the rock—because they have perverted their Christo-mimetic role as *head of the body of the Church*.

"Io son venuto al punto de la rota," then, is a microcosm of the *Commedia*. That Dante proudly inserts into the text of the *Inferno* so many references to the *petrose* should by no means be regarded as a disavowal of their poetics, for it is *in nuce* the poetics of the *Commedia* itself. The birth of the twinned heaven of line 3 is the birth of a new poetics. When Dante says, in the Epistle to Can Grande, "the subject with which the alternative senses are concerned ought to be double," he is describing the allegorical procedures of the *Commedia* in terms of an astronomical metaphor: the double subject of the poem, like the earth encircled by the twin heavens, is circled by double meaning, as the earth is encircled by the *geminato cielo*. To bring out the full implications of this metaphor will require further investigation.

DAVID QUINT

Epic Tradition and "Inferno" IX

When Dante's itinerary stalls before the gates of Dis, he and Virgil stand at a crossroads where two epic traditions of underworld descent diverge in opposite directions. The Furies misapply the typology of Theseus to the pilgrim; but Dante has not come to deprive the infernal kingdom of one of its denizens, nor will he, as the guardians of Dis demand, retrace his steps back to earth by the way he came. Passing through and beyond the underworld, Dante's journey rather imitates the descent of Aeneas. For both protagonists the endpoint of death turns into a point on a continuum: Aeneas moves on to his divinely ordained mission in Roman history, Dante to salvation and the vision of God. But in Canto IX the appropriation and parodistic inversion of the classical texts of Lucan and Statius point towards a second Stygian literary topos: the raising up of dead souls.

Virgil informs Dante of a prior descent from Limbo to lower Hell.

> . . . I was down here once before, conjured by that fell Erichtho who recalled shades to their bodies. My flesh was not long naked of me when she made me enter within that wall to draw forth a spirit from the circle of Judas, the deepest and darkest place, farthest from the heaven that encircles all. Well do I know the way, therefore be reassured.
>
> (22–30)

Shortly after his death but before the Crucifixion, Virgil had been conjured by Erichtho, the Thessalian sorceress of Lucan's *Pharsalia*, with

From *Dante Studies*, vol. 93. Copyright © 1975 by *Dante Studies*.

instructions to draw forth a spirit from the circle of traitors. His statement, accounting for his knowledge of infernal geography, recalls the moment in *Aeneid* VI, 564–565, when the Sibyl claims a similar expertise. But if the passage reasserts the Dante-Aeneas analogy, it simultaneously suggests its inversion. Erichtho is a structural opposite to Beatrice. Beatrice summons Virgil up to earth to lead Dante down through Hell. Erichtho sends Virgil to the bottom of Hell to bring a spirit up to earth. This double movement, coming and going, is repeated at v. 82 where the heavenly messenger brushes aside the heavy air of the Stygian swamp; his action imitates Mercury at the opening of Book II of the *Thebaid* (1–6). But while Dante's messenger descends to Dis, Statius's Mercury is ascending, bringing the soul of Laius beside him to earth; the souls in Hades speculate whether Laius has been called to earth by a witch of Thessaly (II, 21–22). Dante quotes Statius precisely where Statius alludes to Erichtho, both here and in the description of Tisiphone (*Theb.* I, 103) echoed at v. 41; the glow in Tisiphone's eyes resembles the moon under the witch's spell (*Theb.* I, 104–106). Statius clearly admired the Erichtho episode, for he made it the model for Tiresias's conjuration and prophecy in *Thebaid* IV.

During their demonic invocations, both Erichtho and Tiresias run into temporary opposition from the infernal spirits. The conjurors threaten the recalcitrant shades with higher authority. . . . [The *Pharsalia* and the *Thebaid*] occupy an important place in the history of the literary imagination. Together they form the textual authority for Boccaccio's figure of Demogorgon, the all-powerful creator and master of the gods.

The tradition of Demogorgon, however, predates Boccaccio. The fourth or fifth century *Thebaid* scholiast Placidus Lactantius found in Tiresias's menacing words an allusion to the *demiourgos* of Plato's *Timaeus*. . . . Carlo Landi notes the distortions that take place in the Latin translations of δημιουργός in the manuscript tradition of Lactantius's commentary. Citing instances of *demogorgon* and *demogorgona*, Landi plausibly argues for a fusion or confusion of *demiourgos* with the analogous passage in Lucan: "qui Gorgona cernit apertam." Indeed, I have found a reference to a recognizable predecessor of Boccaccio's Demogorgon in the gloss to Erichtho's speech in the twelfth-century commentary on the *Pharsalia* of Arnulfus of Orleans. . . . This is Demogorgon the divine progenitor as Boccaccio would later describe him. Dante appears to have been aware of this interpretative tradition behind the conjuration passages of Lucan and Statius, particularly of the Demogorgon's ability to withstand the gorgon's glance, from which one half of his composite name derived. The gorgon in question, as Arnulfus makes clear, is Medusa, the supreme barrier halting the pilgrim in Canto

IX. The heavenly messenger who arrives to let Dante *into* Dis thus parodies "Demogorgon," invoked to free the conjured shades *out* of Hades. The messenger descends from above while Lucan's chthonic deity would rise from the primeval depths beneath the underworld. The up and down trajectories converge at the walls of Dis.

By now the pattern of literary allusion in the canto is clear. The two alternatives which the uncertain pilgrim faces outside Dis—to continue his descent or to return to earth—both have precedents in the epic tradition. Dante makes the first correspond to the journey of Aeneas, the second to the conjuration of Erichtho. The heavenly messenger breaks the impasse and decisively reaffirms the Virgilian model. Yet the messenger himself, by his allusive associations with Statius's Mercury and with "Demogorgon," draws attention to the road not taken.

When Dante represents the rejection of one epic model that is implicit in his choice of another, he reverses the history of late Latin epic, where conjuration is, in fact, a conscious poetic substitution for the Virgilian *topoi* of the underworld descent and the intervention of the divine messenger. These latter episodes in the *Aeneid* provide moments for the poem to interpet itself, to assert the ideology of Roman destiny which gives meaning to the violence of the epic agon. These interpretative moments lie *outside* the human world of the poem and dramatize its claim to an extratextual significance: Anchises predicts the future greatness of his race from the timeless perspective of death, Mercury brings down the pronouncements of the gods. When Lucan and Statius invert Virgil's fictions, they are attacking not only his political ideology but also the authority of such privileged moments: they are attacking ideology itself.

The Erichtho episode, which takes place in the sixth book of what was to be a twelve-book epic, occupies the same position as Aeneas's underworld journey in the *Aeneid*. The reanimated Pompeian soldier evokes the same catalogue of distinguished Roman souls whom Anchises had pointed out in their embryonic state to his son: the Decii, the Gracchi, Scipio, Camillus, Cato the Censor, etc. But there is no joy in their vision of the future: they are weeping for the carnage of the civil wars and the demise of the republic. Moreover, the soldier's prophecy is vague, aside from its threat of punishment to Caesar and promise of reward to Pompey in their respective afterlives. It is tinged with Stoic renunciation: death is the only certainty. The attempt to contact superhuman authority not only fails to arrive at an interpretative statement, but is in itself an act of horrible and most un-Virgilian impiety. Lucan dwells lovingly upon the stomach-turning details of the witch's rite in order to emphasize the monstrosity of the *literary* incarnation of a "divine" voice in the human poetic text. Paradoxically, the *Pharsalia* makes history its subject matter in order to demonstrate the inauthenticity of poetic inter-pretations of history. The poetic text remains either "disembodied" or "inanimate," its authority self-contained.

In Book II of the *Thebaid*, we have seen that Statius makes explicit the obverse relationship between the descent of the heavenly messenger and the demonic conjuration by conflating the two conven-tions. Recalling still a third epic topos, the journey to the realm of Sleep, Statius's Mercury descends not to earth but to the underworld in order to raise up the soul of Laius. His mission is not the revelation of meaning but the instigation of further violence. The episode illustrates emblematically the *Thebaid*'s adaptation of the epic machinery of the *Aeneid* to the *Pharsalia*'s climate of demystification. The interrelationship of the three epics derives in large part from their common inspiration in the Roman civil wars.

Civil conflict, with its reciprocal violence and interchangeable victims, poses what René Girard has recently characterized as a crisis of undifferentiation. According to Girard, each contending faction claims divine sanction for its violence in order to distinguish itself from its opposition. Suppressing their human sameness, the sacred becomes the sign of the conqueror over the vanquished and oscillates according to the vicissitudes of battle. With its Aeneas-Augustus analogy, Virgil's mytho-logical poem proposes an ideological interpretation to recent history. The victorious imperial party has the last word: its poet-propagandist discovers in the ascendancy of Augustus the fulfillment of a divine historical plan. When Lucan dramatizes those same events as the spokesman for the lost republican cause, he cannot, of course, change their outcome, but he can at least remove the divine machinery which masks their undifferentiated structure. The Olympic gods of the *Aeneid* recede into the background of the *Pharsalia* and leave the wars to the play of Fortune. Statius's recourse to myth is a return to Virgilian form that only reiterates the insights of the *Pharsalia*. Beginning and ending in fratricide, the Theban cycle is *the* archetypal myth of civil warfare. The gods of the *Thebaid* become figures for that very Violence which indiscriminately consumes the rival factions and refuses to explain its own origin.

The confrontation of epic traditions in *Inferno* IX pits the Virgilian underworld descent and heavenly messenger against the conjura-tion scenes of Lucan and Statius. The former are conventions by which divine significance enters the poetic universe, while the latter renounce the possibility of such extratextual authority. It is not hard to see why the

Christian poet Dante chooses the Virgilian model, for he is assured of the spirit beyond the letter.

Looking at the classical environment of Canto IX, Benvenuto da Imola identifies the heavenly messenger as Mercury. . . . Both Benvenuto and Pietro di Dante assimilate the *verghetta* of verse 89 with the caduceus of the god. The two commentators follow the allegory of the *De Nuptiis Mercurii et Philologiae* and identify Mercury with Eloquence. But they also understand him in his traditional epic role as the angel of mediation. Pietro cites St. Augustine's etymology. . . . The descent of this Christian Mercury is analogous to the "condescension" of Scripture which Beatrice describes in *Paradiso* IV. The revelation of the Word sanctions the *Commedia*'s converse poetic ascent towards reunion with the Word; in the dramatic representation, the heavenly messenger opens the gates of Dis and allows the resumption of the pilgrim's journey. During the frightening impasse which halts the Virgilian descent outside the walls of the infernal city, the "other" tradition of Lucan and Statius is recognized as an inversion of Dante's poetics, a literary alternative which must be confronted and discarded before the pilgrim-poet may proceed.

JOHN FRECCERO

Manfred's Wounds and the Poetics of the "Purgatorio"

In the third canto of the *Purgatorio*, one of the excommunicants calls to Dante to ask if the pilgrim recognizes him:

> biondo era e bello e di gentile aspetto
> ma l'un de' cigli un colpo avea diviso.

(Fair was he and beautiful and of gentle aspect, but one of his brows had been cleft by a blow.)

The mark is not enough to identify him, so that the spirit names himself:

> . . . 'Or vedi';
> e mostrommi una piaga a sommo 'l petto.
> Poi sorridendo disse, 'Io son Manfredi,
> nepote di Costanza imperadrice . . .'

('Look here,' and he showed me a wound at the top of his chest. Then smiling he said, 'I am Manfred, the grandson of the Empress Constance . . .')

The episode marks one of the most famous moments of the *Purgatorio*: a generic description of masculine beauty, slightly skewed by rhetorical distortion, is interrupted by the adversative 'but' that suffices to mar the ideal with what appears to be an accident of history. That cleft brow helped to make Manfred a romantic hero in the nineteenth century and serves as testimony today of Dante's prodigious power of representation.

From *Centre and Labyrinth: Essays in Honour of Northrop Frye.* Copyright © 1983 by University of Toronto Press.

At first glance, the representation might appear to be an example of what Erich Auerbach referred to as mimesis, especially since his classic work on the subject began with a chapter entitled 'Odysseus' Scar.' Manfred's wounds are equally unforgettable and perhaps for some of the same reasons, but they serve a deeper purpose than Dante's desire to hold up a mirror to reality. In fact, the wounds are an anomaly in the representation, a flaw that seems to undermine the bases of Dante's fiction: we learn, later on in the *Purgatorio*, that the souls wending their way up the mountain have aerial bodies, fictive replicas of their real bodies and exact reflections of the soul itself. Wounds are inexplicable on such bodies, because they seem to be accidental intrusions into the ideal corporeity of the afterlife. If Manfred's wounds are reminiscent of Odysseus' scar, it cannot be at the level of descriptive detail. Odysseus' scar, Auerbach tells us, is an example of Homeric realism, described by the poet because it is *there*; Manfred's wounds, on the other hand, demand an interpretation. They are *there*, on a body made of thin air, and ought not to be.

The basis for associating the two texts is mythic, rather than mimetic, and becomes clear when we challenge Auerbach's reading of Odysseus' scar. The thesis of Auerbach's essay seems undermined by its title. The purpose of the essay was to reveal 'the need of the Homeric style to leave nothing which it mentions half in darkness and unexternalized.' In the style that 'knows only a foreground, only a uniformly illuminative, uniformly objective present, . . . never is there a form left fragmentary or half-illuminated, never a lacuna, never a gap, never a glimpse of un-plumbed depths.' Yet Odysseus' scar is itself precisely all of those things: an indelible mark of the past within the present, an opaque sign healed over a hidden depth. The scar is the mark of Odysseus' identity and manhood, or there could be no recognition. In a passage whose significance Auer-bach does not discuss, Homer tells us that the hero, when hunting as a boy, was gored in the thigh by a wild boar which he then killed with his lance. Almost seventy lines are devoted to describing the nobility of his lineage and his youthful courage, so that the scar remaining from the hunting accident takes upon itself a meaning never hinted at by Auer-bach: it is a sign of Odysseus' coming-of-age, almost a ritual scar, and it identifies him in the eyes of his former nurse, not fortuitously, but rather as the sign at once relating him to his ancestors and distinguishing him from them. In the succession of fathers and sons, Odysseus' scar marks his place precisely, bracketing him between his ancestors and Telemachus, his son, who is about to undergo his own baptism of blood.

At some level, of course, Auerbach knew that the primordial drama of male identity was hidden beneath the apparently innocuous and realistic detail. When he turned for contrast in the same essay to an equally ancient epic in a totally different tradition, he chose the story of Abraham and Isaac, the foundation story for Israel and a foreshadowing of the circumcision. Odysseus' scar is also a kind of circumcision. It bears the same relationship to Adonis' fatal wound (in Northrop Frye's masterful reading of the myth) that circumcision bears to castration. For all of the irreducible differences between the two epics, they are united by a common theme: the rites of violence that have traditionally been used by males to mark their identity and manhood.

Manfred's wounds hide a similar story, for they signify his relationship to his father, yet, by an ironic reversal of earthly values that is one of the functions of Dante's other-worldly perspective, they mark his passage away from patrilinear succession toward the mother. Critics have noticed that Manfred identifies himself only as the grandson of the Empress Constance; in fact, he was the son of Frederick II Hohenstaufen, known in Dante's day as *Stupor Mundi*. This pointed reticence has been explained in various ways: psychologizing critics have suggested that Manfred, although Frederick's favourite, was a natural son and not the legitimate heir of the mighty emperor. It is indelicate, according to this line of reasoning, for a bastard to name his father. A slightly more sophisticated view, the thematic interpretation, insists that Frederick is in Hell, with the rest of the Epicureans, and thus is erased from the memory of his son. The contrast between Manfred's radiant smile and his ghastly wound serves as a contrast between the vicissitudes of history and the power of grace for the late repentant.

A more interesting thematic reading of the passage involves Dante's own political ideals. Frederick was the founder of the Ghibelline imperial dream, but was by Dante's time totally discredited as a heretic and an excommunicant. The fictive salvation of his son, mortally wounded at the battle of Benevento, might then represent a survival of the Ghibelline ideal, to which Dante clung against all the evidence of his senses. On this reading, Manfred's insistence on Grace, 'mentre che la speranza ha fior del verde,' might then mask a much more specific hope for Dante's own political dream. In the *Purgatorio*, Manfred remembers his daughter, 'la mia buona Costanza,' the honour of Sicily and Aragon, and asks the pilgrim to tell her that he has been saved, in spite of his excommunication. Manfred is therefore bracketed between the two Constances, his grandmother in Paradise and his daughter on earth. The ideal of Empire lives on, but in matrilinear succession, outside the city of man, and reconciled at last to *Mater Ecclesia*. Manfred's message to his daughter repeats, yet transforms, the popular oracle that was said to have kept

Germany dreaming imperial ideals for centuries after the death of Frederick II: 'He lives not; yet he lives.' The body of the father is entombed in porphyry, the monument to imperial aspirations in Palermo or, for that matter, in Paris, but Manfred's bones are scattered to the four winds:

> Or le bagna la pioggia e move il vento
> di fuor dal regno, quasi lungo 'l Verde,
> dov' e' le trasmutò a lume spento.

(Now they are drenched by the rain and the wind shifts them *outside of the realm*, along the course of the river Verde, to which the Bishop brought them, with extinguished candles.)

The dispersion of Manfred's corpse suggests that, in so far as he is still a hero of a realm, the kingdom is not of this world.

Manfred's wounds are the scars of history, but his smile is a revisionist smile, belying the official versions of his fate. In spite of the fact that he was excommunicated by the Church, Dante places him among the late repentant, who will ultimately reach Paradise. Manfred tells us that the Bishop who had his body disinterred had misread that page in God's book; the implication seems to be that the poet, unlike the Church, has read God's book correctly. Manfred's salvation therefore represents an interpretation of the brute details of history, an allegorical reading of those wounds that belies the horror that they literally imply. As Manfred survived extinction, so Dante's political ideal survives historical contradiction by assimilation into the unity of his vision.

If Manfred's real body is dispersed, then it is clear that his fictive body is a representation, bearing symbolic wounds, diacritical marks slashed across the face of his father. Frederick's beauty won for him the title of *Sol invictus*: the adjectives *biondo, bello e di gentile aspetto* might have been taken from contemporary chronicles describing the Emperor. At the same time, Frederick's *persona* is the mystical body of Empire, the head of state, as we still say, whose heart is the law. The dazzling incongruity of Manfred's smile serves to affirm the triumph of the ideal in spite of the apparently mortal wounds to both the head and heart. Like the scar of Odysseus, the adversative 'ma' serves to affirm sameness with a profound difference—that is to say, the syntax performs the function of ritual scarring. The wounds incurred in his father's name win for him his own: 'Io son Manfredi'—so that the mortal wounds are in fact a baptism, a rebirth into a new order, with what Saint Paul called 'a circumcision of the heart' (Romans 2:2).

For all of the apparently mimetic power of Dante's verses, there can be no doubt that corporeal representation in the poem is self-consciously symbolic. In this respect the *Purgatorio* does not differ greatly from the *Inferno*. The recognition of Manfred has its infernal counterpart in Mohammed among the schismatics, who bares his cloven chest as an emblem of theological schism and is introduced by similar syntax—'vedi com'io mi dilacco.' In the same canto (XXVIII), Bertrand de Born's decapitated body suggests the schism in the political order. The clinical horror—Bertrand carrying his head like a lantern—lends horror to the more abstract political enormity. Bertrand is said to have set father against son:

> Perch'io parti' così giunte persone,
>   partito porto il mio cerebro, lasso!
>   dal suo principio ch'è in questo troncone.
> Così s'osserva in me lo contrapasso—

(Because I divided persons who were so conjoined I carry my brain separated from its source in this trunk. Thus is observed in me the counterpass—.)

Applying the same figure, we may say that the marks on Manfred's fictive body also stand for his relationship to a wounded theological and political order which he has survived and, in a sense, redeemed.

The representation of Manfred is meant to bear witness of this redemption within the fiction of Dante's purgatorial journey. His wounds, apparently accidental, are in fact signs of his identity and distinction. They are like the marks of *history*, which cannot be accommodated by the abstract mimetic claim of a one-to-one correspondence between the aerial bodies of the Purgatory and the souls which produce them. At some level, the disfiguring marks of history mark the soul as well. Like writing itself, they deface in the name of significance. Their presence in the *Purgatorio* is at the same time the poet's mark, his intervention in the fiction that otherwise purports to be an unmediated representation of the other world. As wounds are inexplicable on an aerial body, so writing is inexplicable on what is claimed to be an exact representation of an other-worldly vision. Paradoxically, the text 'mirrors' the other world only by virtue of its cracks.

Lest the parallel between Manfred's wounds and the text itself seem too ingenious for a medieval text, it should be pointed out that such an analogy is implied in what is probably the most famous and most solemn of recognition scenes. The newly risen Christ shows his wounds to Thomas so that he may believe what he has *seen*: 'Thomas, because thou hast seen me, thou hast believed: blessed are they that have not seen, and yet have believed.' Christ's wounds, made manifest to Thomas, bear witness to the Resurrection. The solemnity of that moment leads to the representation of

Manfred a theological force that serves to underscore the strength of Dante's Imperial faith.

It is, however, the passage immediately following Thomas' recognition in the gospel of John that I wish especially to recall in this context. The narrative of Jesus' works ends with his remark to Thomas and, almost as if to end *his* work, John adds these words: 'And many other signs truly did Jesus in the presence of his disciples, which are not written in this book, but these are written, that ye might believe that Jesus is the Christ, the Son of God, and that believing, ye might have life through his name.' The writer of the gospel thereby establishes a parallel between the wounds of Christ's body and his own text, filled with signs that demand of the reader the same assent that is demanded of the doubting Thomas. As Christ's scarred body is *seen* by the disciples, so John's text is *read* by the faithful. That analogy is operative in Dante's poem. Manfred's wounds, slashed across a body made of thin air, stand for Dante's own intrusion into the course of history. They are, as it were, writing itself, Dante's own markings introduced across the page of history as testimony of a truth which otherwise might not be perceived. It is this parallelism between the text and the aerial body of the *Purgatorio* that establishes the fiction of the *Purgatorio*, the vision of the pilgrim translated by the writing of the poet, scars of history erased and assimilated into God's Book, where the Truth is finally conveyed, according to Saint Augustine, without letters and without words.

The analogy between the aerial body and the poem itself is consistently developed throughout the *Purgatorio*. It underlies the apparently gratuitous account that Dante gives us in canto XXV of the formation of the body in the afterlife. The question is how the souls in this circle can speak of nourishment or grow thinner in their askesis when there is no need of food. Virgil answers with generic theories of mimesis and poetic representation: the bodies of the *Purgatorio* are related to real bodies as the torch was related to the life span of Meleager in the eighth book of the *Metamorphoses* or as an image in a mirror is related to what it reflects. This statement of the relation of the aerial bodies to nature—like a mirror or like a lamp—establishes the context as unmistakably aesthetic, with ancient figures for doctrines of poetic inspiration that have become particularly familiar to us since they were studied by M. H. Abrams. If the bodies of the Purgatory are related to nature as either mirror or lamp, then the poem itself is either a mimetic or metaphoric representation of nature. This is as far as Virgil will go in his explanation, asserting that a complete understanding of the process transcends human understanding. He then defers to Statius for a fuller explanation than he can provide.

At this point, Dante enters upon a digression that has been something of a scandal in the history of Dante criticism, not only because of its apparent irrelevance, but also because of its reputed technical aridity. In the midst of six cantos of the *Purgatorio* that deal more or less explicitly with poetry, Dante now embarks upon what amounts to a lesson in medieval embryology. This occurs when Statius chooses to answer the question about the fictive bodies of the Purgatory with a discussion of the general relationship of body and soul, on earth as well as in the afterlife. As we shall see, the lesson has at least as much to do with poetics as it has with embryology. Like an analogously technical discussion in the *Paradiso* on the nature of moon spots, this scientific disquisition can be skipped over by the general reader only at the risk of missing something essential about the nature of Dante's poetic theory.

To anticipate somewhat, I should like to suggest that Statius' discussion about conception and reproduction in canto XXV also serves as a gloss on canto XXIV, where the subject is *literary* creation and conception. More than that, it seems to suggest strongly an analogy between the act of writing and the act of procreation. Dante begins with the clinically obvious and proceeds to explain its metaphysical significance. Sexuality is, for Dante, nature's expression of creativity, rather than the repressed subject matter of literary expression. This is one important sense in which it may be said that art imitates nature. As the soul is inspired in the foetus, so the inspiration of the poet comes from God. The body, however, is the work of parenthood. In the same way, the poetic corpus is sired by the poet, who provides the vehicle for God's message.

Statius begins by telling us how the seed is formed. A small portion of blood is stored and purified in the heart of the male and is eventually transformed into the male seed, which contains within it an informing power, *virtute informativa*, that will gradually mould the blood of the female into a human body, with all of its organs. When this power is released into the female, the two bloods unite and the foetus is formed. The foetus then naturally grows into a vegetative and then into a sensitive soul. As yet, there is no human life at all, strictly speaking; it is not until the brain is completely formed, in about the sixth month of pregnancy, that God directly inspires the intellective soul into the embryo:

> . . . sì tosto come al feto
> l'articular del cerebro è perfetto,
> lo motor primo a lui si volge lieto
> *sovra tant' arte di natura, e spira*
> *spirito novo, di vertù repleto,*

> che ciò che trova attivo quivi, tira
> in sua sustanzia, e fassi un'alma sola,
> che vive e sente e sé in sé rigira.

(. . . as soon as the brain of the foetus is perfectly formed, the prime mover turns joyfully to such a work of nature's art and inspires in it a new spirit, filled with power, so that what it finds active there it draws into its substance and makes of itself a single soul, that grows and feels and reflects upon itself.)

Statius then moves directly to a discussion of the formation of the fictive body in the afterlife. At the moment of death, the soul falls to the shore to which it is destined and there the informing virtue which it possesses irradiates the surrounding air, as a ray of light irradiates moist air to form a rainbow, in order to form its aerial body. The soul *imprints*, 'suggella,' the surrounding air with its own form and so creates the ghostly body that the pilgrim sees.

Except for a passing reference in Hugh of Saint Victor, there does not seem to be a precedent in specifically Christian thought of the Middle Ages for the belief that the soul could unite with the air in order to form an aerial body, although that demons had such power was a commonplace of popular and learned belief. Neo-Platonic thought might well admit such a possibility, but the Christian emphasis on the indissoluble unity of the human composite and the Aristotelian theory of hylomorphism to which Dante subscribed rule out the possibility that Dante means us to take the fiction seriously as metaphysics. It does not require a great deal of the reader's imagination to see in this fiction a disguised poetic claim. The seal of reality is stamped upon the dreamlike medium of the Purgatory as the seal of the soul is affixed to the wax of the body. Dante's poem seems to make a claim for a kind of mimetic essentialism—realism in the medieval sense of the word.

The 'realistic' quality of the *Purgatorio* is the central theme of this portion of the poem. It has often been remarked that the second realm of the poem is the most lifelike, the most modern part of the vision. Here souls are on the move, on pilgrimage as they were on earth, possessed of a temporality that is measured by the imagination of the pilgrim. His subjectivity is the stage of the action here. Unlike the claim of objective presence in the *Inferno* or the ethereal non-representation of the *Paradiso*, the surrounding world is here filtered through the pilgrim's *fantasia*, which is itself the power that creates images in the form of dreams, out of thin air. The action of *fantasia* is exactly analogous to the process of the afterlife as Dante imagines it. The bodies of the *Purgatorio* are of the same order of reality as the bodies of the imagination, quite literally the 'stuff that dreams are made on.' The pilgrim's initial question about the mode of existence of the bodies here amounts to a question about the relationship of his poem to the real world.

With this hypothesis in mind, Statius' discussion of conception takes upon itself a new dimension of meaning. There are echoes, in Statius' speech, of Dante's doctrine of poetic inspiration contained in the canto immediately preceding this. In canto XXIV, Bonagiunta da Lucca asks the pilgrim if he is the man who drew forth, 'trasse fore,' the new rhymes of the sweet new style. The verb unmistakably suggests childbirth and the adjective *new*, repeated several times, prepares the way for the discussion of the infusion of the intellective soul by God: 'spirito novo, di vertu repleto.' Most interesting, however, is the pilgrim's reply, which for centuries has been taken as Dante's definition of his own art:

> I' mi son un che, quando
> Amor mi spira, noto, e a quel modo
> ch'e' ditta dentro vo significando . . .

(As for me, I am one who, when love inspires me, take note ["noto"], and in the manner that it is written within, I go signifying . . .)

The moment of poetic inspiration exactly matches the moment of inspiration of the new soul: 'sovra tant' arte di natura . . . spira spirito *novo*.' The work of art is not nature's art but that of the poet, although the source of inspiration, *spirito novo*, is the same. The forcefulness and syntactic isolation of the verb 'noto,' etymologically, 'I mark,' seems to highlight the moment of inscription; given the analogy with procreation, it would seem to correspond with the moment of conception, recalling Jean de Meung's playful references to 'nature's stylus' in the sexual act. Dante's emphasis is however on the unitary source of spiritual inspiration, the soul of the foetus or the spirit of the text. At the same time, the gerund 'vo significando' suggests that literary creation is not a moment but a process, a constant approximation approaching but never quite reaching God's text within as its limit. The construction used in that sense has since been hallowed by literary tradition. When the Romantic Leopardi wrote his own lyric on the subject of literary inspiration, invoking the wind rather than God's spirit, he used a similar construction to describe his own effort: in 'L'Infinito,' the act of writing is rendered 'vo comparando'—'I am comparing'—presumably the present text with Nature's own. For Dante, the gerund depicts the *process* of writing, the askesis that will bring the 'body' of the text closer and closer to the spirit which informs it. The words suggest that the poem, like the pilgrim, is still en route in the *Purgatorio*.

Manfred's wounds constitute the marks that must be expunged in order for history to be brought into conformity with God's will, just as sin must be purged in order for the soul to be made 'puro e disposto a salire alle stelle.' At the same time, the wounds have served a providential purpose, in much the same way that sin can prepare the way for conversion. In this respect, both history and sin are analogues for writing itself. As history *disfigures* the face of Manfred with apparently accidental marks that in fact give him his significance under the aspect of eternity, so writing progressively disfigures the page ('vo significando') in order paradoxically to make it clear. The process of interpretation, like the process of purgation, is an assimilation and a gradual *effacement* of the marks, like melting footprints in the snow: 'così la neve al sol si disigilla.' The phrase from the *Paradiso* signals the ending of the poet's work and the vision of God's Book, 'legato con Amore in un volume, ciò che per il mondo si squaderna.'

Readers of the *Purgatorio* will remember that its central action, for the pilgrim, is the *erasing* of his sins, sins that are at once *wounds* and *letters*. The instrument is not nature's stylus, nor that of the poet, but history's pen. The angel guardian of the Purgatory draws seven letter P's on the forehead of the pilgrim with his sword, as a representation of his history:

> Sette P ne la fronte mi descrisse
> col punton della spada e 'Fa' che lavi
> quando se' dentro, queste piaghe' disse.

(He drew seven P's on my forehead with the point of his sword and 'see that when you are within, you wash these *wounds*,' he said.)

The penitential process for the pilgrim consists in the eradication of wounds inflicted by a sword. We may imagine this also to be the case with Manfred's wound, eternally there in the space of canto III, but effaced in the process of refinement toward the resurrected body. Later on, Statius describes the whole penetential process in this way: 'Con tal cura conviene e con tai pasti, / che la piaga da sezzo si ricucia.' (With such care and with such a cure will the wound be completely healed.) Underlying these images is the affirmation that the poem we read has its counterpart in Manfred's face.

In God's Book, Manfred's brow is clear. This is implied by a verse that has always presented a certain difficulty for commentators. Speaking of the Bishop who had his body disinterred and thrown into the river, Manfred says that had the pastor realized that Manfred was saved, he would have spared his body. The difficult sentence reads: 'Se 'l pastor di Cosenza . . . avesse in Dio ben letta questa faccia,' and the difficulty resides in the translation of the word 'faccia,' which means either 'face' or, as Charles Singleton has translated it, 'page.' 'Had the pastor of Cosenze well *read* that page of God.' Our discussion thus far suggests, however, that one might equally well have translated the word 'faccia' as 'face,' thereby giving more force to the Bishop's misreading and more concreteness to the demonstrative adjective 'questa': 'Had the pastor of Cosenza well read *this face* in God.' God's Book has no marks that are subject to misinterpretation; Manfred's wounds, however, might have been taken as signs of his damnation when read from a purely human perspective, without benefit of that radiant smile.

Finally an additional nuance of meaning can be derived from comparing this passage with what is undoubtedly its source. There is a culminating moment at the end of Book VI of the *Aeneid* when Anchises points out to his son the shadow of a soul who might have been a hero of Rome equal to Marcellus had he not died prematurely. Scholars tell us that he was the adopted son of the Emperor and Octavia is said to have fainted with grief when Virgil first recited his lines. They describe the handsome boy in terms that recall, if only by contrast, the description of Manfred, even to the adversative *sed*, which serves to indicate not a wound, but an enveloping darkness suggestive of premature death:

> A man young, very handsome and clad in shining armour, *but* with face and eyes down cast and little joy on his brow . . . What a noble presence he has, *but* the night flits black about his head and shadows him with gloom . . . Alas his goodness, alas his ancient honour and right hand invincible in war! . . . Ah poor boy! If thou mayest break the grim bar of fate, thou shall be Marcellus. Give me lilies in full hands . . .
>
> (*Aeneid* VI. 860–85)

The foreboding darkness contrasts with the smile of Manfred in the same way that Virgilian pathos contrasts with the hope of the *Purgatorio*; even the eternity of Rome must bow before the death of this beautiful young man. He too is an emperor's son, but the success of Empire cannot mitigate individual grief. We are left with Anchises' futile funereal gesture.

From Dante's standpoint, of course, this is the Virgilian misreading of death; Manfred's smile, with an imperial dream in shambles, is in a sense a smile at Virgil's expense. It happens that this passage contains the only verse from the *Aeneid* literally quoted, in the original Latin, in the *Divine Comedy*: 'Manibus O date lilia plenis!' It occurs in a very different context, toward the end of the *cantica*, as Beatrice approaches for the first time. The angels sing out for the lilies of the Resurrection and Anchises' funereal gesture is turned into a note of triumph.

This deliberate misreading of Virgil brings me to the final point I want to make concerning the effacement of heterogeneity in Dante's text.

I have said that Dante's doctrine of poetic inspiration cannot account for what may be called the 'body' of his text as opposed to its spirit. If the inspiration is claimed to be God-given, the poetic *corpus* is very much Dante's own. To extend the procreative image that Dante has established, we may say that the claim of inspiration does not account for the ancestry of the text, especially for the influence of Virgil, whom Dante refers to as his 'dolcissimo patre' at precisely the moment when he quotes the *Aeneid* verbatim, thereby acknowledging Virgil's part in the genesis of his own poem. Once more, heterogeneity is assimilated by an effacement before our eyes. The foreignness of the Virgilian sentiment here at the top of the mountain, underscored by the foreignness of the original language, is neutralized by the otherwise seamless context; death is transformed into resurrection, leaving behind the distinctive mark of the disappearing father, his text in Latin like a foreign element. Like Manfred's wound, the sign of the father is most in evidence at the moment of the son's triumph and, again like Manfred's wound, it is about to be effaced.

After that quotation from Virgil's text, the pilgrim trembles at the approach of Beatrice and turns to tell Virgil, 'Conosco i segni dell'antica fiamma,'—'I recognize the signs of the ancient flame'—which is, not a direct quotation this time, but a literal translation of Dido's words of foreboding when she first sees Aeneas and recalls her passion for her dead husband while she anticipates the funeral pyre on which she will die: 'Agnosco veteris flammae vestigia' (*Aeneid* IV.23). Dante transforms those words as well, for he uses them to celebrate the return of his beloved and a love stronger than death. He turns to Virgil for support and finds him gone. Calling to him three times, the text evokes the merest allusion to a Virgilian text, the disappearance of Eurydice in the Fourth Georgic: 'Eurydice, Eurydice, Eurydice':

> Ma Virgilio n'avea lasciati scemi
> di sé, Virgilio dolcissimo patre,
> Virgilio a cui per mia salute die'mi.

(But Virgil had left us bereft of himself, Virgil sweetest father, Virgil to whom I gave myself for my salvation.)

The calling out to Eurydice is the culmination of Virgilian pathos, lamenting death that is stronger than poetry, as it is stronger than love and even than Rome. Dante's adversative *ma* [but] records the loss, yet transcends it with an affirmation. The progression from direct quotation to direct translation to merest allusion is an effacement, further and further away from the letter of Virgil's text, as Virgil fades away in the dramatic representation to make way for Beatrice. It is at that point, for the first time, that the poet is called by name: 'Dante!' The intrusion of Virgil's words into Dante's text is at that point the mark of poetic maturity.

SUSAN NOAKES

The Double Misreading of
Paolo and Francesca

The episode of Paolo and Francesca is
no doubt the most widely known episode of Dante's *Commedia*. Endeared
to the hearts of many for what is taken to be a highly sentimental
presentation of the force of romantic love, it now enjoys a currency
among participants in "the attack on literature." The famous final phrase
that Dante puts into Francesca's mouth—"Galeotto fu il libro e chi lo
scrisse"—has nearly reached the status of a proverb in literary circles. I
find it often alluded to by colleagues who warn, with a wink and a certain
sense of glee, against the perils of literature. The phrase has even made it
into twentieth-century American popular culture, in the novel *Fear of
Flying*.

When Dante is taken over so straightforwardly in the service of a
twentieth-century critical fashion, any reader who is concerned for the
historicity of Dante's text must become uneasy. What I would like to show
here is that such an adoption of Dante's line as a motto in the attack on
literature involves not only considerable over-simplification but also out-
right historical inaccuracy. Interpretation of the passage is by no means
inappropriate, but such interpretation must stress, at least, two characteristics of the period in the history of reading in which the work was
written: the alert and relatively sophisticated interest, on the part of the
educated reading public, in what is now termed "intertextuality," and the
concern about the effects of the inclusion in that audience of laymen and

From *Philological Quarterly* 2, vol. 62 (Spring 1983). Copyright © 1983 by University of
Iowa.

laywomen. When read with these characteristics in mind, the line "Galeotto fu il libro . . ." emerges as an ironic comment on the woman depicted as speaking it.

Traditionally, the line has not been read as ironic. What is striking about most of the scholarly discussions of *Inferno* V, is their focus on the morality of the episode. Any treatment of the canto's possible reference, ironic or otherwise, to a theory of reading or of literature has consistently been made subsidiary to this moral concern. The questions most often raised about *Inferno* V, are these: (1) Are Francesca's actions, if not right, at least justifiable? (2) Is it the author of the Lancelot romance who is to blame for Francesca's eternal damnation? (3) Should the reader empathize with her and with the pilgrim's pity for her?

Commentators who find her behavior understandable, under the circumstances, lament her tragic fate and sometimes draw from it a moral lesson. Other commentators become almost ferocious on the subject of Francesca's moral laxity. Charles Grandgent exemplifies the first group. Calling Francesca "this unhappy lady," he judges her as follows: "It is not alone the undying passion of Francesca that moves us, but even more her gentleness and modest reticence. In her narrative she names none of the participants. . . . Everything in her story that could mar our pity is set aside, and nothing remains but the quintessence of love. Amid the tortures of Hell, where all is hatred, her love does not forsake her, and she glories in the thought that she and Paolo shall never be parted." Mark Musa's view, representing the second group, seems very different from Grandgent's:

> Like Eve, who tempted Adam to commit the first sin in the Garden of Eden, Francesca tempted Paolo . . . [who is] surely not happy with their state. . . . Francesca cooly alludes to Paolo with the impersonal "that one" . . . or "this one" . . . She never mentions his name. Line 102 indicates her distaste for Paolo: the manner of her death (they were caught and killed together in the midst of their lustful passion) *still* offends her because she is forever condemned to be together with her naked lover; he serves as a constant reminder of her shame and of the reason that they are in Hell. . . . Their temporary pleasure together in lust has become their own particular torment in Hell. . . . Perhaps we should not blame the pilgrim for being taken in by Francesca; dozens of critics, unaware of the wiles of sin, have also been seduced by her charm and the grace of her speech.

The contrast between these two interpretations reflects the passage of sixty-two years more than it reflects *Inferno* V. Both scholars, for example, focus on Francesca's substitution of "*costui*" and "*questi*" for Paolo's name, but, for one, that substitution indicates gentility, for the other, coldness. An "impersonality" that in 1909 (the year Grandgent's commentary first appeared) could be interpreted as a lady-like reticence could be seen, by the seventies, as vindictive callousness.

Alongside this purely moral approach to *Inferno* V, another interpretive tradition has, indeed, flourished, a tradition which seems to focus on the canto's possible reference to a theory of reading or of literature. According to this tradition, the pilgrim's fainting reveals the poet's recognition of the seductive nature of literature, especially literature of a particular kind. Current since the beginning of the century, this view found its most sensitive and learned exponent in Renato Poggioli. In an article, basically New Critical in approach, and first published in 1957, Poggioli paraphrases the "literary moral" of *Inferno* V, as follows: "writing and reading romantic fiction is almost as bad as yielding to romantic love. This obvious and almost naive truth is all contained in the famous line, 'Galeotto fu il libro e chi lo scrisse,' by which, as Francesco d'Ovidio says, the poet confesses his horrified feeling at the thought that he too 'could become a Gallehaut to somebody else.'" But this interpretation is still essentially moral in character. It wears the semblance of a literary interpretation since it is "about" literature; but lurking under the guise of a focus on the self-reflexiveness of literature there remains a moral teaching. If it no longer implies that literature can teach diffidence about adultery, it still implies that literature can teach diffidence about literature. In other words, this interpretation still sees literature as a moral tool; the question to which it responds is a question about how people should behave, not about how literature works. Moreover, Poggioli's "literary moral," by his own admission, represents the poet as making a superfluous gesture: "But there is no reason for [the fear that Dante could become a Galahad], since that line helps to destroy the very suggestion on which it is built."

The gesture is not superfluous, however, if what is sought is not a "literary moral" but rather an implicit theory of reading. Such a theory of reading can readily be discovered by exegesis; this requires attention to the particular details of the way in which reading is represented in *Inferno* V. There is more to it than the simple narrative structure which makes reading precede and cause adultery. This structure is used in so many permutations in the late Middle Ages that it attains the status of a commonplace, one which expresses the concern of those who use it with the increasing number of lay readers—that is, readers who might lack the moral guidance and discipline of clerical readers. So often does the author of the *Commedia* criticize the literary attitudes of others and so seldom does he imitate their themes and commonplaces unquestioningly that it seems unlikely he would simply adopt the topos which connected lay reading, especially by women, with the temptation to seduction, without a re-consideration of its meaning and implications.

Dante does not present this topos in general terms; he depicts Paolo and Francesca as reading, not just an example of romantic fiction, but a specific text. Philologists agree that the text in question must be from the Vulgate cycle *Lancelot del Lac*. The passage from it which Paolo and Francesca read also has to do with a love based in reading, or, more precisely, in the interpretation of words: using this passage, Dante creates a kind of "mise-en-abîme." The details of Paolo and Francesca's reading of this text may be briefly summarized: What Paolo and Francesca read about Lancelot is "how love seized him" (v. 128). They are represented as being "conquered" by a particular passage: "solo un punto" (v. 132). That single point is the one at which a "desired smile" is kissed by "cotanto amante," a lover of masculine gender; the only possible inference, then, is that it is the point at which Lancelot kisses Guinevere which conquers them. Furthermore, Paolo and Francesca are represented as not getting any farther in their reading of the Lancelot story than that kiss: at the moment they read of it, they mimic it, stopping their reading, and consequently do not find out how the story ends.

As early as 1902, scholars pointed out a major discrepancy between what Dante gives as Francesca's paraphrase of the episode of the kiss in the Lancelot romance and that episode itself. . . . In *Inferno* V, Francesca is represented as recalling the fatal kiss as follows:

> . . . when we read that the longed-for smile was kissed by so great a lover, he who never shall be parted from me, all trembling, kissed my mouth. A Galeotto was the book and he that wrote it; that day we read in it no farther.

(vv. 133–38)

In the romance, it is clear that Lancelot, repeatedly described as trembling, is kissed by Guinevere. In the *Commedia*, the roles are reversed; Francesca's mouth is kissed by Paolo. Unless one makes the dangerous assumption that Dante was being careless here, one must infer that the character, Francesca, is depicted by Dante as either deliberately misrepresenting or unconsciously misreading the *Lancelot* text.

Various efforts to explain the significance of this discrepancy have been made. Two of the most recent are, in 1957, Poggioli's and, in 1968, Musa and Anna Hatcher's. Poggioli wisely keeps his discussion of the matter quite brief; he asserts that Francesca "*unconsciously* re-shapes the literary kiss to make it better agree with the real one" (emphasis added). This suggestion, first made by Francesco Torraca, must be received sceptically because of its evident anachronism. Dante does not attribute to his characters unconscious motivations any more often than he makes them speak in Freudian slips. Poggioli adds that "Dante cared more for the spirit than for the letter of his text" and had a "scorn for literalness." This is an extremely refined way of attributing to Dante a careless mistake, a distressing suggestion whose premise Poggioli himself must reject later in the same article, asserting that Dante's ". . . ethical message may be easily read not in the spirit, but in the very letter of his tale." Poggioli does not urge either of these explanations for the discrepancy too strongly, however; he quickly turns from this to other matters, and the rest of his interpretation does not depend on his remarks on this issue.

Musa and Hatcher are not quite so reticent. In their view, Francesca is to be condemned for more than simple adultery. Much interested in the question of whether (presumably in some pre-textual world they posit) Francesca "took the initiative," they accuse her of a "cover-up," meant to "put the blame on Paolo" and ask "did she try to force his glance?" Although the pilgrim invites both Paolo and Francesca to speak, only Francesca actually does; Musa and Hatcher present this as evidence that Francesca is rather more forward than a lady who speaks the language of the *dolce stilnovo* might be expected to be. On the other hand, they ask rhetorically, does Paolo stand by and weep silently because he is "too timid to contradict her words, still under her domination?" Their analysis culminates in still another rhetorical question: "Why did Dante choose as a supposed parallel to the behavior of his lovers the love scene from the Old French romance when he had at hand a much closer parallel in the first love scene of Tristram and Iseult? . . . Perhaps he chose the Lancelot romance in order to trap Francesca, or to allow her to entrap herself. . . . Why this subtly cruel auctorial trick in the first canto devoted to the punishment of sinners in Hell?"

It is possible, however, to explain the discrepancy between *Inferno* V and *Lancelot del Lac* without such extravagant speculative questions and without attributing to Dante either cruelty or carelessness. To do this, it is necessary to read the Lancelot romance, in order to find out two things: (1) "how love seized Lancelot" and (2) what the context of the "single point" which conquered Paolo and Francesca was. I will deal with the second and broader question first.

As the narrator of the prose *Lancelot* moves toward the kiss episode, he makes it clear that neither Lancelot nor Guinevere is to be seen in the glamorous light which modern interpreters of Dante cast upon them. Lancelot is presented as foolish and bumbling, while Guinevere is manipulative and disdainful. As she watches Lancelot and a companion approach across a meadow, she insults him by remarking to Galahad that he does not look as impressive as she had expected. . . . Once he reaches her, things go from bad to worse. As she interrogates him at length about his identity and achievements, his terror far exceeds the conventional bounds of knightly reticence, and he is embarrassed to the point of swooning by the presence of a former mistress, the Lady of Malohaut.

Dante represents Paolo and Francesca as ignorant of the outcome of this interview, for they stop reading at the point of the kiss. Because they do not read on, they do not find out that the Guinevere Lancelot kisses in the prose *Lancelot* is not Arthur's queen at all, but rather an impostor, something of a witch. Nor do they learn that Lancelot is severely punished for his lustful faithlessness to a holy mission. Energetically berated by a priest for his impurity, he cannot succeed in his quest for the Grail, and his role in that quest must be assumed by Galahad.

The traditional Lancelot story, already condemned by the papacy a hundred years before the *Commedia* was written, had in the prose *Lancelot*, been transformed into a religious attack on chivalric values. Since 1960, a good deal of textual criticism of the *Lancelot en prose* has appeared, and its attribution has been much debated. This research has led to an entirely new view of the romance, presented in 1972 by Henri de Briel and Manuel Hermann. They suggest that it was composed by Templars, Templar sympathizers, or Cistercians, for religious ends: "The authors of the Vulgate version, far from glorifying this affair, condemned it consistently. . . . They utilized such love to show that it only led to failure."

This, then, is the context of the "single point" in the *Lancelot* text at which Dante represents Paolo and Francesca as falling into sin. The *Lancelot* text is quite lucid, even overstated, in its condemnation of adultery. Paolo and Francesca are depicted as reading a text which provides the spiritual guidance potential adulterers presumably need to stay out of Hell. Dante shows that these readers, everlastingly unfortunate, do not have the ears to hear the guidance they need most when it is offered; in other terms, he shows that they are blind to the text's meaning.

That their torment is the result of a misreading of a text which intends to edify, Dante emphasizes with the line "di Lancialotto *come amor lo strinse*" (v. 128, emphasis added). Francesca reports that she and Paolo were reading about the way in which love took hold of Lancelot; the important moment in any courtly encounter known, technically, as the *amoris accensio*. Their curiosity about the *amoris accensio* of Lancelot is paralleled by the pilgrim's curiosity about their own:

> . . . how and *by what occasion (come)* did love grant you to know your
> uncertain desires?
>
> (vv.119–20, emphasis added)

The *"come"* in both v. 119 and v. 128 means "in what way"; the
repetition of the word marks the parallel.

Lancelot's account of the *amoris accensio* is the turning point of the
kiss episode in the prose romance and, indeed, according to him, the
ground of the entire narrative. In the *Commedia*, the importance of this
moment is further highlighted when the poet alludes to Guinevere's
inquiry about Lancelot's *amoris accensio* as the "primo fallo scritto di
Ginevra" (*Par.* XVI, v. 15). The question, not the kiss, is her first
recorded fault. And the story Lancelot tells Guinevere is indeed striking
enough to bear all this narrative weight.

Lancelot explains that it was she who elicited his love for her
when she named him her "ami." . . . Guinevere, who is represented as not
even recognizing Lancelot at his approach, expresses shock at this assertion of verbal intimacy. . . . The lines which follow Lancelot's citation of
Guinevere's mode of address to him . . . may properly be described as a
litany in praise of a word, a word with magical powers. The word "ami,"
pronounced by Guinevere, he describes as not only awakening his love
but also protecting him in tribulation and enabling him to perform all the
feats which are the stuff of the romance.

At this response, Guinevere is even more shocked than at first.
She is rather like the ladies who, Prufrock fears, will reply:

> "That is not it at all,
> That is not what I meant, at all."

. . . Although she thinks it well that Lancelot has been motivated to
become a valiant knight, she is amazed that he has taken a word from a
general and conventional context and interpreted it as having an individual and intimate meaning. She makes it clear that, for her, words may be
nothing but words, with no relation to feeling, no relation to anything
"fors le dit." To read about "how love seized Lancelot," then, is to read
about how the naive may mistake words intended to have only a conventional sense for words intended to have a personal sense. Although
Lancelot's misinterpretation of what Guinevere says leads, in the short
run, to desirable results, in the long run he suffers for it.

This, then, is Lancelot's "misreading": he mistakes a phrase spoken
many times ("a maint cheualier") for one spoken only once, uniquely
for him. Thus, the text, and the particular passage of the text, which
Dante presents Paolo and Francesca as reading voices two warnings:

against adultery and against misinterpretation, as words directed uniquely to one individual, of words which are repeated as part of a convention. Dante depicts the pair as blind to both warnings and condemned eternally for their blindness. The misreading of detail which Dante attributes to Francesca and Paolo—reversing the roles of Lancelot and Guinevere—points to their dual misreading on a larger scale.

The first form their misreading takes is indicated by their committing adultery, precisely the sin against which the entire prose *Lancelot* warns. Even considering only this first form, and leaving the second aside for the moment, it is clear that Francesca's famous exclamation, "Galeotto fu il libro, e chi lo scrisse," is much more horrifying than it has seemed to previous interpreters to be. Appallingly, she and Paolo have undone themselves by misreading a work meant to edify them. The pilgrim's fainting "come corpo morto cade," too, becomes more understandable. There is very little reason for the pilgrim-poet to faint upon hearing Francesca's accusation if she is merely condemning romances. The Church had been pointing out their dangers for a century, and to condemn them would have been nothing new or shocking—but instead a repetition of a tired late medieval commonplace about literature and morality. Moreover, since Dante had never written a romance and was not just then writing one, he and his pilgrim would not be personally implicated by Francesca's accusation, if Dante intended it to condemn romances. What he had written, with the *Vita Nuova*, and was just writing, with the *Commedia*, were literary works with moral, as well as poetic, ends. Both are works which use literary themes and devices known to appeal to contemporary audiences in order to attract a public for the ideas which form their moral and spiritual foundation. They thus belong to the same literary category as the prose *Lancelot*, although they are certainly of a much higher quality. What makes the pilgrim faint is the recognition that such works, despite the intentions of their authors, can be misread, even in a sense which changes the meaning the authors intended into its opposite. Specifically, the pilgrim faints "from pity" for Paolo and Francesca; Dante depicts him as directing his attention toward them, not himself and his literary aspirations. Their situation is indeed extraordinarily pitiful: they have been lost just when an effort was being made to save them, or, in other terms, lost by receiving improperly what is endowed with salvific properties. There are few situations more genuinely pitiful than this.

The second aspect of their misreading consists in their mistaking a literary convention for something having special meaning in their own "reader's moment"—to apply Singelton's phrase to Dante's characters. This second kind of misreading, which mirrors Lancelot's, is of greater interest to students of literature than the first, though it is the first which has received the most attention from critics. It is particularly surprising that Francesca (one knows little about Paolo) should misread in this second way. The love of the characters Lancelot and Guinevere in the fiction she and Paolo read is just one of many examples of a conventional love narrative, one in a long line of texts about love and its consequences, which deal with the passions and griefs of Dido, Helen, Paris, and Tristan—all of whom are named as Francesca's companions in Hell. Dante shows that Francesca is familiar with the conventions of literary love by having her speak, as many of Dante's readers have noted, the language of the *dolce stilnuovo*. But, in Dante's account, instead of realizing that what she reads is literature and not life, a convention with no necessary and direct applicability to her own "moment," Francesca tries to transform her life into literature.

The situation seems to have given Dante pause. After all, he was doing the same thing. He was making himself, a poet, into a pilgrim; transforming his autobiography into a *speculum* of all human and divine history. It was, I think, because the situation he represented by means of Francesca was so disturbing to him that he had his pilgrim character interrogate her rather closely and had Francesca respond in terms which Dante then took up again later in the poem, in a passage on the relation between human time and interpretation, and one on the temporal difference between human love and divine love.

It will therefore be useful to review the terms of the pilgrim's interrogation and Francesca's response. The pilgrim first addresses Paolo and Francesca by alluding to their mode of punishment, which is the inability to find rest, to stand still in the face of the winds which buffet those condemned to this part of Hell: "O anime affannate" (v.80). This stress on their inability to stand still is continued in Francesca's first speech, which, as Poggioli noted, is as obsessed with "pace" (vv. 92, 99), quiet and repose, as it is with "amor." In response to her general account of her love and death, the pilgrim asks for more details. Francesca's reply is prefaced with a close paraphrase of the opening lines of *Aeneid* II, the only prominent change being a reversal of sexual roles— here the Dido-figure speaks, whereas in the *Aeneid* she is spoken to:

And she answered me: "There is no greater pain than to recall the happy time in misery. . . ."

(vv. 121–23)

But, despite her pain, she does go on to remember the time of her happiness. She interprets the pilgrim's request as a desire to learn "*la prima* radice / del nostro amor" (vv.124–25) and equates this "prima radice" of love with "solo un punto": ". . . solo un punto fu quel che ci vinse" (v.132). (The "punto" is reading of the kiss, which, as noted above, is presented as a misreading). She concludes her reply by stating that their reading stopped at that "punto," the narration of the kiss: ". . . puì non vi leggemmo avante." All these terms and themes are reintroduced, developed, and, in fact, turned upside-down, in the *Paradiso:* the desire for a place of repose, the difficulty of remembering a joyful moment, the first root of love, the "solo . . . punto," and the interruption of reading.

A major step in this reversal of the Paolo and Francesca motifs is accomplished in the *Paradiso* XIII, where the pilgrim finds himself, no longer among the damned victims of Eros, speaking with a daughter of Eve, but among the blessed spirits of wise men, speaking with St. Thomas Aquinas. Before going to the heart of the canto, Thomas's lecture on the methods and perils of interpretation, it is important to note the image within which this lecture is presented. It is the dominant image of the *Paradiso*'s fourth heaven, that of the sun: the circle and its center. The wise doctors form a circle around the pilgrim and Beatrice as center (*Par.* X, 65): "far di noi centro e di sè far corona"). In the canto in which Thomas lectures on interpretation, Dante describes this center, where the pilgrim and Beatrice stand as the doctors dance around them, as a "punto": "de la doppia danza / che circulava il punto dov'io era" (*Par.* XIII, 20–21). This geometric image of center and circumference is again emphasized at the end of Thomas's lecture as *Paradiso* XIV opens with a line that associates Beatrice and her next speech with the point at the center of the circle and Thomas and his concluded speech with its circumference: "Dal centro al cerchio, e sí dal cerchio al centro. . . ."

As Thomas begins the explanation which will resolve the pilgrim's doubt, he uses the framing image of center and circle to represent something other than the relation between the wise souls and their visitors: he uses it to describe the relation that will exist between the pilgrim's opinion and Thomas's own utterance when the explanation is concluded.

> Open now thine eyes to the answer I give thee and thou shalt see that
> thy belief and my words meet in the truth *as the centre of the circle.*
>   (vv.49–51, emphasis added)

The relation between center and circle thus suggests completeness, perfection, truth. In the body of his lecture itself, Thomas uses the word "punto" in what would seem to be an entirely different sense, one which would never seem to be related to that of the "punto" as the center of the circle if there were not, in the framework of the passage, such a strong emphasis on the image that any appearance of a key word associated with it necessarily resonates with the framing image: "Se fosse a punto la cera dedutta . . ." (v. 73). Thomas is here describing the unattainable case in which the earthly material ("cera") in which heaven stamps its imprint would be at such a state of perfection ("a punto") that the light of heaven would appear in that earthly material with no impairment or diminution. The word "punto" is associated, once again, with the attainment of perfection, though here it is a perfection not anticipated as attainable at the end of Thomas's lecture, or indeed at any time.

The doubt which Thomas undertakes to resolve in this canto has arisen in the pilgrim's mind in response to a statement Thomas himself made just a bit earlier, citing Scriptural authority (X, 113–14, based on 3 Kings 3:12). The pilgrim's doubt is this: how can what Thomas and the Old Testament Jehovah have said about Solomon—that no one wiser than he lived before or after him—be true, since both Adam (still in God's image before the Fall) and Christ must have been as wise or wiser? Thomas's resolution of the pilgrim's doubt has two parts. In the first (vv. 52–87) Thomas argues that Adam and Christ, created directly by God, are to be understood to be in an entirely different category from Solomon's. In the second (vv. 92–108), Thomas goes on (note the phrase "avanti piue," indicating a forceful and sustained interpretive effort, which contrasts with Paolo and Francesca's going no further: "non . . . più avante") to distinguish Solomon's wisdom as kingly from, for example, theological wisdom or dialectical wisdom.

But it is not Thomas's argument about Solomon itself which is of particular interest in this discussion of Dante's development in the *Paradiso* of themes associated with Paolo and Francesca. What is of interest is the imagery which Thomas uses in his argument and the lengthy peroration (vv. 112–42) on Scriptural interpretation and misinterpretation with which he concludes. I have already stressed the role of the image of the center and the circle. In what I have called the first part of Thomas's argument, the most important theme is the difference between mortal and immortal ("Ciò che non more e ciò he può morire"), between that which is eternally one ("etternalmente rimanendosi una") and that which is reflected ("specchiato") and contingent ("brevi contingenze"). Also prominent is the basic notion that everything in the universe is generated by God's love (v. 54). This divine love is the source of divine light, which is reflected throughout the universe in various ways, reflecting itself in the mortal realm only to a diminished degree. That inferior material, the earthly "cera" mentioned earlier, can give forth this light only in an impaired form is emphasized by Dante's Thomas by means of one of the purposely skewed similes with which Dante so often jolts the mind of the reader of the *Paradiso*: the inadequacy of the material heaven has to make do with is compared to the inadequacy of the hand of the talented human artist in shaping his material (vv. 77–78). The implication is that the artist's material is not, for example, paints, words, or notes, but his hand, himself.

Thomas's concluding general counsels, on the interpretation and misinterpretation of Scripture and of the Book of the World, are sufficiently pertinent to the problem raised by Paolo and Francesca to be quoted in full:

> And let this always be lead on thy feet to make thee slow, like a weary man, in moving either to the yea or the nay where thou dost not see clearly; for he ranks very low among the fools, in the one case as in the other, who affirms or denies without distinguishing, since it often happens that a hasty opinion inclines to the wrong side and then the feelings bind the intellect. Far worse than in vain he casts off from the shore, for he does not return the same as he sets out, who fishes for the truth without the art. And of this manifest proofs to the world are Parmenides, Melissus, Bryson, and many who knew not whither they went; so were Sabellius and Arius and these fools who were to the Scriptures like swords that give back the natural face distorted.
>
> So also let not the people be too sure in judging, like those that reckon the corn in the field before it is ripe. For I have seen the briar first show harsh and rigid all through the winter and later bear the rose upon its top, and once I saw a ship that ran straight and swift over the sea through all its course perish at the last entering the harbour. Let not Dame Bertha and Master Martin, when they see one rob and another make an offering, think they see them within the divine counsel; for the one may rise and the other fall.
>
> (vv. 112–142)

Thomas's condemnation of those who distort Scripture and "fish for the truth without knowing the art" of fishing, locked by emotion into a hurried judgment, culminates in one central principle: skill in the art of interpretation depends upon a proper understanding of time. This principle is enunciated in a series of three images, involving the maturation of plants, the duration of a voyage, and the Resurrection and Last Judgment. In these images (which may also be taken to form a quasi-palinode or at last a qualifier with respect to Dante's own allocation of the sinners and the saved), Dante's Thomas makes clear that no interpretation of Scripture or of human events may be accepted as final until time stops, at the Resurrection—until, to paraphrase Paul (1 Cor. 4:5), the Lord comes to throw light on shadows and to show forth the counsels of hearts. When Thomas warns the pilgrim always to move slowly in interpretation, he is advising slowness according to a divine rather than a merely human clock.

Indeed, there would be some difficulty in measuring this, since one day and a thousand years are, for God, equal (1 Pet. 3:8). In any case, it is clear that when Dante suggests that Paolo and Francesca's misreading was the result of a reading of insufficient duration, he does not mean merely that they should have read through to the end of the book before deciding to interpret. For him, all interpretation is provisional, pending the Second Coming.

This basic correlation between temporal understanding and validity in interpretation is developed further in the last two cantos of Dante's poem. Here again, the seemingly banal word "punto" reappears, three times, finally demonstrating fully the nature of Paolo and Francesca's error in making what they saw as a single point in a text the "first root" of their love. In *Paradiso* XXXII, the word first appears as St. Bernard of Clairvaux explains to the pilgrim that, in Paradise, all is fixed by eternal law (v. 55), and there is no room for the contingent or accidental: "casüal punto non puote aver sito" (v. 53). Here "punto" clearly falls within the category of the temporal rather than the eternal. The second appearance of the word in the canto begins with an allusion to time, though it goes on, startlingly, to the realm of tailoring:

> But since the time flies that holds thee sleeping we shall stop here, like a good tailor that cuts his coat according to his cloth; and we shall direct our eyes to the Primal Love. . . .
>
> (vv. 139–42)

Here "punto" is part of the idiom "fare punto," that is, "to stop"; but, since the idiom and indeed the entire simile is startling in Bernard's mouth, preceding his invitation to lift the eyes to the vision of God, I think it must be assumed that Dante wished very much to use the word *punto* just here. I take the first line of the tercet cited to refer, not merely to the fact that the poet is running out of time or out of cantos, but to the fact that he is a mortal, who must, in the image of sleep, die.

But it is only in the next and final canto that the word "punto" as used by Francesca ("un punto fu quel che ci vinse") is completely inverted:

> A single moment (*punto*) makes for me deeper oblivion than five and twenty centuries upon the enterprise that made Neptune wonder at the shadow of the Argo.
>
> (vv. 94–96)

The speaker is the poet, as narrator, and the "punto" he refers to is the vision of God, conceived not only spatially, as the center and circumference of the circle (cf. vv. 127, 129, 134, 138, and esp. the last three lines of the poem), but also temporally. Indeed the association of "punto" with time in *Paradiso* XXXIII is more prominent than any geometric meaning, because the "punto" is described as creating a greater obstacle to memory than twenty-five centuries have to the memory of the Argonauts. Again, as he did with the allusions to Dido, Helen, and Tristan in *Inferno* V, Dante cites an ancient literary tradition, but this time for the purposes of contrast rather than comparison. His "letargo" (from "Lethe" with "argos"), which I take to be an inability to remember, a kind of sleepy ineffectiveness, confirms Bernard's observation in the previous canto that time was making the pilgrim drowsy:

> But since the time flies that holds thee sleeping we shall stop here . . .
> (qui farem punto . . .)
>
> (vv. 139–40)

In this final canto, Dante also explicitly compares his divine vision to the reading of a book of a kind which does not exist on earth or indeed anywhere else in creation:

> In its depth I saw that it contained, bound by love in one volume, that which is scattered in leaves through the universe, substances and accidents and their relations as it were fused together in such a way that what I tell of is a simple light.
>
> (vv. 85–90)

The contrast is between, on the one hand, the scattered pages which are, of necessity, the only reading material the created world provides, and, on the other, the unified volume, bound together with love, which is available only in God. In other terms, reading in the created world is necessarily discontinuous; a complete, continuous text and interpretation is attainable only in union with God. This is only one of several places in the *Purgatorio* and *Paradiso* in which insight into the divine is compared to reading in a book unlike earthly books. For example, in *Paradiso* XV, learning God's purposes is described as

> . . . the reading of the great book where there is never change of black or white.
>
> (vv. 50–51)

The stress is on the mutability of what is written in the "books" of the contingent world.

The "punto solo" conquers the poet, for it is easier to remember back through 2500 years to the Argonauts than to "remember" what he saw in it; Francesca, though in an entirely different sense, has also been conquered by "solo un punto." The inadequacy of the poet's mind to the task of "remembering" his final vision, of calling it into the present from the past, is rendered in temporal terms. If one accepts the repeated injunctions of Vergil and Beatrice to gloss one part of the poem by another, this suggests that Francesca's failure in making one "punto" into the "prima radice" of a criminal love is to be thought of temporally, too. This possibility is, moreover, also suggested by her complaint that it is painful to recall and recount lost happiness, alluding, like the narrator here, to the temporal theme of memory. How her misreading of the "punto" could be temporally caused, in more than the banal sense of the cessation of reading before the book is done, should become clearer after a brief review of one other theme in the poem, the central theme of love.

To say that love is the central theme of the *Commedia* is to say many things in one word. The transformation of the first everlasting sin encountered by the pilgrim, Paolo and Francesca's misdirected love, into the final blessing he receives, the vision of divine love, is encapsulated in the contrast between Francesca's bitter though clever "Amor condusse noi ad un*a morte*" (emphasis added), the culmination of a series of three lines she begins with "Amor," and the final line of the *Commedia*, "l'amor che move il sole e l'altre stelle." When she speaks of love, it is equivalent to death ("un*a morte*"), a death which cannot even look forward to the Resurrection. When the narrator speaks of it at the end of the poem, "amor" is eternal life, the source of all life, guiding and moving everything in the universe.

But this abbreviated contrast between the two forms of love is not sufficient to explain this inversion. Its basis is best seen in what is literally the center of the poem, the middle of purgatory, where Marco Lombardo explains to the pilgrim the nature of love (XVII, 91–139). Love, Marco says, is the source of all human action, whether good or ill. Every creature is born loving "il primo ben," its creator, but soon is distracted by other objects in which it thinks it sees love reflected and in which it hopes to find rest for the soul (v. 128). There thus develops a contrast between properly directed love, whose fruit is happiness (vv. 134–35), and misdirected love, which brings neither happiness nor peace, but merely the never-fulfilled promise of them.

Dante describes the transmission of God's love primarily through the image of light. For example, in *Paradiso* XVIII, he represents the pilgrim as delighting in the reflection of love in the "mirror" of Cacciaguida's soul (vv. 1–2), and then, at Beatrice's command, turning to gaze at it in her eyes (v. 9), where it shines brightly because of her "proximity" to God. In *Paradiso* V, Beatrice describes the relationship of all objects of love to love's original source quite clearly, again using the image of light:

eternal light which, seen, alone and always kindles love; and if aught else beguile your love it is nothing but some trace of this, ill-understood, that shines through there. Thou wouldst know if with other service it is possible so to make good for a vow unfulfilled that the soul is secure from challenge.

(vv. 7–12)

There is, then, in the *Commedia*'s terms, only one "point" of love, from which all its reflections radiate. The movement of the pilgrim's eyes, or of the soul, from one reflection to another is depicted as a successive process, a process that occurs across time, the goal of which is its own cessation, the attainment of repose. The only point in which there is the "pace" for which Francesca longs is God: "e 'n la sua volontade è nostra pace" (*Par*. III, 85). It is Francesca's misapprehension of the "punto" of the kiss as the "primo radice" of "amore" that causes her downfall. It may seem outrageous, today, to make divine love and erotic love inversions of one another, but indeed, Dante's lifelong poetic quest was for an understanding of the continuity of these two. His best known sinner, Francesca, is damned because she privileges a human "punto" in an attempt to rebel against the nature of time. By the endpoint of the poem, the nature of her sin is clear: no human "punto" is static; every moment is one of change and process. To try to give the "reader's moment" a duration its nature does not permit is to try to falsify time: clearly, a form of rebellion against the workings of the divine.

Yet Paolo and Francesca's form of rebellion against the temporal structure of reading is an extremely familiar, even a necessary one. The Paolo and Francesca episode deals with an aspect of what might be called the double structure of literary language. Indeed, the episode itself has a double structure, which provides the ground for both the reading of the passage I have presented here and the traditional reading of it as non-ironic. The kind of model of misreading the episode offers is by no means the only one to be found in the *Commedia*. One thinks immediately of the counter-model, Statius, whose misreading, one which flagrantly violates human temporal norms, brought him the possibility of eternal salvation. Dante's views on the relation of reading to history are extremely complex, much too complex to be set forth in their entirety here. It should, nonetheless, be kept in mind that they are far too complex to be reduced to one simplistic shibboleth, which "Galeotto fu il libro" has often been misinterpreted to be. To rewrite another famous line: In the Paolo and Francesca episode, Dante suggests that "The fault" is not in the book, nor in the author, nor even "in ourselves": it is inherent in the nature of the temporal relationship among the three, a relationship mortals cannot change but can ignore quite conveniently, at considerable risk.

TEODOLINDA BAROLINI

Autocitation and Autobiography

One of the *Comedy*'s most debated moments, [is] the culminating phase of the encounter between the pilgrim and the poet Bonagiunta da Lucca. If we briefly rehearse the dialogue at this stage of *Purgatorio* XXIV, we note that it is tripartite: Bonagiunta asks if Dante is indeed the inventor of a new form of poetry, which begins with the poem "Donne ch'avete intelletto d'amore" (49–51); Dante replies by apparently minimizing his own role in the poetic process, saying that he composes by following Love's dictation (52–54); Bonagiunta then claims to have finally understood why the poetry practiced by himself, his peers, and his predecessors is inferior to the new poetry, which he dubs—in passing—the "sweet new style" (55–63).

Bonagiunta's remarks, which frame the pilgrim's reply, are grounded in historical specificity: his initial query concerns Dante's personal poetic history, invoked through the naming of a precise canzone; his final remarks concern the history of the Italian lyric, invoked through the names of its chief practitioners, " 'l Notaro e Guittone e me" (56). The concreteness of Bonagiunta's statements contrasts with the indeterminate transcendentality of the pilgrim's reply, in which poetic principles are located in an ahistorical vacuum. Not only are the famous *terzina*'s only protagonists the poet and Love ("I' mi son un che, quando / Amor mi spira, noto . . ."), but the absence of any external historical referent is emphasized by an insistent subjectivity, articulated in the stress on the first person ("I' mi son un") at the outset.

Structurally, Dante's reply functions as a pivot between Bonagiunta's first question and his later exclamation. The "Amor mi spira" passage thus enables the poet of the Comedy to accomplish that shift in subject matter that has so puzzled critics: from the problematic of an individual poet to that of a tradition. Indeed, precisely the neutrality of the pilgrim's reply allows it to serve as a narrative medium conferring significance both on what precedes and what follows; because of its lack of specific content, the pilgrim's statement—"I am one who takes note when Love inspires me"—is able to provide a context first for the composition of "Donne ch'avete," and then for the emergence of the "sweet new style" as a poetic school. Both are defined in terms of a privileged relation to Amor.

By the same token, however, that the central terzina confers significance, it also generates ambiguity, by obscuring the terms of the very transition that it facilitates and by deliberately failing to clarify the application of the key phrase "dolce stil novo." Reacting against what they consider the reflex canonization of a school on the basis of a misreading of Bonagiunta's remarks, recent critics have insisted that the expression "dolce stil novo," as used in Purgatorio XXIV, is intended to apply only to Dante's own poetry. In other words, they refer Bonagiunta's latter comments back to his initial query. From this point of view (one which seeks to disband, at least within Dante's text, the group of poets known as stilnovisti), the "new style" begins with "Donne ch'avete," and it encompasses only Dante's subsequent poetry in the same mode.

Whereas the historiographical potential of Bonagiunta's concluding statements has sparked controversy, critics have not been similarly divided in their reaction to his earlier remark on "Donne ch'avete." Perhaps one reason for the general consensus regarding the status of "Donne ch'avete" is the unusual consistency in Dante's own attitudes toward this canzone as displayed throughout his career, from the Vita Nuova to the De Vulgari Eloquentia to the Comedy. As the first of the Vita Nuova's three canzoni, it marks a decisive moment in the libello: in narrative terms it signals the protagonist's total emancipation from the Provençal guerdon, and in poetic terms it signals his liberation from the so-called tragic, or Cavalcantian, mode. In the Vita Nuova, where aesthetic praxis is viewed as a function of ethical commitment, developments in form are strictly coordinated with developments in content; a stylistic triumph can only exist within the context of a conceptual breakthrough. Nowhere is this procedure more observable than in the chapters describing the genesis of "Donne ch'avete."

The account begins with an impasse in the poet's love for Beatrice. In Vita Nuova XIV Dante attends a wedding where he sees the gentilissima;

his resulting collapse is ridiculed by the ladies present. In the aftermath of this event, Dante writes three sonnets: the first is a direct appeal to Beatrice for pity ("Con l'altre donne mia vista gabbate" [chap. XIV]); the second details his physical disintegration upon seeing her ("Ciò che m'incontra, ne la mente more" [chap. XV]); the third further chronicles the state to which he has been reduced by the erotic conflict "questa battaglia d'Amore," waged within him ("Spesse fiate vegnonmi a la mente" [chap. XVI]). All share an insistence on the self (the three incipits all contain the first-person pronoun), a tendency to self-pity ("e venmene pietà" from "Spesse fiate"), and a preoccupation with death. Moreover, they presume the lover's right to air grievances and ask for redress; the first two sonnets are directly addressed by the lover to the lady, who is implicitly viewed as responsible for his suffering.

The last of these sonnets is followed by a strikingly brief chapter consisting of only two sentences, in which the poet quietly announces a major transition; whereas the preceding poems deal obsessively with his own condition, he shall now undertake to write in a new mode, selflessly:

> Poi che dissi questi tre sonetti, ne li quali parlai a questa donna però che fuoro narratori di tutto quasi lo mio stato, credendomi tacere e non dire più però che mi parea di me assai avere manifestato, avvegna che sempre poi tacesse di dire a lei, a me convenne ripigliare matera nuova e più nobile che la passata.

> After I had composed these three sonnets, in which I had spoken to this lady since they were the narrators of nearly all of my condition, deciding that I should be silent and not say more because it seemed that I had revealed enough about myself, although the result would be that from then on I should cease to write to her, it became necessary for me to take up a new and more noble subject matter than the past one.

> (XVII, 1)

We notice that the "matera nuova e più nobile che la passata" is predicated on a double-edged verbal renunciation: he may no longer speak about himself ("credendomi tacere e non dire più"), and he may no longer speak to her ("avvegna che sempre poi tacesse di dire a lei"). The result of blocking both traditional outlets and traditional responses will be a new poetry.

The archaic dialogue imposed by the poet on the lady is thus replaced by a monologue whose morphology is based on a poetics of sublimation, a poetics illuminated for the poet by the Florentine Muse of chapter XVIII. Here the topos of the *gabbo* is replayed, but with positive results; both lover and poet are provoked into defining new goals. Rather than locating his supreme desire ("fine di tutti li miei desiderii" [XVIII, 4]) in an event outside of his control (Beatrice's greeting) whose presence is transformational but whose denial induces narrative lapses into self-pity and poetic lapses into regressive modes, the lover learns to use the lady to generate a happiness ("beatitudine") that cannot fail him ("che non mi puote venire meno" [XVIII, 4]) because it is under his own governance. Such total autonomy from referentiality—true beatitude—translates, in poetic terms, into the praise-style; by placing his poetic happiness "in quelle parole che lodano la donna mia" ("in those words that praise my lady" [XVIII, 6]), the poet foregoes the traditionally dualistic mechanics of love poetry and discovers a new mode.

The privileged status of the first poem written in the new style is immediately apparent. Only on this occasion does Dante chronicle the birth of a poem, a birth that is described as a quasi-miraculous event, a creation *ex nihilo*: "la mia lingua parlò quasi come per sé stessa mossa, e disse: *Donne ch'avete intelleto d'amore*" ("my tongue spoke as though moved by itself, and said: 'Donne ch'avete intelletto d'amore' " [XIX, 2]). The inspirational emphasis of this statement from *Vita Nuova* XIX foreshadows the poetic credo of *Purgatorio* XXIV; both texts present "Donne ch'avete" as deriving from a divinely inspired exclusionary relation existing between the poet and a higher authority. The *De Vulgari Eloquentia* also sanctions, albeit in less mystical terms, the special status of "Donne ch'avete": in a text where Dante uses many of his later poems to serve as exempla of excellence in various stylistic and metrical categories, he nonetheless chooses the youthful "Donne ch'avete" as the incipit to follow the formal definition of the canzone, thus establishing this early lyric as emblematic of the entire genre.

The testimony of the *Vita Nuova* and the *De Vulgari Eloquentia* clarifies the appearance of "Donne ch'avete" in *Purgatorio* XXIV, where Bonagiunta invokes the canzone as a badge of poetic identity:

> Ma dì s'i' veggio qui colui che fore
> trasse le nove rime, cominciando
> '*Donne ch'avete intelletto d'amore.*'

But tell me if I see here him who brought forth the new poems, beginning "Donne ch'avete intelletto d'amore"?

(*Purg.* XXIV, 49–51)

In fact, Bonagiunta both revives and integrates each of the canzone's previous textual roles: in that "Donne ch'avete" is an inaugural text ("le nove rime") he recapitulates the *Vita Nuova*; in that the canzone sets a standard by which to measure other poetry (" 'l Notaro e Guittone e me") he recapitulates the *De Vulgari Eloquentia*. But Dante does not limit himself to recapitulation; in cantos XXIII and XXIV of the *Purgatorio* he constructs a sustained tribute to "Donne ch'avete" that effectively designates this canzone his supreme lyric achievement.

The episode surrounding the citation of "Donne ch'avete" is complicated by the fact that it involves a double set of characters, issues, and retrospective allusions, for the statements of *Purgatorio* XXIV acquire their full significance only when viewed on the backdrop of *Purgatorio* XXIII. The first sign directing us to a contextual reading of canto XXIV is the apparent absence of the requisite autobiographical marker, an absence rectified by the figure of Forese Donati, the friend Dante meets in canto XXIII. As we shall see, the encounter with Forese provides the necessary prelude to the conversation with Bonagiunta. Structural considerations further support reading canto XXIV in tandem with canto XXIII; we do well to bear in mind that the entire Bonagiunta episode takes place literally within the meeting with Forese.

Purgatorio XXIII begins with a description of the pilgrim peering through the green boughs of the tree he and his guides have discovered on the terrace of gluttony, "like one who wastes his life chasing little birds": "come far suole/chi dietro a li uccellin sua vita perde" (2–3). The emphasis on loss in "sua vita perde" sets the canto's tone; as well as initiating the episode, the verb *perdere* will also bring it to a close, in Forese's final words in canto XXIV:

> Tu ti rimani omai; chè 'l tempo è caro
> in questo regno, *sì ch'io perdo troppo*
> venendo teco sì a paro a paro.

Now you remain behind, for time is dear in this realm, *so that I lose too much* by coming thus with you at equal pace.

(*Purg.* XXIV, 91–93; italics mine)

The encounter with Forese is precisely about loss, a loss which is recuperated through that redemption of history which is the chief matter of the *Purgatorio*. It is no accident that this of all episodes is used to articulate the fundamental relation of the *Purgatorio* to time. Forese's remark on the importance of time in Purgatory, "ché 'l tempo è caro/in questo regno," echoes the crucial definition of the previous canto, where the pilgrim comments that he had expected to find his friend down below, in Ante-Purgatory, where time is restored for time: "Io ti credea trovar là giù di sotto,/dove tempo per tempo si ristora" (XXIII, 83–84). Although the pilgrim's maxim refers directly to the Ante-Purgatory, with its formulaic insistence on literal time, it in fact glosses the whole of the second realm.

Time is the essential commodity of the *Purgatorio*, the only real eye for an eye that God exacts. The *Purgatorio* exists in time because the earth exists in time; time spent sinning in one hemisphere is paid back in the other. Because earth is where "vassene 'l tempo e l'uom non se n'avvede" ("time passes and man does not notice" [*Purg.* IV,9]), Purgatory is where "tempo per tempo si ristora." Climbing Purgatory allows the reel of history to be played backward; the historical fall of the race through time, symbolized by the Arno in Guido del Duca's discourse as it was in Hell by the Old Man of Crete, is reversed. The journey up the mountain is the journey back through time to the place of beginnings, which is in turn the new ending; it is a journey whose goal is the undoing of time through time. The fall that occurred in history can only be redeemed in history; time is restored so that with it we may restore ourselves. This reversal of the fall, most explicitly reenacted in the ritual drama of *Purgatorio* VIII, finds its personal and autobiographical expression in the meeting with Forese Donati.

If Purgatory is the place where we are given the chance, desired in vain on earth, to undo what we have done, the Forese episode is chosen by the poet as the vehicle for articulating these basic principles of the canticle because it is emblematic, more than any other episode, of a fall in Dante's own spiritual biography. The episode's thematics of loss rehearse at a personal level what will later be fully orchestrated in the Earthly Paradise, where Matelda reminds Dante of Proserpina in her moment of loss ("Proserpina nel tempo che perdette / la madre lei, ed ella primavera" "Proserpina in the time when her mother lost her, and she lost spring" [*Purg.* XXVIII, 50–51]), and where Eve, signifying loss, is continually insinuated into the discourse. Indeed, the opening simile of *Purgatorio* XXIII may be seen as an anticipation of Beatrice's Edenic rebuke; the vain pursuit of little birds finds its metaphorical equivalent in another distracting diminutive, the *pargoletta* of canto XXXI:

> Non ti dovea gravar le penne in giuso,
> ad aspettar più colpo, o pargoletta
> o altra novità con sì breve uso.

No young girl or other novelty of such brief use should have weighed your wings downward to await further blows.

(Purg. XXXI, 58–60)

The fall that Forese Donati marks in Dante's life is redeemed in cantos XXIII and XXIV of the *Purgatorio*, both biographically and poetically. The moment of failure is placed before the moment of triumph, the encounter with Forese before the dialogue with Bonagiunta. Thus, Dante's so-called *traviamento morale*, as remembered in canto XXIII, is ultimately seen from the perspective of an enduring conquest, as formulated in canto XXIV. The poetic correlative of Dante's spiritual fall is the *tenzone* of scurrilous sonnets exchanged by him and Forese; the *tenzone* stands in contrast to the *stil novo*, celebrated here as the pinnacle of Dante's lyric form in the canzone "Donne ch'avete." There is no further autocitation in the *Purgatorio* because "Donne ch'avete" is the end-term in the search for the purgatorial mode of pure love poetry; like the Earthly Paradise, the beginning is revealed to be the end.

As a poetic experience, the *tenzone* is present only obliquely, in Dante's encounter with his former verbal antagonist. The lexical gains of the uncompromisingly realistic *tenzone* are registered less in the second canticle than in the first, where we find, for instance, the exchange between Sinon and Maestro Adamo. Far from containing a particularly realistic lexicon, *Purgatorio* XXIII is saturated with lyric elements like the antithesis. As the lyric figure par excellence, Dante uses antithesis in canto XXIII to chart the lyric's transcendence of itself. From a tradition-ally private and rhetorical figure, it stretches to accommodate the deepest moral significance; in narrative terms, we move from the Petrarchism *avant la lettre* that describes the gluttonous souls in the first part of the canto ("piangere e cantar" [10]; "diletto e doglia" [12]; "piangendo canta" [64]) to the passion of Christ, expressed through an antithesis whose rigor is foreign to the lyric experience:

> E non pur una volta, questo spazzo
> girando, si rinfresca nostra pena:
> *io dico pena, e dovria dir sollazzo,*
> ché quella voglia a li alberi ci mena
> che menò Cristo lieto a dire 'Elì,'
> quando ne liberò con la sua vena.

And not just one time as we circle this space is our pain refreshed—*I say pain, and I ought to say pleasure*, for that desire leads us to the trees which led Christ happy to say "Elì" when He freed us with His blood.

(Purg. XXIII, 70–75; italics mine)

That most banal of amatory expedients—pain that is pleasure—thus ren-ders the sublime. The rhetorical achievement of line 72 is concretized in two further antithetical expressions, again radically new: "buon dolor" in "l'ora / del buon dolor ch'a Dio ne rimarita" ("the hour of the sweet grief that rewds us to God" [80–81]), and "dolce assenzo" in "a ber lo dolce assenzo d'i martìri" ("to drink the sweet wormwood of the torments" [86]). Thus, in the *Purgatorio* "sweet wormwood" describes not the contradictory love of the poet for his lady (as in Petrarch's *Canzoniere*, where his lady's eyes can make honey bitter, or sweeten wormwood: "e 'l mel amaro, et addolcir l'assenzio" [CCXV, 14]), but the soul's paradoxical attachment to the martyrdom of purgation.

Through such textual strategies the poet sets the stage for the elaboration of a new poetic category in *Purgatorio* XXIV, that of the transcendent lyric. Indeed, as though to underscore the importance of canto XXIII for our reading of canto XXIV, Dante introduces the souls of the terrace of gluttony, at the beginning of XXIII, in a *terzina* that proleptically glosses the role of the canzone "Donne ch'avete":

> Ed ecco piangere e cantar s'udìe
> 'Labïa mëa, Domine' per modo
> tal, che diletto e doglia parturìe.

And suddenly in tears and song was heard "Labia mea, Domine" in such a way that it gave birth to delight and sorrow.

(*Purg.* XXIII, 10–12)

Embedded within lyric antitheses is a verse with enormous resonance for Dante's conception of the lyric, from the Vulgate's Fiftieth Psalm: "Domine, labia mea aperies; et os meum annuntiabit laudem tuam" ("Lord, open my lips, and my mouth will announce Your praise"). Thus, the gluttons pray to the Lord to open their once closed mouths so that they may sing forth His praises, a fact that illuminates the positioning of Bonagiunta and his poetic discourse on this terrace. As a poet, Bonagiunta also failed to "open his mouth" in praise; he is emblematic of an archaic poetics that stopped short of discovering the praise-style, the "matera nuova e più nobile che la passata" of *Vita Nuova* XVII.

The gluttons of canto XXIII have turned their mouths from the basest of concerns—"eating," or unrelieved self-involvement—to praising God, in the same way that the discovery of the *stil novo* turns the Italian lyric from the conventional poetics of the "I" to the deflection of the "I" in the poetry of praise. Thus, the gluttons chanting their Psalm are described as souls who are loosening the knot of their obligation, "forse di lor dover solvendo il nodo" (XXIII, 15), in a phrasing that anticipates the loosening of Bonagiunta's "knot" (his uncertainty regarding the reasons for his poetic failure) by the pilgrim. The artifact that symbolizes the conversion that the gluttons have only now achieved—away from the self toward a disinterested focusing on the Other—is "Donne ch'avete," which attains its prominence within the *Comedy* precisely because it marks the moment in which Dante first opens his mouth in a song of praise.

Within the new order imposed by the *Comedy*'s confessional self-reading, in which literal chronology becomes irrelevant, Forese signifies the fall preceding the conversion to Beatrice. Moreover, the pilgrim will specify, in the detailed account of his journey that he offers at the end of canto XXIII, that he proceeded directly from the experience shared with

his friend to the meeting with Vergil; thus, we can state that Forese
signifies, within the *Comedy*'s ideal scheme, no less than the final fall
before the final conversion. That this fall is connected to the displacement of Beatrice is suggested by the fact that Dante's friendship with
Forese seems to correspond to the period of depression following Beatrice's
death, a period documented by the *Convivio* (and perhaps by Cavalcanti's
sonnet rebuking Dante for his *vile vita*), in which Beatrice was replaced by
other interests to a degree later judged intolerable.

In the absence of precise indices regarding the years after 1290, the
decadence of the *tenzone* (dated by internal evidence to 1293–1296) was
originally viewed as symptomatic of a literally dissolute period in Dante's
life. The illegitimate biographical status once assumed by these texts has
been defused by studies insisting that the low style of the *tenzone* is just as
conventional as the high style of the courtly lyric. As a result, Dante's
straying after the death of Beatrice is now generally interpreted in a more
metaphorical light, as a phase of moral and political secularism, involving
a philosophical and/or religious deviation from orthodoxy. To the extent
that any strictly personal or erotic failure is involved, it is viewed as part
of a larger problematic; the *pargoletta* cited by Beatrice is not only a rival
lady (as witnessed by her place in the *Rime*), but is also the central
symbolic node of a cluster of transgressions. Among these transgressions
are the poems to the *donna gentile*, composed at this time, most likely in
1293–1294. The episode of his life to which Dante later attached the
rubric "Forese Donati" is, therefore, a synthesis of the deviations cata-
logued by Beatrice: the moral ("o pargoletta / o altra novità" [*Purg.* XXXI,
59–60]), and the philosophical ("quella scuola / c'hai seguitata" [*Purg.*
XXXIII, 85–86]).

Beatrice forecasts her more specific rebukes with a single compact
charge, that of turning away from her to someone else: "questi si tolse a
me, e diessi altrui" ("he took himself from me and gave himself to
another" [*Purg.* XXX, 126]). Indeed, the hallmark of Beatrice's personal
discourse throughout the Earthly Paradise is negative conversion. She
concentrates insistently on the illicit presence of the other: "altrui" is
echoed by "altra novità," and finally by "altrove" in the verse "colpa ne la
tua voglia altrove attenta" ("the fault of your will elsewhere intent" [*Purg.*
XXXIII, 99]). To the thematics of negative conversion is opposed the
positive conversion of canto XXIII, where the pilgrim registers the
forward turn of *Inferno* I:

> Di quella vita mi volse costui
> che mi va innanzi, l'altri' ier, quando tonda
> vi si mostrò la suora di colui . . .

From that life he who goes before me turned me the other day, when the
sister of him [the sun] showed herself round to you . . .

(Purg. XXIII, 118–120)

The full moon over the selva oscura marks the poet's tryst with the
conversion that will take him, as he explains to his friend, ultimately to
Beatrice, "là dove fia Beatrice" (Purg. XXIII, 128).

When Dante says to Forese "Di quella vita mi volse costui," he
defines the new moment with Vergil ("mi volse") in terms of the old
moment with Forese ("quella vita"), the conversion in terms of the
preceding fall. The words "quella vita" refer literally to the past life shared
by the two friends, a past whose memories are still burdensome (the flip
side of Casella's song, which is still sweet):

> Se tu riduci a mente
> qual fosti meco, e qual io teco fui,
> ancor fia grave il memorar presente.
> Di quella vita mi volse costui . . .

If you call to mind what you were with me and I with you, the present
memory will still be grievous. From that life he turned me . . .

(Purg. XXIII, 115–118)

The life-experience shared by Dante and Forese thus assumes a metaphoric
value in the Comedy that bears little relation to anything we know about
the two men. Forese stands in Dante's personal lexicon for his own
compromised historical identity, the past—"qual fosti meco, e qual io teco
fui"—brought painfully into the present—"il memorar presente." Their
life together represents everything the saved soul regrets before being
granted forgetfulness: the sum total of personal falls, little deaths, other
paths. For Dante, this is everything he left behind when he turned to
Beatrice.

In directly linking his friendship with Forese to the encounter with
Vergil, in casting the Florentine traviamento as the immediate predecessor
to the dark wood, Dante far outstrips the literal content of the tenzone,
which (with its gluttonies, petty thieveries, and untended wives) tells of a
more social than spiritual collapse. Nor is he concerned with strict chronology; Forese, who died in 1296, had been dead for four years when the
pilgrim wanders into the first canto of the Inferno. Such underminings of
the factual record, combined with the evasion of textual echoes from the
tenzone, underscore the metaphorical significance of the Forese episode in
the Comedy.

The paradigmatic value assigned to the episode necessarily extends
to the poetic sphere as well. The conversion from "that life" with Forese

to "new life" with Beatrice is also the conversion from the fallen style of the *tenzone* to the new style of "Donne ch'avete." In this ideal chronology, the *tenzone* occupies a position antecedent even to Bonagiunta's old style; it is as complacently rooted in fallen reality as the *stil novo* is free of it. As Dante's personal fall—"quella vita"—is redeemed by the restorative time of Purgatory, so the poetic fall—the *tenzone*—is redeemed by the converted style of the *stil novo*. This poetic conversion takes place in a context of lyric antitheses so overriding that they embrace even the episode's personnel; in the violent contrast between Forese's chaste wife Nella and the "sfacciate donne fiorentine" ("brazen women of Florence" [XXIII, 101]) one could see a continuation of the canto's antithetical mode, carried from the lexical to the figural level. In fact, the terrace of gluttony is played out on a backdrop of contrasting women, good and bad, courtly and anti-courtly: not only Nella and her Florentine opposites, but Beatrice, Piccarda, Gentucca, Mary (from the exempla at the end of canto XXII), and (mentioned in XXIV, 116) Eve.

An episode that deals with lyric themes is thus sustained by the genre's narrative prerequisites, by women. It is not coincidental that in the course of this episode Dante should ask his friend about the location of his sister, or that Bonagiunta should prophesy the aid of a young woman from Lucca; both Piccarda and Gentucca are historical correlatives of the terrace's true heroines, the "ladies who have understanding of love." Most important is the fact that only here does the pilgrim take the opportunity to name Beatrice as the term of his voyage, thus relinquishing his usual practice of indicating her through a periphrasis. He names her because Forese—unlike the majority of the souls he has encountered—knows her, a simple fact with less simple implications. Precisely Forese's historical identity, his connection to a literal past, makes him valuable to a poet whose metaphors require grounding in reality. The fall must have a name, Forese, as salvation has a name, Beatrice, and as conversion occurs under the aegis of Vergil, specifically five days ago, when the moon was full. The irreducible historicity of this poem—the radical newness of its style— retrospectively guarantees all those other poems, and the newness of their style: "le nove rime, cominciando / 'Donne ch'avete intelletto d'amore.' "

KENNETH GROSS

Infernal Metamorphoses: An Interpretation of Dante's "Counterpass"

This is an essay in the poetics of pain and punishment, in the symbology of sin. I do not have anything new to add, as might otherwise be expected, to scholarly accounts of the philosophical system which informs the horrific, orderly landscape of Dante's *Inferno*, and the machinery of suffering deployed within it—the progression downwards, that is, from sins of Incontinence to those of Violence and Fraud, from Lust to Treachery. Rather, I want to explore a way of describing the conceptual and metaphoric logic underlying Dante's mode of representing such suffering, a logic which must bridge the gap or muddle any easy distinctions between the theological and the poetical. My investigation starts from the realization that the pains of the damned are in truth their own living sins, but sins converted to torturing images by what Dante would persuade us is the allegorizing eye of eternal Justice. These pains become portions of a total metaphoric vision of human evil, one in which the damned souls' existence is doubly circumscribed, first by the orientation of their affections—which defines the individual nature of their transgression—and second by the fact of their being dead and placed in a realm beyond that of ordinary life. This implies in turn, as I shall argue more fully below, that it is the states or powers of Death and Love

From *Modern Language Notes* 1, vol. 100 (1985). Copyright © 1985 by The Johns Hopkins University Press. All citations and translations are from the edition of Charles S. Singleton, 6 vols. (Princeton, 1970).

which become the progenitors of all allegorical representation in the punishments themselves. Such speculations are grounded not only in the theological background of Dante's ideas about sin (especially in Augustine and Aquinas), but emerge from a study of the more purely literary sources of the poet's fantastic inventions. My arguments about the ways in which Dante transforms such a mixed genealogy may produce some unusual conclusions. Nevertheless, the picture of what I have called Dante's "infernal metamorphoses" fundamentally interprets the familiar dynamics of that mode of ironic judgment known as the counterpass, or *contrapasso*.

Since Dante himself introduces this term into Italian, a preliminary discussion of its context in the *Commedia* is necessary. Indeed, it may be a useful way of defamiliarizing and for a moment putting into question a term which critical tradition has idealized into too neutral a descriptive term. The word's first and only appearance is at the very end of *Inferno*, XXVIII, where it closes the *apologia* of Bertran de Born, whom Dante and Virgil discover in the circle of the schismatics. Decapitated by a sword-wielding angel, healed as he marches around his circle, and struck again as he repasses that angel, Bertran provides the pilgrims with the following commentary on his situation:

> Perch'io parti' così giunte persone
> partito porto il mio cerebro, lasso!
> dal suo principio ch'è in questo troncone.
> Così s'osserva in me lo contrapasso.

"Because I parted persons thus united, I carry my brain parted from its source, alas! Thus is the retribution [*contrapasso*] observed in me."
(XXVIII, 139–142)

Contrapasso is derived from the Latin *contrapassum*, used in Aquinas's translation of the *Nichomachean Ethics* to render a Greek phrase meaning "he who has suffered something in return"; hence the Latin sense of the word as "retribution" or "retaliation." (An oddity which will become significant for Dante is that the translator chose to join the prefix *contra* with the noun *passum*—"pace" or "step"—rather than with the more likely *passio*, "suffering.") Aristotle, in his discussion of civil justice, asserts that retaliation is a part of commutative but not of distributive justice, and is thus only a portion of the larger scheme by which punishments are to be meted out in a just society. Aquinas, in his *Summa Theologica*, though following Aristotle's lead in severely limiting the scope of retaliation in the workings of justice, does at least claim that "this form of Divine judgment is in accordance with the conditions of commutative justice, insofar as rewards are apportioned to merits, and punishments to sins." He also associates retaliation with the Old Testament *lex talionis:* "I answer that, Retaliation (*contrapassum*) denotes equal passion repaid for previous action; and the expression applied most properly to injurious passions and actions, whereby a man harms the person of his neighbor; for instance, if a man strike, that he be struck back. This kind of justice is laid down in the Law (Exod. xxi:23,4): 'He shall render life for life, eye for eye, etc.' " Despite the first passage cited, there is really no evidence that Aquinas would have found the word fitting for an eschatological scheme like Dante's, where no single, particular action is repaid, and where the "equal passion" is really a highly metaphorical rendering back of suffering for the soul's entire career of sin. Furthermore, the term's direct association with a tenet of the Old Law specifically overturned by Christ (see Matt. 5:38–9) suggests that the idea of punishment by *contrapassum* falls somewhat outside the Christian dispensation of Grace and Love.

That the word is supplied by a damned soul should give pause to those critics who have appropriated the term to refer to Dante's entire theory of punishment. For by Canto XXVIII the reader should have learned that even the most eloquent of the damned have major blind spots in their understanding of religion, philosophy, and language. So if Bertran does invoke the word strictly in Aquinas' sense, one may suppose that he is subtly misreading his situation. Although I will continue to use the word "counterpass" in this essay—both for simplicity and because I do not think that Bertran is completely mistaken—I want at the outset to point to the possible mixture of error and unwitting accuracy in his speech, if only to remind critics of how strange a conceptual trope the word offers up to us. To do this, however, it will be necessary to look briefly over two relevant medieval theories regarding the workings of sin, and to point out their influence on Dante.

The phenomenological totality which one might call the "state" of each of the damned in Dante's Hell—a condition embracing body, mind, language, landscape, and weather—is a complex reflection of and on the sinful disorder of his soul. As Charles Singleton has suggested, Dante's view of the proper order and motion of the soul may derive from Aquinas, in his Christian re-reading of Aristotle's central assertion that every organism is bound by an inner drive to fulfill its own generic form. Aristotle himself applied this principle metaphorically in his *Ethics*, where he asserts that the authentic "form" of human life lay in our realizing an inner justice, the "inner rule of the rational part of the soul over the other parts." Aquinas raises this further to a spiritual principle, so that sin would be defined as a state wherein the soul is misdirected or halted in its movement toward its true form: the justice of subjecting itself to God's will and the reception of sanctifying Grace. The "punishments" of the *Inferno*, then, insofar as they reflect sin, show this deviation of the soul's proper motion. The worm of the human soul, "nato a formar l'angelica farfalla, / che vola alla giustizia sanza schermi" (*Purg.* X, 125–26, slightly altered), is hindered in its spiritual morphosis. It acquires a monstrous, mutated form, "quasi entomata in difetto, / sì come vermo in cui formazion falla" (X, 128–29), instead of realizing itself as a blessed *psyche*. This half-generated form—which yet retains evidence of the soul's original deviation—is in a sense the shape of the soul's suffering after death.

Augustine provides a related but, for the purposes of this essay, more usefully dialectical model of the workings of sin. As Kenneth Burke has shown in *The Rhetoric of Religion*, *The Confessions* describes the soul's motion in relation to God in terms of a series of "turnings." Thus the sinful soul is one that has wrongly turned itself aside or askew (*perversus*), that has turned away (*aversus*) from God and so has turned against (*adversus*) the true, rational, and divine good. True Christian love, *caritas*, leads the soul toward this good, but is changed into sinful *cupiditas* when the soul turns from God in order to seek a false or limited object. Because Hell is the domain of those who have lost the good of the intellect by subjecting rational love of God to mere desire, the structure of punishment is patterned on that of human appetite.

This aspect of the problem brings us closer to Aquinas, but there is more. Implicit in Dante is also the conviction that sin inverts or parodies two processes that are central to Augustine's theology: the divine act of Grace, symbolized by the Incarnation of Christ, and the human act of conversion. These two acts, which always entail each other in the work of salvation, represent respectively the turning of love from God to man, and the turning or returning of love from man to God. The states of the damned, then, can be read not so much as simple retributive punishments, but instead as various incarnations of false love or as emblems of false, downward, or parodic conversions. For after death the sinful soul loses all chance of real conversion, and so exists "in bondage to an incessant repetition of its own slavery to finite objectives." Thus the perverse love that in life was a result of free will and the cause of the soul's loss of Grace, becomes in Hell an inescapable state of being.

The Augustinian model will become more significant later in this essay. But neither Aquinas nor Augustine will help us finally if we do not see the ways in which Dante's idea of the infernal state transforms theological concepts of sin into central poetic principles, or, perhaps more accurately, exposes the allegorical or figurative logic that is already at work in traditional accounts of the negative, imitative, or grotesque processes of sin. As I have said, the pains of the damned are more revelation than retribution; they compose difficult moral emblems which shadow forth sin's inward nature. The Gluttonous, for example, who neglected their souls to pleasure their bodies, their "muddy vesture of decay," wallow eternally in mud—like the pigs which are also emblems of their crime. Tempestuous lovers are whirled forever in a mad, windy storm. Hypocrites walk weighed down by leaden cloaks with ornate gilded surfaces, symbolizing the sinful, false exteriors which burdened their souls in life. Dante's didactic method becomes less objectionable when one realizes that the fallen reader is to be deterred from sin not by threat of retroactive punishment, but by seeing how horrifying his crimes are in themselves, from the perspective of God or the poet. Dante does not predict a future but says, with prophetic literalness, "this is what you are." More generally, we might suggest that the forms of punishment, whatever their pathos, have the ironic structure of satirical images, reflecting Augustine's notion (as explicated by Burke) that sinful "perversity" equals "parody"—the fatal turning of sin yielding a demonic turn or trope on the authentic forms of Christian virtue. For rather than correcting sin, Dante's symbolic ironies show how the infernal states actually perpetuate the spiritual disorder which constitutes sin.

In this sense, we should observe that the moral function and metaphoric structure of the punishments in the Inferno are not strictly commensurable with those of the sufferings meted out in Dante's Purgatory. There, the burdens of the souls eventually blessed are not so much ironic allegories of sin as antithetical, curative conditions: the proud are weighed down with stones, the gluttonous are gaunt and starving, and the envious—the name of whose sin, *invidia*, derives from the Latin for evil or improper looking—have the eyes with which they sinned sewn shut. The Purgatorial states are simpler than those of Hell; they never involve any complex or grotesque reshaping of the human form; and they allow for real spiritual change, as the sufferings of Hell do not. The damned souls are described in corporeal imagery of great vividness, but the forms they inhabit are only like a body which is a dead thing, a torture house, and not something with the potential for future resurrection. If in life the *anima* is the *forma corporis*, in Hell the body is a corpse which deforms the soul.

This long excursus puts us in a better position to judge the implications of Bertran's speech. If he uses the word *contrapasso* to refer to some sort of retaliatory punishment which he suffers under the hand of the Old Law, then he is clearly wrong. Bertran alone bears responsibility for the shape of his soul. However, his choice of the word would reveal a limitation of vision quite appropriate to a worldly, politically-minded troubadour. Part of his counterpass, in the broad sense, is to use the word *contrapasso*. Furthermore, Dante's idiosyncratic use of a virtual calque of the original Latin, *contrapassum*, especially in the context of Bertran's puns on "parti" and "partito," makes for an expanded awareness of the word's etymological implications. Thus one is conscious that *contrapasso* literally means something like a "step against," a "reverse step" or even a "step away from." This recalls Augustine's depiction of the sinfully turned soul as *adversus*, *perversus*, and *aversus*. In the context of an allegorical narrative which images the conversion of the soul as a long walk, Bertran's term thus becomes an uncannily accurate description of the motions of sin which the counterpass is supposed to represent.

If nothing else, Bertran retains enough of his poetic insight to see that his punishment makes out of his sensible, corporeal form a symbol of the divisions he had formerly wrought within the body politic. Indeed, he sets up this image of himself with a punning wit that suggests a similar rhetorical or etymological key to many other punishments in the *Inferno*: "I parted men, thus I carry my head parted from its base, my trunk." Still, he seems to consider his condition as the grim joke of a vengeful God, rather than as the inevitable form of his soul—hence his assertion regarding "retaliation." It is also important that his reading of the allegory behind his decapitation does not exhaust the possible meanings of his counterpass. For instance, one recent critic has argued that Bertran is made to stand for his own poetics of strife and division; his being "*due in uno*" embodies among other things his tendentious joining of the unifying poetry of love and the divisive poetry of war.

Bertran's mistakes and incapacities point to one other important aspect of the counterpass. That each damned soul knows only the partial truth about his or her moral and symbolic state is a consistent feature of experience in the *Inferno*. But the *conversio* of the pilgrim and the trial of the reader depend largely on the continual effort to bridge the gap between the remarkable things which the self-limited souls say about themselves, and the ironic qualifications or additional knowledge which arise from a more detached view of their words and sufferings. (That this is the point of view of any self-conscious reader as well as that provided by the higher perspective of Christian truth effectively dramatizes Augustine's assertion that the labor of interpretation is implicitly a labor of divination, a means of recognizing God.) In some sense, then, the damned souls are like those condemned prisoners in Kafka's parable, "In the Penal Colony," criminals who are strapped to an intricate ancient machine (the "harrow") which incises into the back of each an exact account of his transgressions, executed in elaborate, hieroglyphic script. Ideally, the sufferer deciphers the inscription only at the moment of death, and then with a dark rapture of recognition which, says the Warden, "would tempt one beneath the harrow oneself." Likewise, those souls trapped in that machine which is the Inferno have been turned into animated hieroglyphs of sin, pages written on by the hand of God. But in Dante, only the pilgrim and the reader seem to have the potential for real enlightenment; the damned cannot fully decipher themselves, since they have lost true *caritas*, the key to all divine coding. They also lack the free will necessary to pursue fully any restorative act of interpretation. Nor, as in Kafka, will the machinery break down or they die into oblivion, since Hell is eternal and the sinners already dead.

II

Our chief concern in dealing with the counterpass is to locate the inward crossing of image and idea for each of the pains of Hell. Iconographic source-hunting is of some use here, but only if it proceeds within a larger conceptual framework, even a semimythic one. One might begin by saying that, while it is the shape of a soul's love which defines the trajectory of its sin, it is the singular event of human death which is responsible for the transformations of appearance by which that sin is represented in the *Inferno*. Only by dying into Eternity does the damned soul discover and become the emblematic form of its inward life; Dante himself gains access to such forms only by entering and moving through the realms of eternal death. Death, the portal of divine vision, the threshold of revelation, is then the mother of trope, if not (as Stevens said) the mother of beauty. Indeed, to say that Death and Love, by dint of an obscure marriage, generate between them the allegorical imagery of Dante's Hell, is not merely to play with personifications, especially in the context of a theology which sees sinful love as death or recognizes a sacrificial death as the great type of love. In any case, it is only by reflecting on such a strange marriage that I can connect some of my remarks on the theology of sin to arguments about a more strictly literary source for Dante's treatment of the counterpass, one in which the powers of death and love are similarly intertwined. This subtext should also illuminate numerous other aspects of infernal suffering: its symbolic ironies, its binding together of life and after-life, its fatality, repetitiveness, and endlessness. The source I have in mind is no Christian eschatological work, but the *Metamorphoses* of Ovid, or, more precisely, the principle of symbolic change which gives life to that poem.

Let me say now that the influence which I am suggesting does not necessarily depend on any particular body of allegorical exegesis attached to the *Metamorphoses*. Nor need such influence appear only in details specifically drawn from Ovid's own fables. Certainly Dante may have found precedent in works like the *Ovide Moralisé* for reading the various metamorphoses as allegories of conversion or sinful perversion. Such is the case with the story of Io, who is first loved by Jupiter (God the Father), but then turned into a cow (falls into sinful, carnal desires), and kept from her freedom by Argus (Satan). Liberated by Mercury (Christ), she is restored to human form when, through the merciful offices of Juno (the Church), she reaches the waters of the Nile (Scripture). One of the limitations of this basically homiletic mode of exegesis, however, is that it must flatten out and schematize the Ovidian tales, more often than not wholly ignoring their affective power as literary narratives. While the allegorists are able to shift quite serenely between reading the same myth now *in bono*, now *in malo*, they seem incapable of distinguishing when Ovid is being serious and when he actually parodies the high rhetoric of the mythological mode, or in any way manipulates the decorum of pastoral or epic narrative. Even setting aside the oppressively doctrinal thrust of the allegories—the emphasis on salvation through the sacraments of the Church, the work of good and bad preachers, and so forth—there is no sense of dialectic, and no feeling for the real poetic risks of mythological representation. The *Ovide Moralisé* shows no direct interest in Ovidian change as an intricate metaphoric language in its own right; nor does that poem examine, as Dante's does, both the strengths and limits of such a complex, grotesque, and often arbitrary language for symbolizing either false or true forms of conversion.

I will yet be making some reference to the commentary tradition below. If, however, one for the moment takes Ovid's poetic machinery as a relatively self-sufficient, if sometimes ironic and fragmentary grammar of myth, one sees at least three aspects of his treatment of metamorphosis that find precise reflection in Dante's counterpass.

First, the event of transformation usually represents a kind of death, and at the same time a substitution for or evasion of death brought about through the agency of some supernatural power (though often such a power is only *implicit* in the fantastic turns of the narrative itself). Such a death does not mean total annihilation but rather survival in a new form. The changed individual may eventually rise into a transmundane realm, deified like Hercules or Julius Caesar, but more often he or she falls out of humanity into the cycle of a merely natural growth and decay. The metamorphosis is then not so much a rebirth as a debasement of human life; at least in problematizes the threshold between human life and human death, even (as Harold Skulsky argues) raising an epistemological crisis by straining our habitual ways of relating mind or personality to bodily form. Given the fluidity and arbitrariness of both identity and change in Ovid, the images of "the mind in exile" are as often comic or parodic as they are tragic. But though the pathos of metamorphosis may be minimal, still in those cases where the transformed figure puts on the merely generic or mortal immortality of an animal or plant we have, if not a loss of life, then a loss of self. He or she is reduced to a form which cannot truly develop or transcend its being (pre-Darwinian species did not evolve). As part of nature, the new being only commemorates or repeats the occasion of its original change, like the damned souls who repeat the form of their false conversions of value. Metamorphosis, that is, becomes a perverse form of stasis. Thus in Ovid, the nightingale Philomel exists only to lament (VI. 668ff); the daughters of Cadmus are turned to stone, caught in their violent positions of mourning (IV. 564); the flower Narcissus always grows by the banks of streams (III. 510); the violet or heliotrope, originally Phoebus's lover Clytie, always turns its face to the betrayed and betraying sun (IV. 268); and Hyacinth, whose stained petals spell out the Greek AI AI, perpetually echoes the wailing of the dead youth's divine lover, Apollo (X. 217).

We have here, then, what Northrop Frye schematizes as the tragic or elegiac side of the mythic world-picture, where the activity of original creation is converted into merely

> a recreation of memory and frustrated desire, where the spectres of the dead, in Blake's phrase, who inhabit the memory take on living form. The central symbol of the descending side is metamorphosis, the fall of gods or other spiritual beings into mankind, of mankind, through Circean enchantments, into animals, of all living things into dead matter.

Such a tragic structure partly informs the second relevant aspect of Ovidian transformation, one that accounts as well for much of the naive aesthetic and moral interest in metamorphosis. I am referring to the severe, ironic logic and inevitability reflected in many of the changes, something pointed up by the fact that they are often divinely imposed, and function either as reward or punishment. As in Dante, death is the threshold of metaphor, and while Ovidian metamorphosis does entail the loss of a flexible, human self, yet it may also be a grotesque sort of self-realization, since men and women "die" into emblems of their own moral characters. A grim and bloodthirsty man becomes a wolf; a steadfast servant of Jove becomes an adamant; a faithful husband and wife become an intertwining oak and linden; a chattering tattletale becomes a voice which can only repeat what it hears. The randomly allegorical structure of metamorphosis comes out even more directly in the case of the stories of Erysichthon (VIII. 738ff.) and Aglauros (II. 740ff), both of whom encounter early in the narrative personifications of the passions—Hunger and Envy respectively—which will later transform them. Many of the changes, of course, show no precise metaphoric or thematic continuity, being little more than supernatural flourishes which close tales of purely dramatic interest. But even here Ovid may provide a kind of conceptual coherence through proleptic or teleological naming: Hyacinthus becomes a hyacinth (X. 217), Myrrha a myrrh tree (X. 489), Lycaon a *lycus* or wolf (I. 237), and Cygnus a *cygnus*, or swan (XII. 145). Thus if a human being does not quite become an impersonal symbol, at least an individual name turns, through Ovid's invented etiologies, into a generic one. Dante is more problematic in this respect, no doubt, since the generalizing symbolic structures of punishment, which often tend to level all sinners within a particular circle, are played off against the highly individualized presentation of historical characters, each of which usually retains his or her own name.

Thirdly, and here we approach the more disturbing center of Ovid's metamorphic fictions, the characters' confrontations with literal or symbolic death are linked to the transforming power of love. Daphne's conversion into a laurel evades an unwanted love (I. 525ff); Philomel's pricking thorn and lamenting song speak of love's fierce, corruptive power (VI. 668ff); the fusing of Salmacis and Hermaphroditus becomes a grotesque figure for the sexual union (IV. 373ff); while Pygmalion's miracle, accomplished by Venus (X. 243ff), is both a myth of love's sublimation into art and a reflection on the relation between erotic love and idolatry. Not only are the forms of love, like death, most often a crossing of boundaries—incest, narcissism, hermaphroditism, divine rape, etc.—but it is the encounter with *eros*—human or divine, creative or destructive, ennobling or perverted—which is the direct occasion of most metamorphoses, and hence the key to their moral and psychological meanings. Indeed, it is the love-goddess Venus who in Ovid speaks of metamorphosis as a penalty "midway between death and exile." Dante merely replaces Ovid's focus on the multitudinous forms of pagan *eros* with a parallel attention to the perversions of Christian love classifiable under the term *cupiditas*, which derives from the Roman name for the god of love. For it is *cupiditas*, as the Christian rereading of *eros* and the antithesis of *caritas* or *agape*, which animates the strange shapes of punishment in Hell.

GIUSEPPE MAZZOTTA

The Light of Venus and the Poetry of Dante: "Vita Nuova" and "Inferno" XXVII

My title refers to the passage in *Convivio* in which Dante classifies the seven liberal arts according to a conventional hierarchy of knowledge. Grammar, dialectic, rhetoric, music, geometry, arithmetic and astronomy are the disciplines of the *trivium* and *quadrivium*, and each of them is linked to one of the planets in the Ptolemaic cosmology. Venus is the planet identified with Rhetoric because the attributes of Venus, like those of rhetoric, Dante says, are:

> the brilliancy of its aspect which is more pleasant to behold than that of any other star; the other is its appearing at one time in the morning, at another time in the evening. And these two properties exist in Rhetoric, for Rhetoric is the pleasantest of all the Sciences, inasmuch as its chief aim is to please. It "appears in the morning" when the rhetorician speaks directly of the surface view presented to his hearer; it "appears in the evening," that is, behind, when the rhetorician speaks of the letter by referring to that aspect of it which is remote from the hearer.

The definition alludes, as is generally acknowledged, to the traditional double function of rhetoric, oratory and the *ars dictaminis* or letter-writing. What the definition also contains is the notion of the *ornatus*, the techniques of style or ornamentation whereby rhetoric is said to be the art that produces beautiful appearances. The term, "chiarezza," one might add, translates *claritas*, the light that St. Thomas Aquinas conceives to be the substance of beauty and the means of its disclosure.

In *Convivio*, Dante does not really worry the issue of the beautiful as an autonomous esthetic category. Although the beautiful can be an attribute of philosophy (Dante speaks, for instance, of "la bellissima Filosofia") or the synonym of morality, the importance of both the beautiful and of rhetoric is decisively circumscribed in this speculative text of moral philosophy. To grasp the reduced value conferred on rhetoric in *Convivio*, where it is made to provide decorative imagery, one should only remember its centrality in the *De Vulgari Eloquentia*. The treatise, which straddles medieval poetics and rhetoric, was written with the explicit aim of teaching those poets who have so far versified "casualiter" to compose "regulariter," by the observance of rules and by the imitation of the great poets of antiquity. This aim reverses, may I suggest in passing, Matthew of Vendôme's judgement. In his *Ars Versificatoria* Matthew dismisses the lore of the ancient poets, their rhetorical figures and metaphors as useless and unworthy of emulation. But for Dante rhetoric, which begins with the Greeks, is the very equivalent of poetry. The concern with style and taste, which occupy a large portion of the *De Vulgari Eloquentia*, dramatizes the identification of rhetoric and poetry. At the same time, as the art of discourse, the art of pleading political or juridical causes, rhetoric is also in the *De Vulgari Eloquentia* the tool for the establishment of political, legal and moral authority. In this sense, Dante's notion of rhetoric re-enacts the concerns of a cultural tradition that ranges from Cicero to Brunetto Latini.

It comes as something of a surprise that scholars, who have been remarkably zealous in mapping the complex implications of rhetoric in the *De Vulgari Eloquentia* have not given equal critical attention to its role in Dante's other major works. In the case of the other texts rhetoric is treated as a repertory of figures, but not as a category of knowledge, with unique claims about authority and power. The statement, in truth, ought to be tempered somewhat in the light of the extensive debates to which the question of allegory in both *Convivio* and the *Divine Comedy* has been subjected. Yet even then the relationship between rhetoric and the other arts or the way in which rhetoric engenders reliable knowledge and may even dissimulate its strategies is not always adequately probed. It is not my intention to retread here the research that scholars such as Schiaffini, Pazzaglia, Tateo, Baldwin and others have carried out about the various influences on Dante's thinking about rhetoric, or their systematic analyses of the places in Dante's *oeuvre* where rhetoric is explicitly mentioned. I shall focus instead on *Convivio*, *Vita Nuova* and *Inferno* xxvii to show how rhetoric works itself out in these texts, but I will also submit some new evidence that might shed light on Dante's position in the liberal arts,

namely, the thirteenth century polemics which involved the secular masters of theology at the University of Paris and the anti-academism of the
early Franciscans.

There is no significant trace of this polemic in *Convivio*. The point
of departure of this unfinished treatise, and the principle that shapes its
articulation, is the authority of Aristotle, who in his *Metaphysics*, which
Dante calls "la Prima Filosofia," states that "all men naturally desire to
have knowledge." The reference to Aristotle may well be the enactment
of the technique of exordium which rhetorical conventions prescribe. But
the reference also announces what turns out to be the central preoccupation
of the four books: namely, that knowledge is made available by and
through the light of natural reason. This recognition of man's rationality
allows Dante to argue that it can be the choice of man to pursue the way
to achieve the good life on this earth. In spite of the initial *sententia*, the
Convivio is explicitly modeled not on Aristotle's *Metaphysics*, which deals
with pure theoretical knowledge, such as the knowledge of spiritual entities, but on Aristotle's *Ethics*. This is, as Isidore of Seville refers to it, the
practical "art of living rightly," which casts man in the here and now of
his historical existence and which demands that man exercise the choices
(without which no ethics can be conceived) appropriate to a moral agent.

It is this philosophical optimism about human rationality that
accounts for the thematic configuration of *Convivio*. The narrative is
punctuated, for instance, with references to one's own natural language to
be preferred to Latin, which is at some remove from one's own life; it is
clustered with insistent discussions on the moral virtues and on nobility,
whether or not it is contingent on birth, wealth or customs; it focuses on
the value of political life and the justice which the Roman Empire, a
product of human history, managed to establish in the world. What
sustains the textual movement, above all, is the belief in the allegory of
poets as a technique that affords the thorough interpretability of the
indirections of poetic language. Running parallel to the notion that poetry
can be the object of a full philosophical investigation, there is an insistence on the knowability of the moral and rational operations of man.

This acceptance of the natural order is the principle that lies at the
heart of two related and crucial gestures which shape the intellectual
structure of *Convivio*. The first, as Gilson has argued, is the revolutionary
re-arrangement, within the confines of *Convivio*, of the dignity of aims:
ethics rather than metaphysics is placed as the "highest good." The
second is the subordination of rhetoric to ethics. The statement needs
clarification. The first treatise, actually, begins by explaining Dante's own
shift away from the *Vita Nuova* to *Convivio*:

> The teachers of Rhetoric do not allow any one to speak of himself except on ground of necessity. And this is forbidden to a man because, when any one is spoken of, the speaker must needs either praise or blame him of whom he speaks. . . . I affirm . . . that a man may be allowed to speak of himself for necessary reasons. And among necessary reasons there are two specially conspicuous. One may be urged when without discoursing about oneself great disgrace and danger cannot be avoided. . . . This necessity moved Boethius to speak of himself in order that, under the pretext of finding consolation, he might palliate the lasting disgrace of his exile. . . . The other necessity arises when from speaking about oneself great advantage to others follows in the way of teaching. This reason moved Augustine to speak of himself in his *Confessions*, because by the progress of his life . . . he gave us example and teaching.

The passage is primarily a dismissal of what is known as epideictic rhetoric, one of the three classical divisions, along with the deliberative and the forensic, or rhetoric proper. Epideictic rhetoric, says Cicero in *De Inventione*, is the branch of oratory ". . . quod tribuitur in alicuius certae personae laudem aut vituperationem; . . ." This epideictic mode, quite clearly, is identified with the autobiographical writing of Boethius and St. Augustine. But for all the acknowledgement of the utility and exemplariness of the *Confessions*, Dante's passage is overtly anti-Augustinian: the point of *Convivio* is that the natural order, of which St. Augustine had too narrow an appreciation, is the locus of a possible moral-social project. More importantly, the passage marks an anti-Augustinian phase in Dante because it signals the limitations of autobiographical writing in favor of a philosophical discourse that would transcend private concerns and squarely grapple, as *Convivio* will do, with the issue of the authority of intellectual knowledge and its relationship to political power.

The departure from the *Confessions* is, in reality, a way of taking distance from Dante's own Augustinian text, the *Vita Nuova* and its rhetoric. It could be pointed out that in the *Vita Nuova* there is an occasional resistance to the excesses of self-staging. Yet the rhetoric of the self remains the path through which the poet's own imaginative search is carried out. The exordium of the *Vita Nuova*, consistently, stresses the autobiographical boundaries of the experiences about to be related:

> In that part of the book of my memory before which little could be read is found a rubric which saith: *Incipit Vita Nova*. Beneath which rubric I find written the words which it is my purpose to copy in this little book, and if not all, at least their substance.

The exordium is a poem, as Dante will call it later in the narrative, in the technical sense of a *captatio benevolentiae*. What one could also point out is the technical resonance of the term "sententia." Though the *Glossarium* of Du Cange refers only to the juridical sense of the word and neglects the meaning of moral lesson, which one can find in the *Rhetorica ad Herennium*, it hints that the text is also a plea for oneself in the presence of one's beloved. But what is central in the poem is the textual presence, which had gone unnoticed by the editors, of Guido Cavalcanti's *Donna me prega*.

As is known, Cavalcanti wrote his poem in response to the physician Guido Orlandi's query about the origin of love. Orlandi's sonnet, "Onde si move e donde nasce amore?" proceeds to ask where is it that love dwells, whether it is "substance, accident or memory," what is it that feeds love and climaxes with a series of questions as to whether love has its own figural representation or it goes around disguised. Cavalcanti replies that love takes its dwelling place in that part where memory is, a formulation which Dante's exordium unequivocally echoes.

The echo compels us to place the *Vita Nuova* as conceived from the start in the shadow of Cavalcanti's poetry, but it does not mean that the two texts are telling the same story. The most fundamental difference between them is their antithetical views of rhetoric and the nature of the esthetic experience. For Guido memory, which is in the sensitive faculty of the soul, is the place where love literally resides. In his skeptical materialism there is no room for a visionariness that might relieve one's dark desires. The deeper truth, so runs Cavalcanti's argument, is imageless and Guido's steady effort in the poem is to unsettle any possible bonds between poetic images and love, or love and the order of the rational soul. The scientism of *Donna me prega* literalizes desire and makes it part of the night: its poetry, with its overt anti-metaphysical strains, turns, paradoxically, against poetry and assigns truth to the idealized realm of philosophical speculation.

For Dante, on the contrary, the truth of love is to be the child of time—as Venus is—and, hence, under the sway of mutability and death. The temporality of desire links it unavoidably to memory, but memory is here—and this is the main departure from Cavalcanti—a book or the "memoria artificialis," which is one of the five parts of rhetoric. The parts are usually identified as *inventio, dispositio, elocutio, memoria* and *pronuntiatio* and memory is defined as "a strong perception of things and words by the soul." The rhetoricity of memory makes the quest of the *Vita Nuova* into an interrogation of the value of figures. More precisely, memory is not the refuge of a deluded self, the a-priori recognition of appearances as illusive shapes, the way Cavalcanti would have it. For Dante, memory is the visionary faculty, the imagination through which the poet can question the phenomena of natural existence and urge them to release their hidden secrets. It can be said that Cavalcanti makes of memory a sepulcher and of death the cutting edge of vision: he broods over the severance death entails and it thwarts his imagination. He is too much of a realist, too much of a philosopher to be able to soar above the dark abyss into which, nonetheless, he stares.

But the poet of the *Vita Nuova* is impatient with this skepticism, this dead literalism, and from the start he seeks to rescue visionariness out of the platitudes of the materialists. The figures of love are not irrelevant shadows or insubstantial phantoms in the theatre of one's own mind as Cavalcanti thinks when he ceaselessly beckons Dante to join him on the plain where the light of ideas endures. Nor are women part of an infinite metaphorization, always replaceable (hence never necessary), as the physician Dante da Maiano, who tells Dante that his dream of love is only lust that a good bath can cure, believes.

The contrivance of the lady of the screen, related in chapter four, which literally makes a woman the screen on which the lover projects and displaces his own desires, is rejected because it casts doubt on Beatrice's own uniqueness. At the same time, chapter eight, which tells of the death of one of Beatrice's friends, allows Dante's sense of poetry in the *Vita Nuova* to surface. The passage is undoubtedly meant to prefigure Beatrice's own future death. Retrospectively, however, it is also another put-down of the materialists' belief that love is reducible to the mere materiality of bodies. Dante refers to the dead woman as a body without a soul. The poem he then proceeds to write is "Piangete, amanti, poi che piange Amore," which turns out to be, quite appropriately, a lament over the dead figure, "la morta imagine." But this poet can glance heavenward, "where the gentle soul was already located . . ." In short, Dante installs his poetry at the point where Cavalcanti's poetry, where most poetry, for that matter, stops: between the dead body and the soul's existence. Images are not, a-priori, mere simulacra of death, and the "stilo de la loda," which re-enacts the principles of epideictic rhetoric, strives for a definition of Beatrice's felt but unknown essence.

This concern with metaphysics, with the links between rhetoric and the soul, comes forth in chapter twenty-five, where metaphor is said to be the trope that animates the face of the world. The meditation on metaphor, which is the burden of the chapter, is carried out as an attempt to grasp the nature of love. Here we see why Venus should be coupled to Rhetoric. The question Dante raises has a stunning simplicity: is love a divinity, as the Notaro suggests, or is it a mere rhetorical figure as Guido Cavalcanti in his *pastorella*, "In un boschetto," states. Dante defines love, in only partial agreement with Cavalcanti, for whom love is "un accidente-che sovente-è fero," as "accident in substance." The metaphoricity of love is then discussed in terms of a movement from the animate to the inanimate and vice-versa. Metaphor is given in the guise of *prosopopeia*, the orphic fiction whereby that which is dead is given a voice or, more correctly, a face.

With the actual death of Beatrice, related from chapter twenty-eight on, the fiction that poetry is capable of providing a simulation of life is no longer sufficient. To be sure, Beatrice was described as the living figure of love, but now that she is physically dead, the metaphors for her seem to be another empty fiction. If the question, while Beatrice was alive, was whether she is and how she is unique, now that she is dead, the question is finding the sense of metaphors that recall her. Dante's imaginative dead-end at this point (it induces tears, but Dante records no poetry) narrows in the prose to the vast image of general darkness, the death of Christ. An analogy is established between Beatrice and Christ in the effort to invest the memory of Beatrice with a glow of material substantiality. As is known, Charles Singleton views this analogy as the exegetical principle of the *Vita Nuova*, the aim of which is to portray the lover's growing awareness of the providentiality of Beatrice's presence in his life.

But the tension between the Christological language, the status of which depends on the coincidence between the image and its essence, and the poetic imagination, which in this text comes forth in the shifty forms of memory and desire, is problematic. There is no doubt that the poetic imagination aspires to achieve an absolute stability which only the foundation of theology, which has its own visionariness, can provide. But Dante marks with great clarity the differences between his own private world and the common theological quest. The penultimate sonnet of the *Vita Nuova* addresses exactly this predicament.

> Ah ye pilgrims, that go lost in thought, per-
>   chance of a thing that is not present to you,
>   come ye from folk so far away as by your
>   aspect ye show forth?
>
> For ye weep not when ye pass through the
>   midst of the sorrowing city, even as folk who
>   seem to understand naught of her heaviness.
>
> If ye tarry for desire to hear it, certes my heart
>   all sighing tells me, that ye will go forth
>   in tears.

> She hath lost her Beatrice; and the words that
> a man can say of her, have power to make
> one weep.

The sonnet is an apostrophe to the pilgrims who are going to Rome there to see the true image, literally a prosopopeia, Christ has left on the veil of the Veronica. The pilgrims are unaware of the lover's own heart-sickness and, in effect, the poet's mythology of love, that Beatrice is an analogy of Christ, comes forth as too private a concern. More precisely the sonnet is built on a series of symmetrical correspondences: the pilgrims are going to see Christ's image and are caught in an empty space between nostalgia and expectation, away from their homes and not quite at their destination; the lover is in his own native place, but like the pilgrims, away from his beatitude. But there is another contrast in the sonnet which unsettles the symmetries: the motion of the pilgrims, who are on their way, is in sharp contrast to the poet's invitation that they stop to hear the story of his grief. In the canzone, "Donne ch'avete intelletto d'amore," the Heavens vie with the lover to have Beatrice; now the terms are reversed: the lover seeks to waylay the pilgrims, begs them to stop for a while, a gesture that is bound to remind us of the repeated temptations the pilgrim himself eventually will experience in *Purgatorio*.

The vision of the pilgrims' journey to Rome triggers the last sonnet, "Oltre la spera" ["Beyond the sphere"], which tells of the poet's own pilgrimage. This is an imaginative journey to the separate souls, which the intellect cannot grasp. In this most visionary text, at the moment when a revelation is at hand, the eye is dazzled by the sun and the essences remain hidden behind their own inapproachable light. The perplexing quality of the image is heightened by the fact that it was used by both Averroes and Aquinas to describe the separate souls. Doctrinally, the text evokes and is poised between two opposite metaphysical systems. More poignantly, the phrase, "the sigh that issues from my heart" echoes another phrase which is patterned on a line in a sonnet by Cavalcanti. In this sonnet Cavalcanti restates the absolute separation of desire and its aim; Dante, instead, yokes rhetoric to metaphysics, makes of rhetoric the privileged imaginative path to metaphysics, though rhetoric can never yield the spiritual essence it gropes for.

Convivio picks at the very start the reference to Aristotle's *Metaphysics* on which the *Vita Nuova* comes to a close. But Dante challenges, as hinted earlier, the traditional primacy of metaphysics and replaces it with ethics. The move is so radical that Dante dramatizes in the first song, "Voi che 'ntendendo il terzo ciel movete" the shift to ethics. Written in the form of a *tenso*, a battle of thoughts within the self, and addressed to the angelic intelligences that move Venus, the planet of Rhetoric, the poem tells the triumph of the "donna gentile," Philosophy over Beatrice. With the enthronement of Philosophy, rhetoric is reduced to an ancilliary status: it is a technique of persuasion, the cover that wraps within its seductive folds the underlying morality.

The confinement of rhetoric to a decorative role in philosophical discourse is not unusual. From Cicero to Brunetto Latini rhetoricians are asked to link rhetoric to ethics because of rhetoric's inherent shiftiness, its power to argue contradictory aspects of the same question. In a way it is possible to suggest that the voice of Dante in *Convivio* is a Boethian voice, for like Boethius, who in his *De Consolatione Philosophiae*, banishes the meretricious muses of poetry to make room for the appearance of Lady Philosophy, under whose aegis poetry is possible, Dante, too, makes of poetry the dress of Philosophy.

This analogy with the Boethian text stops here, for unlike Boethius, Dante does not seek consolation for too long. Philosophy, says Isidore of Seville, is "meditatio mortis." Dante has no intention to be trapped in the grief that the shadow of Beatrice's death caused in him. He turns his back to the past in *Convivio* and ponders ethics, which is not the land of the dead, but the "ars bene vivendi." As a matter of fact, his voice is that of the intellectual, who, exiled and dispossessed, asserts the authority of his knowledge and seeks, by virtue of that knowledge, power. This claim for power by an intellectual does not, obviously, start with Dante. Its origin lies in the revival of another sphere of rhetoric, the *artes dictaminis* elaborated by Alberic of Montecassino and the Bologna school of law and rhetoric where the intellectuals would shape and argue the political issues of the day.

Yet Dante's project in *Convivio* to cast the philosopher as the advisor of the Emperor utterly fails. Many reasons have been suggested by Nardi, Leo and others as to why the project collapsed. The various reasons essentially boil down to Dante's awareness that a text expounding a system of values cannot be written unless it is accompanied by a theory of being. The text that attempts the synthesis is the *Divine Comedy*.

The point of departure of the poem is the encounter with Vergil whose "parola ornata," an allusion to the *ornatus* of rhetoric, has the power, in Beatrice's language, to aid the pilgrim in his quest. But if rhetoric is unavoidably the very stuff of the text, rhetoric's implications and links with the other disciplines of the encyclopedia are explicitly thematized in a number of places. One need mention only *Inferno* xv, where rhetoric, politics, grammar, law and their underlying theory of nature are all drawn within the circle of knowledge; or even *Inferno* xiii, the canto which features the fate of Pier delle Vigne, the counsellor in the court of Frederick II.

I shall focus, however, on *Inferno* xxvii because this is a canto that inscribes Dante's text within the boundaries of the XIII century debate on the liberal arts and, more precisely, on the Franciscan attack against logic and speculative grammar. The canto is usually read in conjunction with the story of Ulysses that precedes it. The dramatic connections between the two narratives, however superficial they may be, are certainly real. It can be easily granted that *Inferno* xxvii is the parodic counter to *Inferno* xxvi and its myth of style. In the *De Vulgari Eloquentia*, in the wake of Horace's *Ars Poetica* and of the *Rhetorica ad Herennium*, Dante classifies the tragic, elegiac and comical styles in terms of fixed categories of a subject matter that is judged to be sublime, plain or low. The canto of Ulysses, with its "verba polita," to use Vendôme's phrase, moral aphorisms and grandiloquence, stages the language of the epic hero whose interlocutor is the epic poet, Vergil. Ulysses' is a high style and it makes his story a tragic text, for Ulysses is, like all tragic heroes, an over-stater and hyperbole is his figure: he is one who has staked everything and has lost everything for seeking everything.

As we move into *Inferno* xxvii there is a deliberate diminution of Ulysses' grandeur. His smooth talk is replaced by hypothetical sentences, or, later, parenthetical remarks swearing, colloquialisms and crude idioms. From the start, Guido's speech draws the exchange between Vergil and Ulysses within the confines of the dialect:

> O thou to whom I direct my voice and who just now spoke in Lombard, saying: "Now go thy way, I do not urge thee more."
>
> (11. 19–21)

Vergil allows Dante to speak to Guido, "Parla tu, questi e latino" (1. 33), because Vergil, too, observes the rhetorical rules of stylistic hierarchy. There is a great deal of irony in shifting from Ulysses' high ground to the specifics of the Tuscan Appennines or Urbino and Ravenna. But from Dante's viewpoint the irony is vaster: degrees of style are illusory values and Ulysses and Guido, for all their stylistic differences, are damned to the same punishment of being enveloped in tongues of fire in the area of fraud among the evil counsellors. Even the image of the Sicilian bull within which its maker perishes (11. 7–9), while it conveys the sense that we are witnessing the fate of contrivers trapped by their own contrivances, it also harks back to Ulysses' artifact, the Trojan horse.

It could be said that Guido is the truth, as it were, of Ulysses. If the pairing of their voices, however, can be construed as a confrontation between the epic and the mockheroic, style is not just a technique of characterizing their respective moral visions. Guido's municipal particularity of style introduces us to the question of political rhetoric—the rhetoric by which cities are established or destroyed—which is featured in the canto. What we are shown, to be sure, is an obsessive element of Dante's political thought: Guido da Montefeltro, as the advisor of Pope Boniface VIII, counselled him on how to capture the city of Palestrina, and this advice is placed within the reality of the temporal power of the Papacy. From this standpoint *Inferno* xxvii prefigures St. Peter's invective in *Paradiso* xxvii and it also echoes *Inferno* xix, the ditch of the Simonists where Pope Boniface is expected.

As in *Inferno* xix, here too, we are given the cause of the general sickness: just as Constantine, the text says (11. 94–99), sought out Pope Sylvester to cure his leprosy, so did Boniface VIII seek Guido da Montefeltro to cure his pride. If leprosy suggests the rotting away of the body politic, pride is the fever of the mystical body and the origin of both is the Donation of Constantine. The chiasmus that the comparison draws (Boniface is equated to Constantine) points to the unholy mingling of the spiritual and secular orders and to the role-reversal of Pope and his advisor.

But there is in the canto an attention to political discourse that goes beyond this level of generality. In a way, just as there was a theology of style, we are now allowed to face the politics of theology. We are led, more precisely, into the council chamber, behind the scenes, as it were, where "li accorgimenti e le coperte vie," (1.76), the art of wielding naked political power is shown. Here big deals are struck, so big that they focus on destruction of cities and salvation of souls. These are the terms of the transaction: by virtue of his absolute sovereignty (an authority that depends on the argument of the two keys which he quotes [11. 103–105]), the Pope promises absolution for Guido's misdeed. Guido's advice is simply to make promises without planning to keep them (11. 110–111).

This advice, I would like to suggest, textually repeats and reverses Brunetto Latini's formulation in *La rettorica*. Commenting on Cicero's statement that the stability of a city is contingent on keeping faith, on observing laws and practicing obedience to one another, Brunetto adds that to keep faith means to be loyal to one's commitments and to keep one's word: "e dice la legge che fede e quella che promette l'uno e l'altro l'attende." The deliberate violation of the ethical perspective, which alone, as Brunetto fully knows, can neutralize the dangerous simulations that rhetoric affords, brings to a focus what the canto on Ulysses unveils:

that ethics is the set of values rhetoric manipulates at will. From Dante's viewpoint, however, the arrangement between the Pope and his counselor is charged with heavy ironies that disrupt the utilitarian calculus of the principles.

The Pope begins by taking literally what is known as his *plenitudo potestatis*, the fullness of spiritual and temporal powers given to him by God, yet he is powerless to act and seize a town. He believes in the performative power of his words, that by virtue of his office his words are a sacramental pledge. Yet, he takes advice to say words that do not measure up to his actions. There is irony even in Dante's use of the word "officio"—a term which for Cicero means moral duty and its appearance in line 91 only stresses duty's dereliction. On the other hand there is Guido, who knows that in the tough political games men play there is a gap between words and reality. Yet he believes in the Pope's "argomenti gravi" (weighty arguments) 91. 106—a word that designates probable demonstration according to logical rules—without recognizing that the Pope does not deliver what he promises, which, after all, was exactly Guido's advice to him.

The point of these ironies is that Boniface and Guido thoroughly resemble and deserve each other. Both believe in compromises, practical gains and moral adjustments, as if God's grace could be made adaptable to their calculus and to the narrow stage of the goings-on of everyday politics. And both are two sophists, of the kind St. Augustine finds especially odious in *De Doctrina Christiana*, those who transform the world of political action to a world of carefully spoken words. As a sophist, Boniface entertains the illusion that he can control the discourse of others and ends up controlling Guido while at the same time being controlled by him. As a sophist, Guido is the character who is always drawing the wrong logical inference from his actions: he mistakenly believes Dante is dead because he has heard that nobody ever came alive from the depth of Hell (11. 61–66); he becomes a friar believing that, thus girt, he could make amends for his past (11. 66–69).

What does it exactly mean to suggest, as I am doing, that Guido is portrayed as if he were a logician? And how does it square with the textual fact, that to the best of my knowledge has so far not been probed by commentators, namely that he is a Franciscan, or, as he calls himself a "cordigliero" (1.67)? The fact that Guido is a Franciscan has far-reaching implications for the dramatic and intellectual structure of the canto. The tongues of fire in which the sinners are wrapped are an appropriate emblem more to a Franciscan like Guido than to Ulysses. The tongues of fire are usually explained as the parody of the Pentecostal tongues, the gift of prophecy that descends on the apostles at the time of the origin of the Church. It happens, however, that in the Constitution of the Franciscans it was established that the friars would convene at the Porziuncola every four years on the day of the Pentecosts. The reason for this ritual is to be found in the Franciscans' conscious vision of themselves as the new apostles capable of reforming the world.

Guido's language perverts the Pentecostal gift and the perversion puts him in touch with the fierce enemies of the Franciscans, the logicians. The possibility for this textual connection is suggested by the canto itself. At Guido's death there is a *disputatio* between one of the "neri cherubini" and St. Francis over Guido's soul (11. 112–117). The devil wins the debate and speaks of himself as a "loico" (1. 123). The debate between a devil and St. Francis is not much of a surprise, for as a fallen angel—one of the cherubim—the devil is the direct antagonist of Francis, who is commonly described in his hagiographies as "the angel coming from the east, with the seal of the living God." Further, the reference to the devil as one of the cherubim, which means "plenitudo scientiae" and is the attribute of the Dominicans, seems to involve obliquely in Dante's representation both orders of friars. But this is not a hidden allegory of a *quaestio disputata* between Dominicans and Franciscans. What is at stake, on the contrary, is the long debate in which the two fraternal orders were engaged in the XIII century—and in which they end up on the side of their opponents, as Dante implies. The debate centered on the value of the Liberal Arts at the University of Paris.

In historical terms the debate saw the preachers and the mendicants opposed by the secular masters of theology. The Dominicans, to be sure, adapted quickly to the pressures of the university circles because they were founded with the explicit intellectual aim of combatting heresies. The Franciscans, on the other hand, in response to the call for evangelical practice, believed that their homiletics had to retrieve without any sophistry the essence of the good news. Francis is an "idiota," given to the cult of *simplicitas* and Paris, the city of learning, is made to appear the enemy of Assisi.

This stress on simplicity did not mean that the Franciscans kept away for too long from the world of learning. There is a strong Augustinian strand, in effect, in their attitude toward academic knowledge. St. Augustine, it will be remembered, encourages Christians in *De Doctrina Christiana* to make good use of pagan rhetoric in order to communicate effectively the message of the Revelation. Secular wisdom, which is crystallized in the liberal arts and which St. Augustine rejected in the

Confessions, is now viewed as a treasure to be booted by the Christians the way the Hebrews booted the "Egyptian gold."

The Franciscans, figures such as Alexander of Hales, St. Bonaventure and Duns Scotus did move into the universities, but by virtue of their voluntarism they adhered to an essential anti-Aristoteleanism. The formal edifice of Aristotelean logic, as a theory of abstract reasoning and as a doctrine that the universe is a logical system of numbers and mathematically measurable order is severely challenged. In *Inferno* xxvii, as the devil is identified as a logician, logic comes forth as the art that deals with judgements about the logical consistency or contradictions within the structure of an argument, but radically lacks an ethical perspective. Appropriately, Guido, who has betrayed his Franciscan principles is now claimed by one of the very logicians the Franciscans opposed.

But the debate between Franciscans and the secular masters is not left in the canto entirely on this academic level. There are political extensions to it which Dante absorbs in his representation. Guillaume de Saint-Amour, a leader of the secular masters had unleashed an attack in his *De Periculis Novissorum Temporum* against the Franciscans as the pseudo-apostles and heralds of the anti-Christ; in their purely formal observance of the externals of faith they are identified as the new Pharisees, who from under the habit of holiness connive with Popes to deceive the believers. As Y. M. J. Congar suggests, the polemic was a clear attempt to contain the power of the Pope, for the mendicants, by being under the Pope's direct jurisdiction, weakened the *potestas officii* of the local bishops. Largely at stake was the issue of confessions, a source of controversy between local priests and friars, which, ironically, was given a firm solution in the bull *Super cathedram* by Boniface VIII.

In *Inferno* xxvii Boniface is "The prince of the new Pharisees" (1.85); he makes a mockery of confession, "Do not let thy heart mistrust; I absolve thee" (11. 100–101), and his *potestas* appears as only temporal power. By the same token, Guido, who as a Franciscan should believe in the power of confession, settles for a pharisaic formula, "Father, since thou dost cleanse me from this sin into which I must now fall" (11. 108–109). He seeks absolution before the commission of sin—an act that makes a mockery of his prior contrition and confession (1. 83). And, finally, he is throughout the Pope's conniver.

In effect, Guido da Montefeltro never changed in his life. The emblem he uses for himself, "my deeds were those, not of the lion, but of the fox" (11. 74–75) gives him away. The animal images, to begin with, are consistent with the unredeemed vision of the natural world in terms of mastiff, claws and young lion (11. 45–50). More to the point, the metaphor of the lion and the fox echoes Cicero's *De Officiis* (I,xiii, 41) and it may be construed in this context as a degraded variant of the *topos* of *fortitudo et sapientia*. But the fox, Guido's attribute, has some other symbolic resonances. In the *Roman de Reynard*, the fox goes into a lengthy confession of his sin and then relapses to his old ways; for Jacques of Vitry, more generally, the fox is the emblem of confession without moral rebirth. More importantly for *Inferno* xxvii is the fact that Rutebeuf, who wrote two poems in support of Guillaume de Saint-Amour, uses the fox as the symbol of the friars; in *Renart-le-nouvel* the fox is a treacherous Franciscan.

These historical events and symbols are brought to an imaginative focus in the digression of the deceits of False Seeming in the *Roman de la Rose* of Jean de Meung. Absorbing the anti-fraternal satire of Guillaume, Jean presents Faussemblant as a friar, a "cordelier," who has abandoned the evangelical ideals of Francis and lives on fraud. Reversing Joachim of Flora's hope that the fraternal orders were providentially established so that history would hasten to a close, Jean sees the mendicants as symptoms of decay: "fallacious is the logic of their claim: religious garment makes religious man." This sense of the friars' deceptiveness ("now a Franciscan, now a Dominican," as Jean says) re-appears in *Il Fiore*, where Falsembiante's steady practice of simulation comes forth as metaphoric foxiness. The sonnet conveys what was Jean's insight: namely, that the only fixed principle in False Seeming's shifty play of concealments (which in the sonnet the technique of enumeration and the iterative adverbs of time mime) is falsification itself.

To turn to the anti-fraternal satirists such as Guillaume and Jean is not equivalent, from Dante's viewpoint, to granting assent to their statement or even giving them the seal of a privileged authority. In *Inferno* xxvii Dante endorses the anti-fraternal rhetoric, for Guido da Montefeltro has clearly betrayed the paradigm of Franciscan piety. But Dante also challenges, as the Franciscan intellectuals did, the logicians' categories of knowledge. When the devil, at the triumphant conclusion of his dispute with St. Francis, appeals to logic's principle of non-contradiction (11. 119–120), the devil is using logic only rhetorically: his is a sophistical refutation by which he sways the opponent. But logical conceptualizations, as has been argued earlier, are delusive because they are not moored to the realities of life and because they establish a *de facto* discontinuity between the order of discourse and the order of reality. More importantly, the devil is claiming as his own Guido da Montefeltro, whose very experience in the canto unveils exactly how the principle of non-contradiction is a fictitious abstraction: like Faux-Semblant, the Pope and the Devil himself, Guido is Proteus-like, to use Jean de Meung's metaphor for the friars, shifty and always unlike himself.

This rotation of figures and categories of knowledge is the substance of a canto in which, as this paper has shown, prophecy is twisted into rhetoric, theology is manipulated for political ends, politics and ethics are masks of desire for power, and logic is deployed rhetorically. From this perception of how tangled the forms of discourse are comes Dante's own moral voice, both here and in his attacks against the sophistry of syllogisms immediately after the Dominican St. Thomas Aquinas celebrates the life of St. Francis.

Because of this movement from theory to practice and back again to theory and from one order of knowledge to another, it appears that the liberal arts can never be fixed in a self-enclosed autonomous sphere: each art unavoidably entails the other in a ceaseless pattern of displacement. Ironically, what, from a moral point of view, Dante condemns in Guido da Montefeltro, becomes, in Dante's own poetic handling, the essence of knowledge itself, whereby the various disciplines are forever intermingled. The idea that the arts cannot be arranged in categorical definitions is not only a poet's awareness of how arbitrary boundaries turn out to be. Medieval textbooks and compendia are consistent, so to speak, in betraying the difficulty of treating each of the liberal arts as crystallized entities. If Isidore views dialectic as logic, John of Salisbury in his *Metalogicon* considers *logica* an encompassing term for "grammatica" and "ratio disserendi," which, in turn, contains dialectic and rhetoric. For Hugh of St. Victor, who follows St. Augustine in the *City of God*, *logica* is the name for the *trivium*.

These references are valuable only if we are ready to recognize that what is largely a technical debate never loses sight of the spiritual destination of the liberal arts. What the technicians may sense but never face, however, is that which rhetoricians and poets always know: that knowledge may be counterfeited. Small wonder that Dante in *Convivio* would repress, in vain, rhetoric. But in the *Vita Nuova* and the *Divine Comedy* we are left with the disclosure that rhetoric, in spite of its dangerous status and, ironically, because of its dangerousness, is the only possible path the poet must tread on the way to, respectively, metaphysics and theology. Whether or not the poet delivers genuine metaphysical and theological knowledge or dazzles us with luminous disguises is a question which lies at the heart of Dante's poetry.

Chronology

1265?	Dante Alighieri born in Florence.
1266	Guelph victory at Benevento over Ghibellines.
1274	Meets Beatrice, believed to be daughter of Folco Portinari.
1277	Engaged to Gemma di Manetto Donati.
1283	Between this date and 1295 marries Gemma and has three children.
1290	Death of Beatrice.
1292–93	*Vita Nuova*; begins study of philosophy.
1295	Enrolls in Guild and enters political life.
1300	Becomes prior for bimester; June 15–August 15.
1301	Opposes extension of troops consignment to Boniface VIII in July. In October sent with two other emissaries to Pope in Rome. Takeover of Florence by exiled Black Guelphs in November.
1302	Dante ordered to appear to answer charges; sentenced to death on March 10 when he fails to do so. Begins exile from Florence under pain of death.
1304–07?	*De Vulgari Eloquentia* and the *Convivio*.
1310?	*De monarchia*.
1314	*Inferno* completed.
1315	Dante rejects possibility of pardon; settles in Verona with Can Grande della Scala.
1319?	Dante moves to Ravenna with Guido Novella da Plenta. *Purgatorio* and part of *Paradiso* completed.
1321	Dante dies in Ravenna; September 13–14.

Contributors

HAROLD BLOOM, Sterling Professor of the Humanities at Yale University, is the author of *The Anxiety of Influence, Poetry and Repression* and many other volumes of literary criticism. His forthcoming study, *Freud: Transference and Authority*, attempts a full-scale reading of all of Freud's major writings. A MacArthur Prize Fellow, he is the general editor of *The Chelsea House Library of Literary Criticism*

CHARLES S. SINGLETON is Professor of Humanistic Studies at Johns Hopkins University.

ERICH AUERBACH (1892–1957) was Sterling Professor of Comparative Literature at Yale University at his death. His work on the Middle Ages has been highly influential.

ROBERT E. KASKE is Professor of English at Cornell University.

FRANCIS X. NEWMAN is Professor of English and of Cinema at the State University of New York at Binghamton.

MARGUERITE MILLS CHIARENZA is Professor of Hispanic and Italian Studies at the University of British Columbia at Vancouver.

JOHN FRECCERO is Professor of Italian at Stanford University.

ROBERT DURLING is Professor of Italian and of English at the University of California at Santa Cruz.

DAVID QUINT is Associate Professor of Comparative Literature at Princeton University.

SUSAN NOAKES is Assistant Professor of French and Italian at the University of Kansas.

TEODOLINDA BAROLINI is Associate Professor of French and Italian at New York University.

KENNETH GROSS is Assistant Professor of English at Rochester University.

GIUSEPPE MAZZOTTA is Professor of English at Cornell University.

Bibliography

Abrams, Richard. "Illicit Pleasures: Dante Among the Sensualists (*Purgatorio* XXVI)." *Modern Literary Notes* 100 (1985).
———. "Inspiration and Gluttony: The Moral Context of Dante's Poetics of the 'Sweet New Style'." *Modern Literary Notes* 91 (1976).
Anderson, William. *Dante the Maker.* London: Routledge & Kegan Paul, 1980.
Auerbach, Erich. "Farinata and Cavalcante." In *Mimesis: The Representation of Reality in Western Literature.* Translated by Willard Trask. Princeton: Princeton University Press, 1953.
———. *Dante, Poet of the Secular World.* Translated by R. Manheim. Chicago: The University of Chicago Press, 1961.
Barbi, Michele. *Life of Dante.* Translated by Paul G. Ruggiers. Berkeley and Los Angeles: University of California Press, 1954.
Barolini, Teodolinda. *Dante's Poets: Textuality and Truth in the Comedy.* Princeton: Princeton University Press, 1984.
Bergin, Thomas G. *Dante. Riverside Studies in Literature.* Boston: Houghton Mifflin, 1965.
———. *Dante's Divine Comedy.* Englewood Cliffs, N.J.: Prentice-Hall, 1971.
———. *From Time to Eternity: Essays on Dante's Divine Comedy.* New Haven: Yale University Press, 1967.
Boyde, Patrick. *Dante Philomythes and Philosopher: Man in the Cosmos.* Cambridge: Cambridge University Press, 1981.
Charity, A. C. *Events and Their Afterlife: The Dialectics of Christian Typology in The Bible and Dante.* Cambridge: Cambridge University Press, 1966.
Cosmo, Umberto. *A Handbook to Dante Studies.* Translated by David Moore. Oxford: Blackwell, 1960.
Davis, Charles T. *Dante and the Idea of Rome.* Oxford: Clarendon Press, 1957.
———. "Dante's Vision of History." *Dante Studies with the Annual Report of the Dante Society* 93 (1975).
Durling, Robert M. "Deceit and Digestion in the Belly of Hell." In *Allegory and Representation.* Selected Papers from the English Institute 1979–80. New Series, Number Five. Edited by Stephen J. Greenblatt. Baltimore: The Johns Hopkins University Press, 1981.
Fergusson, Francis. *Dante's Drama of the Mind: A Modern Reading of the Purgatorio.* Princeton: Princeton University Press, 1953.
Ferrucci, Franco. *The Poetics of Disguise: The Autobiography of the Work in Homer, Dante, and Shakespeare.* Translated by Ann Dunnigan. Ithaca: Cornell University Press, 1980.

Foster, Kenelm. *The Two Dantes and Other Studies*. Berkeley: University of California Press, 1977.

Freccero, John, ed. *Dante. Twentieth Century Views*. Englewood Cliffs, N.J.: Prentice-Hall, 1967.

———. "Dante's Firm Foot and the Journey Without a Guide." *Harvard Theological Review* 52 (1959).

———. *Paradiso* X: The Dance of the Stars." *Dante Studies with the Annual Report of the Dante Society* 86 (1968).

———. "Dante's Prologue Scene." *Dante Studies with the Annual Report of the Dante Society* 84 (1966).

———. "Casella's Song (*Purg.* II, 112)." *Dante Studies with the Annual Report of the Dante Society* 91 (1973).

Gilson, Etienne. *Dante the Philosopher*. Translated by David Moore. New York: Sheed & Ward, 1949.

Hollander, Robert. *Allegory in Dante's Commedia*. Princeton: Princeton University Press, 1969.

———. "*Vita Nuova*: Dante's Perceptions of Beatrice." *Dante Studies with the Annual Report of the Dante Society* 92 (1974).

Leo, Ulrich. "The Unfinished *Convivio* and Dante's Rereading of the *Aeneid*." In *Medieval Studies* 13 (1951).

Mazzaro, Jerome. *The Figure of Dante: An Essay on the Vita Nuova*. Princeton: Princeton University Press, 1981.

Mazzeo, Joseph Anthon. *Medieval Cultural Tradition in Dante's Comedy*. Westport, Conn.: Greenwood Press, 1960.

Mazzotta, Giuseppe. *Dante, Poet of the Desert: History and Allegory in the Divine Comedy*. Princeton: Princeton University Press, 1979.

———. "Dante and the Virtues of Exile." *Poetics Today* 5 (1984).

Quinones, Ricardo J. *The Renaissance Discovery of Time*. Cambridge: Harvard University Press, 1972.

Reade, W. H. V. *The Moral System of Dante's Inferno*. Oxford: Clarendon Press, 1909.

Shapiro, Marianne. "*The Fictionalization of Bertran de Born (Inf. XXVII)*." *Dante Studies* 93 (1975).

Shoaf, R. A. *Dante, Chaucer, and the Currency of the Word: Money, Images, and Reference in Late Medieval Poetry*. Norman, Okla.: Pilgrim Books.

Singleton, Charles S. *Commedia: Elements of Structure*. Dante Studies 1. Cambridge: Harvard University Press, 1954.

———. "The Irreducible Dove." *Comparative Literature* 9 (1957).

———. *Journey to Beatrice*. Dante Studies 2. Cambridge: Harvard University Press, 1957.

———. *An Essay on the Vita Nuova*. Cambridge: Harvard University Press, 1958.

Thompson, David. "Figure and Allegory in the *Commedia*." *Dante Studies with the Annual Report of the Dante Society* 90 (1972).

Williams, Charles. *The Figure of Beatrice: A Study in Dante*. New York: Farrar, Straus & Giroux, 1961.

Acknowledgments

"Two Kinds of Allegory" by Charles S. Singleton from *Commedia: Elements of Structure* by Charles S. Singleton, copyright © 1954 by Harvard University Press. Reprinted by permission.

"Figural Art in the Middle Ages" by Eric Auerbach from *Scenes from the Drama of European Literature* by Eric Auerbach, copyright © 1959 by Meridian Books. Reprinted by permission.

"St. Francis of Assisi in Dante's *Commedia*" by Eric Auerbach from *Scenes from the Drama of European Literature* by Eric Auerbach, copyright © 1959 by Meridian Books. Reprinted by permission.

"Dante's *DXV*" by R. E. Kaske from *Traditio: Studies in Ancient and Medieval History, Thought and Religion*, vol. 17 (1961), copyright © 1961 by Fordham University. Reprinted by permission.

"St. Augustine's Three Visions and the Structure of the *Commedia*" by Francis X. Newman from *Modern Language Notes*, vol. 82 (1961), copyright © 1967 by The Johns Hopkins University Press. Reprinted by permission.

"The Imageless Vision and Dante's *Paradiso*" by Marguerite Mills Chiarenza from *Dante Studies*, vol. 90 (1972), copyright © 1972 by State University of New York Press in cooperation with the State University of New York at Binghamton. Reprinted by permission.

"Medusa: The Letter and the Spirit" by John Freccero from *Yearbook of Italian Studies* (1972), copyright © 1972 by *Yearbook of Italian Studies*. Reprinted by permission.

"Seneca, Plato, and the Microcosm" by Robert M. Durling from *Dante Studies* vol. 93 (1975), copyright © 1975 by *Dante Studies*. Reprinted by permission.

"Epic Tradition and *Inferno* IX" by David Quint from *Dante Studies*, vol. 93 (1975), copyright © 1975 by *Dante Studies*. Reprinted by permission.

"Manfred's Wounds and the Poetics of the *Purgatorio*" by John Freccero from *Centre and Labyrinth: Essays in Honour of Northrop Frye*, copyright © 1983 by University of Toronto Press. Reprinted by permission.

"The Double Misreading of Paolo and Francesca" by Susan Noakes from *Philological Quarterly* 2, vol. 62 (Spring 1983), copyright © 1983 by University of Iowa. Reprinted by permission.

"Autocitation and Autobiography" by Teodolinda Barolini from *Dante's Poets: Textuality and Truth in the Comedy* by Teodolinda Barolini, copyright © 1984 by Princeton University Press. Reprinted by permission.

"Infernal Metamorphoses: An Interpretation of Dante's 'Counterpass' " by Kenneth Gross from *Modern Language Notes* 1, vol. 100 (1985), copyright © 1985 by The Johns Hopkins University Press. Reprinted by permission.

"The Light of Venus and the Poetry of Dante: *Vita Nuova* and *Inferno* XXVII" by Giuseppe Mazzotta, copyright © 1985 by Giuseppe Mazzotta. Published for the first time in this volume. Printed by permission.

Index